D0215830

Black
Women
in the
Workplace

Recent Titles in
Contributions in Women's Studies

BLACK
WOMEN
IN THE
WORKPLACE

Impacts of
Structural Change
in the Economy

BETTE WOODY

Contributions in Women's Studies, Number 126

GREENWOOD PRESS
New York • Westport, Connecticut • London

Library of Congress Cataloging-in-Publication Data

Woody, Bette.
    Black women in the workplace : impacts of structural change in the
economy / Bette Woody.
       p.   cm. — (Contributions in women's studies, ISSN 0147-104X ;
no. 126)
    Includes bibliographical references and index.
    ISBN 0-313-25591-1 (alk. paper)
    1. Afro-American women—Employment—United States. I. Title.
II. Series.
HD6057.5.U5W66   1992
331.4'089'96073—dc20   91-28745

British Library Cataloguing in Publication Data is available.

Library of Congress Catalog Card Number: 91-28745
ISBN: 0-313-25591-1
ISSN: 0147-104X

First published in 1992

Greenwood Press, 88 Post Road West, Westport, CT 06881
An imprint of Greenwood Publishing Group, Inc.

Printed in the United States of America

The paper used in this book complies with the
Permanent Paper Standard issued by the National
Information Standards Organization (Z39.48-1984).

10 9 8 7 6 5 4 3 2

Contents

Tables

Acknowledgments

This study grew out of a project initiated by Jean Fairfax, of the NAACP Legal Defense and Educational Fund (NAACP/LDF), and economist Phyllis Wallace, of the Sloan School of Management at MIT. The project asked whether changes in American industry and particularly larger employers contributed to the persistence of low-wage work among black women. As one of the chief architects of strategies to successfully desegregate public higher education and a respected advocate for opportunity for minorities and women, Jean Fairfax had long held a dream of creating a "woman's project" at the NAACP/LDF. At the suggestion of Professor Wallace, then a member of the Board of Overseers of the Wellesley College Center for Research on Women, several members of the Center research staff, including myself, met and developed a study to examine how low-wage black women fared as wage earners in the context of massive industrial change taking place in the U.S. economy.

The timing of the Wellesley project on the economic status of black women was excellent. The project was begun in the mid-1980s at a time when black women were greatly expanding their role as householders supporting families through their earnings. The research also promised to answer a number of nagging policy questions, such as what is the relation between earnings and income and what government action, if any, really helps women earners and breadwinners? A generous grant was provided by the Legal Defense and Educational Fund, and the project, directed by myself, with the collaboration of Michele Malson, of the Wellesley Center staff; Julienne Malveaux, of the University of California at Berkeley; Karen Fulbright of the New School for Social Research and the Ford Foundation; and Laura Lein, then director of the Center for Research on Women at Wellesley College. The results of the first study were summarized in a working paper, "Uncertainty and Risk: Black Women in Paid Employment" (coauthored by Woody and Malson) and formed the basis of a well-attended

Wingspread Conference in Racine, Wisconsin, in 1984, which subsequently launched the very successful "Women's Project" of the Legal Defense and Educational Fund.

This book represents an extension of the original research project to develop a broader context for examining industrial changes and the workplace status of black women and their future in the U.S. economy. Additional support for the book project was provided by a grant from the William H. Trotter Institute, University of Massachusetts/Boston. Gratitude must be extended to Trotter Institute Director Professor Wornie Reed, the Trotter board, and particularly to James Jennings, who persuasively argued the importance of the project. Others who were important in supporting the research were Massachusetts State Representative Saundra Graham of Cambridge, who worked diligently at the state level to put the special issue of employment opportunity for women on the "mainstream agenda" of state and national policy; Marta Wenger and Terri Ackerman, both of Harvard University, who helped with analysis of the U.S. Census Current Population Survey (CPS) Micro-Data Tapes; Susan Bailey and Carolyn Arnold of the Wellesley College Center for Research on Women helped with suggestions, editing, and insight into many of the issues; Ann Withorn and Elba Caraballo of University of Massachusetts, and Gerald Garrett and Robert Dentler of the Sociology Department at the University of Massachusetts, along with Bennett Harrison of MIT and Martin Kilson of Harvard University, helped me sort out the complex debate over work and dependency. Others who provided valuable comments, suggestions, and contributed time to help me unravel the mysteries of the economy, discrimination, and women included Diane Brown, of Howard University; William Darity, Jr., of the University of North Carolina; Sam Myers, Jr. and Barbara Bergman, of the University of Maryland; and last but not least, Bruce Dunson of Texas A & M.

I am extremely grateful to the four women who shared with me their experiences of a lifetime of work: the disappointments and the joys are all there in their stories, which are a fine measure of the real value of work. I am especially grateful to Evonne Shepphard and Dazizi Baker.

I must express my gratitude to the many Wellesley students for indispensable help with typing and editing a difficult draft. I particularly would like to acknowledge Charlotte Burns, Peggy Lee, and Kim Ellis for their help. Finally, many thanks to Anne Foxx of the Sociology Department at the University of Massachusetts/Boston, without whose help the final draft might still be languishing. Naturally, I alone am responsible for the content.

CHAPTER 1

Black Women in the U.S. Workplace: Gains and Losses

INTRODUCTION

In the recent debate over the growing poverty among blacks, attention has increasingly focused on the role of women heading households as a contributor to, if not a cause of, poverty. Supporters of a conservative political view of the role of households headed by black women appeal to deep American insecurities and guilt about the visible lagging status of racial minorities. This conservative view is also bolstered by such trends as a persistent dependency on public assistance by black families and by the emergence of a permanent class of have-nots. By contrast, liberals show more sympathy for the plight of black women as "victims" of a variety of hardships, and there is considerable criticism of social programs and the "safety net" designed to help. Social policy and programs have been found ineffective, poorly designed and managed, or simply beyond the complexity of the problem.[1] Meanwhile, for liberals too, the cause of poverty may be ignored in the rush to define the symptoms.

Throughout the debate about the declining economic status of blacks and the role of black women, surprising little attention has been paid to the workplace as a cause or cure for the problem. In particular, very little research has tackled the issue of how employment shapes the income, experience, and skills of particular labor forces and, in particular, how work has transformed the status of black women as a case. Thus, while black women led the quiet revolution that transformed the American work force from majority male to majority female during the decades of the 1970s and 1980s, few observations in theory or policy have been made about how this revolution came about and the nature of costs and benefits to the economy and to women.[2] Moreover, the economic impact of the workplace on black households remains unaddressed. The growth in women's employment of the recent past initially resulted in rapid gains in hours of work and compensation. But there is growing evidence that as the workplace status of black women improved, black male income tumbled. It is not clear that gains from female workers offset household income losses resulting from black male unemployment. The improvements to black women wrought by structural changes in the U.S. economy in the past were thus mixed. On the one hand, as the services economy boomed, a range of new opportunities opened to black women in the form of occupations that were previously closed to them such as clerical jobs. A combination of new jobs, equal opportunity laws, and educational gains helped black women move from domestic employment to mainstream work nearly overnight.[3] But by the end of the 1980s, a national economic recession, rising unemployment, and declining wages were being felt by black women just as their need was growing most rapidly.[4]

The evolving economic status of black women since passage of the landmark Civil Rights Act of 1964 reflects economic change but also major political dimensions. Structural change, which transformed the economy from production to services, also reshaped the array of jobs available and working conditions, sometimes creating improvements from the perspective of labor, sometimes reducing opportunity and wages. Political changes reinforcing economic change were no less dramatic during the period. The politics of jobs and opportunity in the United States historically involved a back-and-forth movement between liberalization of opportunity and programs sympathetic to the economically stressed, and a "tightening of the rules" on job opportunity, usually accompanied by a reduction in social programs.

The tradition of viewing the economy exclusively as a "market system," where individual workers compete on a relatively level playing field, has not lent itself to evaluating black women as a "mainstream labor force." On the one hand, evidence indicates that structural change did open opportunity for black women in mainstream work settings. At the same time, there is inadequate evidence on the experience of black women, relative to others, in getting hired and in work and task assignment, hours of work, and levels of compensation.

To fully understand how individuals navigate the market system, it is important to understand how occupations within the new industrial organizations are structured and have some notion of the stability of the occupational array over time. It is also helpful to know the potential mobility built into such jobs. A key is in understanding internal labor markets, or the new job and occupational groupings within major industrial sectors. These job groups are both the essential recruitment tool and the task and work organization vehicle. The job groups implicitly specify contributions to production and revenue for the organization. They also appear to vary by industry, making identification even more complex. Thus, while there has long been an emphasis in U.S. economic theory on the market bargaining position of individuals, based on their human capital or skills (which in turn was related to output, worth to production, and wages), the new re-job and task systems suggest that past concepts of labor are obsolete. There is, for example, less and less match between specialized learning of skills and the successful performance of many of the jobs created in the economy in recent decades. In fact, many of the highly skilled tasks, related to higher status or mid-status white-collar work, for example, have been routinely mechanized, and those that have not are frequently designed with built-in assumptions that they may have very limited futures.

Some recent analysis of the impact of structural change on labor has emphasized "deskilling" the work force, particularly blue-collar workers; however, the problem of deliberate job deskilling as the result of job redesign has received less attention. Given changes in the structure of jobs and work itself on such a large scale, questions can be raised about the real basis for recruitment and hiring of individual workers. Although these issues are complex and raise as many questions as they might answer, they are nonetheless at the core of what determines who works and what they are paid today.

Internal restructuring of the U.S. economy from a production to services economy both helped and hurt black women workers. Initial expansion of the services sector assisted in moving black women from very low-status jobs, particularly domestic household work, into new jobs. With services employment, for the first time black women were provided regular and dependable hours, competitive wage scales, and the possibility for such benefits as overtime and reasonably dignified working conditions. But, by the 1990s, some predicted changes with negative impacts for black women had already occurred. Business consolidations and restructuring increasingly displaced labor. Job losses hit the services industry with patterns similar to the plant closings that forced blue-collar manufacturing workers into unemployment a decade earlier. Bankruptcy and consolidation in the banking, real estate, and insurance industries, as well as in transportation, (particularly the airlines), indicated a future of services industry downsizings and work force layoffs.[5]

Politics and public policy are the second great influences on work opportunity for black women. "Welfare state" politics that shaped programs in the United States since the 1930s produced a layered and complex set of social insurance programs, precariously knit together to sustain support of various provider constituencies such as social workers and medical professionals as well as consumers.[6] By the 1980s, political attacks by "new right" conservative forces gained popular support. Assistance programs were presented by right-wing critics as "black subsidies," designed to discourage work and encourage welfare dependency. Liberals also criticized programs for failing to help the disadvantaged. This U.S. brand of "anti-poor" welfare politics contrasted with Europe, where central economic planning permitted very different responses of the state to similar structural unemployment during the 1970s and 1980s, including specific programs to cushion the transition of the work force from manufacturing to services economies.[7]

The United States has recently elected conservative national administrations. Their leading policies have been to cut programs to help the unemployed and dismantle social programs and subsidies on one hand, and, on the other, to deregulate industry, ostensively to reestablish the ''market system'' as a solution to economic growth.[8] Selective industrial sectors gained special interest deregulation advantages: important were special rates on depreciation of capital equipment, ceilings on imports, and relaxation of controls over the exploitation of raw materials in public trust and environmental waste standards. On the labor side, regulation protecting the health, safety, and right to negotiate compensation and working conditions was similarly relaxed.

By the 1990s, a stock market collapse heralded a full-scale economic crisis. Excessive speculation and the lack of regulatory oversight to set and enforce standards produced a snowballing effect, moving from financial and capital markets to the savings and loan system to the commercial banking system. A credit free-fall tumbled values of massive speculative lending in real estate, energy exploration, and a range of new business investment schemes. The banking system collapse led the economy into a national recession that sent unemployment spiraling. The impact on labor was devastating, as companies justified layoffs as ''scaling back'' and downsizing for ''productivity reasons.'' In many cases, however, layoffs followed an increasingly creative use of federal bankruptcy procedures and Chapter 11 reorganization, which frequently found the courts protecting key assets against labor claims. Black women, like other workers, were mainly victims caught in an economic recession with little in the way of personal resources and savings to tide them over. As critical to these lower income workers, public policy offered almost nothing to help. The safety net of welfare programs and unemployment insurance programs was curtailed and employers were less and less responsible for work force protection in time of crisis.

During the past three decades, the U.S. economy has transformed the status of black men from a low-status position to a role increasingly outside the mainstream economy altogether. Black women breadwinners emerged as part of this transformation. Over 60 percent of all black women of working age were in the work force by 1988 and had drastically increased the share of their contribution to total family income. In fact, by the late 1980s, over half of black families received principal support, or 90 percent of their income, from the earnings of female breadwinners alone. This compares to about 20 percent of white families headed by women where 80 percent of income was derived from work. While the decline in black male employment was an important factor, a key reason for the massive growth in black women as principal family earners was the rapid expansion in job opportunities. This was provided mainly by the rising demand for female workers by American industry throughout the decades of the 1970s and 1980s. A second important force pushing black women into the workplace was a decline in the proportion of black men in the labor force.

Black women have a long history in the paid work force, both as sole earners and for a well-known role as the model of the two-earner American family.[9] In contrast to other labor forces, however, until the mid–1960s black women were almost entirely excluded from mainstream places of employment and, where they did find work, were restricted to marginal, part-time, and irregular work, particularly domestic household employment. In a mere two decades after passage of federal equal opportunity legislation, black women entered mainstream work in unprecedented numbers. With rapid improvement in job opportunity, within the decades of the 1970s and 1980s, black women nearly closed the earnings gap with white women. Individual achievements in education that accompanied the growth in job opportunity also helped. The result was visible improvement in the income of black families. Black women helped reduce overall poverty rates among black families between 1960 and 1980 and may have contributed to the success of entire industry sectors, such as nursing homes, by providing a stable and reliable work force. But there is also evidence of problems with rapid gains. The bulk of the jobs open to black women were limited in mobility, earnings, and benefits (such as health plans and retirement insurance). Despite improvements in family income, gaps increased between the races by the close of the 1980s.

While growth in the numbers of black women earners and their access to better jobs improved the well-being of many families, the lower earning power of women as a substitute for male earners acted to reduce median black family income compared to whites. This was visible in a widening of the black/white family income gap during the 1970s and 1980s.[10] Median earnings of black women working full time in 1980 were reported by the U.S. Department of Labor at $10,862, compared to $16,354 for married-couple black families, $14,856 in black families with male heads, and $21,928 in married-couple white families.[11] By 1980, over half of families headed by black women fell below the federal poverty line.

Several trends in the economy contributed to radical change in the status of black women in the labor force. The most important change, which started in the 1970s, was expansion of the services economy. This fueled a massive expansion of jobs, particularly in entry-level and low-skilled categories. Of the 20 million jobs created between 1960 and 1980, fully three-quarters were in the services industry and an overwhelming majority were in entry-level occupations and those traditionally held by women such as clerical work, retail sales, personal services, and human services (health and education). An escalating demand for women in the labor force followed. A second trend was the restructuring of occupational and work systems to emphasize new work scheduling and wage and compensation systems, which reduced traditional wage and job ladder mobility and encouraged transient status and turnover. Horizontal job clusters replaced more vertical systems and were frequently divorced from mainstream core business activities.[12] Internally such systems provide limited training and skills acquisition and few long-term employment commitments.[13] The new job systems were created without collective bargaining and included high proportions of part-time and temporary work. Even such traditional stable employers for women as the hospital and education industries adopted the new job and wage systems. Despite such disadvantages, the new services economy provided major improvements for most women as individual workers. Black women in particular made improvements over traditional employment and wage levels.

Black women gained from the massive structural changes that characterized the economy of the 1970s by being employed and by having a long and uninterrupted tradition of work force participation. Their long history in the work force enabled black women to respond quickly to the growth of new jobs by moving into a range of new occupational categories. The timing of job expansion helped. Black women were able to gain important employment advantages for several reasons. First there were general labor shortages in industries most likely to hire women workers. Second, job expansion initially occurred in central cities close to where black women lived. Third, the accelerated entry of black women into the workplace preceded that of white women during the 1960s.

The improvements made by black women workers were in part caused by their unique position prior to the 1960s. Almost totally restricted to an informal, irregular, and part-time system of domestic household work, any change was major progress. Domestic work was characterized by low pay, limited work hours, instability, unpredictable task content, and a near total absence of benefits and protection that workers in formal systems take for granted.[14] A second factor that influenced employment trends for black women was dramatic changes taking place in family structure. The proportion of black men heading families declined drastically during the 1970s, from nearly 80 percent in 1960 to less than half by the mid-1980s. Causes for this trend are complex but may relate to a drop in the proportion of black males in the work force and corresponding rises in the unemployment rates among black men. The dramatic change in the economy probably hurt black men more than any other labor force. The erosion of jobs traditionally held by black men such as unskilled production and services work, coupled with the loss of agricultural employment, increased the subemployment rates among black men. One impact on families was that marriage rates among black men plummeted between 1960 and 1980. At the same time, the proportion of families headed by never-married black women rose.

Other factors that added to the complexity of change in the status of black women were some geographic trends and politics. Suburbanization has been recently acknowledged as acting to disperse many of the traditional "mobility" jobs, or those where black men and women were able to enter with few qualifications and gain experience and earnings increases over time.[15] The political side of job distribution and its relation to race has only recently been studied as a factor influencing growth of poverty and income distribution in general during the 1960s and 1970s.[16] What in many cases has been termed a "culture of poverty," with assumptions of internal behavior, standards, and reactions, may reflect political barriers to opportunity that assume racial dimensions where there are geographic concentrations of minorities. The political process, reinforced by social behavior and racially structured institutions, as much as the market system may thus be responsible for rising unemployment and black discouragement.

Both theory and policy have had a strong focus on labor supply and particularly on the qualitative characteristics of the labor force and have neglected the demand or employment base structure of the economy. Traditional labor theory is strongly biased with a view that the qualitative characteristics of labor, or "human capital," measured in terms of skills, education, and "effort" or behavior of individual workers, are the principal determinants of whether or not workers are hired, what their occupational status is, and, above all, the level of wages paid.

This theory has been challenged by analysts emphasizing different perspectives. First, there are those who feel the work organization itself plays a significant role in setting limits on the status of a worker from entry on. Rules set by a corporation act to neutralize or cancel out individual talent or "human capital." Other analysts looking behind the bureaucratic tendencies of corporations tend to set rules mainly for "bottom lines," and to count more on organizational logic in the design of job groups that are structured around tasks to produce specific products or production goals. This bureaucratic picture may more accurately reflect how new systems determine a worker's status and pay at entry, as well as potential for advancement. Finally, many analysts of the new trends in job and occupational formation related to labor utilization see a split in labor markets between high-paid primary markets and low-paid secondary markets. As with human capital theorists, however, institutional analysts have focused mainly on a model that reflects characteristics of traditional manufacturing industry, including a predominately male work force. This severely limits analysis of services as a labor market and may account for the failure to identify some significant labor outcomes resulting from the transformation of the industrial workplace. The change in the nature of work has been the biggest factor influencing a change in demand for a very different type of labor.

U.S. labor and employment policy has also neglected any serious appraisal of the changing nature of employment and workplace and any implications these changes have for the work force and the economy as a whole. Since the 1960s, for example, the principal federal policy and programs focused on the supply side of the employment equation and skills training aimed either at unemployed skilled workers displaced by structural changes or unskilled workers seeking new jobs. Policy that centered more on the demand side, such as job creation and improvement in opportunity in the workplace, has been far more limited. Job creation policy dates from the public works and Works Progress Administration (WPA) programs of the Roosevelt administration during the 1930s, which aimed at stimulating the rebuilding of the private sector that had been devastated by the Depression. Over the years, however, political opposition developed to both public employment, as with the Comprehensive Employment and Training Act (CETA) program of the 1960s, and to regional private-sector stimulus programs, such as the Tennessee Valley Authority (TVA) and the Appalachian Regional Commission programs aimed at rural development.[17] By contrast, both European and Japanese government policies have maintained aggressive policies both for short-term job support and long-term regional employment development needs. Many have adopted full employment policies as well as comprehensive unemployment insurance programs. In addition to responding to local political needs, such policies may help stabilize and maintain a viable labor force and a consumer economy through periods of economic downturn.[18]

This study examines how structural change in the U.S. economy and particularly the rise of the new service sectors have reshaped the work content, opportunity, and wages of one labor group, black women. A central thesis is that while short-term growth in services spurred by market forces and the burgeoning welfare state helped those at the lowest end of the employment ladder by providing low-end employment for large numbers, such growth unaccompanied by social and employment policy presents risks to labor and the well-being of the economy as a whole. Problems lie mainly in an unregulated workplace and the status of workers. The current work systems that dominate the employment structure of many major industries act in some ways to restrict large numbers of workers. Black women, limited to a fairly narrow range of job and wage opportunities, serve to illustrate the impacts of new jobs on labor. With the growth of services, a new subculture of women's work has evolved.

While causes are unclear, outcomes include the seemingly contradictory result of rising income for women but falling income for families. As work and pay systems act to reduce the ability of women of both races to provide the principal source of income for families, the workplace can be said to indirectly erode family income. Job characteristics increasingly define the gap between families supported by women's earnings and those where men are principal breadwinners. To the extent that male wages along with male jobs are expanding far slower than women's, family income declines can be predicted to continue in the future. These are important implications for black women as a labor force, but also for the entire U.S. labor force.

Evidence on which this study is based comes principally from two sources. Statistical data are mainly from U.S. Census data on employment, particularly the Current Population Survey file, a biennial sample of approximately 55,000 households. This data set is used to examine recent trends in employment of black and white women. A second source is interviews conducted with black women with employment histories in several representative industries surveyed in the book. The interviews provide insight into the individual human perceptions of industry and workplace and help bring cold statistics down to the level of the individual worker as she copes with her work aspirations and her family life.

The book is organized around three basic themes into nine chapters. The remainder of this chapter along with Chapters 2 and 3 explore the contradiction between evolving trends in the economy, including the decline in manufacturing, and a government policy that continues to rely on the marketplace to provide jobs and income to the work force. We first examine traditional hypotheses about how labor quality is valued in the marketplace and then how labor markets have failed to produce mainstream jobs, while newer markets have evolved that marginalize labor. We look at the entry of women workers into the workplace and how dissemination and concentrations have occurred. Chapters 4, 5 and 6 explore in more detail the outcomes of the shift from a manufacturing to a services economy. They examine how sectors individually shape job markets that are internal to industries and companies and may in the process either provide mobility and wage gains, or intensify the ghettoization of women and the stratification of women by race. The impact of internal job changes on wages and benefits is also reviewed. Chapter 7 looks at the personal case histories of black women to illustrate some of the real-life experiences behind the statistics. Four women use their own words to describe how they have achieved "success" in the workplace, despite extremely disadvantaged backgrounds, and they clearly identify work as a key element in reinforcing individual ambition. Finally, in Chapters 8 and 9 we look at the future of black women as a labor force by examining the emerging workplace of the twenty-first century. These chapters look at the future of employment and wages and the implications for U.S. labor. Using black women as a case of one segment of labor, we also examine the kind of policy needed to provide a bridge between the household income need and jobs and wages available, as well as a deeper need to reevaluate the organization and design of work and how it relates to new work forces.

RISE OF THE NEW CONSERVATIVE POLITICS OF MARKET SOLUTIONS TO POVERTY AND DISCRIMINATION

Two political factors have hampered fuller recognition of the impact of a changing economy on black earners. One is the absence of government response to the massive shift in the economy from production to services and a corresponding changeover in the gender composition of the American work force. The second is the rise in an aggressive political conservatism in the United States, which uses selective indicators that emphasize social behavior as a cause of poverty to the exclusion of evidence on employment.

A massive change took place over the past three decades in the U.S. work force from predominately male to majority female. Between 1960 and 1980, the proportion of the total female work force expanded from slightly over one-third to over one-half. This change was spurred mainly by services industry growth but also by a more subtle change: a decline in earning power of male breadwinners. While we noted the relative decline in black male earnings, overall earnings by male workers of both races slowed in the mid-1980s with no perceptible growth and some losses, according to recent analyses.[19] The expansion of white women in the labor force thus can be partly attributed to a growing need for two household earners to maintain wage growth enjoyed in the past by single male earners. Another contributing factor to the growth of women breadwinners, however, was the rising rate of family breakup among whites, with visible rises in divorce and separation rates.[20]

By contrast, the expansion of black women in the labor force followed somewhat different patterns. Growth in black women-headed households represented a shift from low-earning black male-headed households and dual-earner households underscored by reduced marriage rates among blacks.[21] Census data indicate that family income for both races in 1982 dollars fell dramatically between 1979 and 1982. The loss among blacks was far more dramatic than among whites, however. An index of median annual earnings compiled by the U.S. Census showed that the annual earnings for white families between 1979 and 1985 was 90.5 percent compared to 85.5 percent for black families, and that the gap between black and white income widened over the period between 1972 to 1982 from 56.6 to 55.28 percent.[22]

Family income decline trends in recent years, however, were far more severe in the case of households headed by women and most dramatic among black women. Although median income of black and white women was similar in 1982, black women were far more likely to fall below the poverty line. In 1982, while the earnings gap between black and white women was closing, 56.2 percent of households headed by black women with no husband present were poor, compared to 27.9 of all white women similarly situated.

Despite growing evidence of economic change impacts in shifting family earners and contributing to poverty, a new conservative mood characterized the United States starting in the late 1970s. A political backlash against social programs occurred that was bolstered by reconstructed myths about the causes of poverty in the failure of individual initiative rather than the marketplace. Poverty became increasingly linked to the individual and particularly to antisocial behavior. Accompanying national conservatism, a political retreat also occurred from the social contract in the workplace between labor and management. Open attacks on government regulations in the workplace included such established standards as increases in minimum wage floors, unemployment insurance, and support of collective bargaining under the National Labor Relations Board. Programs aimed at employment and training for the disadvantaged and unemployed also floundered.

Theories about a "culture of poverty" and an urban underclass that arose during the 1980s reflected a growing conservatism in research as well as policy that refocused the problems of poverty on the individual and away from the economy.[23] During the 1950s, several leading sociologists sought to identify specific behavioral traits, which they then associated with poverty and termed "a culture of poverty." Oscar Lewis, in particular, used the term to explain how urban poverty, visible when Mexican peasants moved to city slums, tended to become institutionalized and passed on intergenerationally.[24] Transferred to the United States, however, the culture of poverty was applied to slum poverty, and particularly to black big-city poverty, to demonstrate "social pathology." It hypothesized essentially that poverty was not only a subculture within the larger society, but that it could be transmitted intergenerationally within such populations isolated within the mainstream of society, even in big cities such as the black ghettos of Chicago. Welfare dependency, social disorganization, crime and antisocial behavior, mental illness, and illegitimacy were all indicators of a culture of poverty whose cause centered not on external discrimination but on the internal culture, which created bad life-styles. Others challenged the theory by arguing that it failed to demonstrate any behavior of the poor that was distinct from the nonpoor when the nonpoor were confronted with similar economic conditions as unemployment or lack of money, in effect confirming the famous Hemingway response to F. Scott Fitzgerald's remark: "The rich are different than you and me." Hemingway is credited with replying, "Yeah, they have more money."[25] There was also criticism about a lack of attention to the problems suffered by racial minorities in the United States. American social theorists who were considered members of the "functionalist" school followed University of Chicago sociologist Robert Park. They argued that the experience of white European immigrants—who first lived outside mainstream culture, then gradually became assimulated—was an appropriate model for the integration of blacks into U.S. society. Critics of this view, however, found major differences in the experience of the races. In contrast to white immigrants, racial minorities had been subject to a long history of legal prohibitions ranging from employment to public accommodation to property ownership. The long history and the intricate shape of legal discrimination tended to legitimize and reinforce the private denial of rights by the majority to minority groups. Perhaps more important, this historial tradition of discrimination invaded the most important economic and social institutions in American society, including business, government, and religion, effectively "freezing" a complexity of inequalities, segregation and discrimination.

Despite criticisms, the theory of individual responsibility for economic status and intergenerational poverty as a cultural barrier to change was resurrected as an important force in policy during the 1970s. The expansion of women heading households and trends in illegitimacy were used to validate the notion that a matriarchal society characterized black families. Further, this matriarchy was intrinsically "defective" and, in fact, a mark of deviancy. As more black families fell below the poverty line, intact or not, conservatives looked to theories of social behavior based on self-perpetuated poverty to justify the retreat from policy initiatives, particularly those that focused on income redistribution, equal opportunity in employment, and various floors on human services from health and nutrition to housing and education. During the 1980s, political conservatism reached its apogee under the Reagan administration and a "new right" sought to legitimize its perspectives through the establishment of toned-down, conservative models of liberal think tanks, like the Brookings Institution and the Urban Institute, with such organizations as the American Enterprise Institute and the Heritage Foundation. In study after study, conservative analysts sought to challenge the effectiveness of human services and income distribution policies and government intervention to regulate labor and market discrimination. The Reagan administration, helped by allies in Congress, dismantled most of the programs of the Kennedy-Johnson years in social assistance, child development, housing, health care, education, and employment and training, principally on the grounds of failure to solve problems, if not to create them.

The new conservatism supported basic institutional changes in public policy that were far more serious, however, than the rollback on subsidies to individuals. First a dramatic retreat was made from the evolving social contract between labor and management in the workplace. The regulatory framework influencing labor in general and black and female labor in particular was attacked. The Reagan administration eroded the power of the National Labor Relations Board to expand and protect collective bargaining in the workplace. Second, specific examples were made in hardline wage contact negotiations with the U.S. Postal Service—one of the largest employers of nonwhite and female labor—to reduce entry wages and restructure the entire occupational wage structure into a "two tier" system of old and new workers. The Air Controllers contract and union were also dissolved following a bitter strike. Regulation of workplace safety and health was curtailed as the Occupational Safety and Health Administration (OSHA) was all but dismantled. The long-standing strategy for periodic raises of the minimum wage by the Democratic Party was successfully fought back by the Reagan administration. Most of all, however, over eight years the Reagan administration systematically attacked affirmative action and equal opportunity regulation and enforcement, using the rubric of "deregulation" and reducing the authority of the Equal Employment Opportunity Commission (EEOC) to regulate private employment. Through judicial and executive appointments, conservative and anti-civil rights policy was guaranteed long into the future.

To illustrate how deeply conservatism penetrated, in addition to reconstructing institutions such as the judiciary and the EEOC, executive power was used to dismantle the detailed, finely tuned regulatory system of equal opportunity built up over a decade. Federal contracting regulations, evolved over the years from successive statutes and executive orders, were rescinded or simply ignored. Included in the equal opportunity infrastructure was the Office of Federal Contract Compliance (FCC) of the Department of Labor which was responsible for overseeing hiring practices of all federal contractors, and the Office of Civil Rights of the U.S. Department of Education which was responsible for enforcement of hiring and educational opportunity for federal grantees or nearly all the U.S. educational system. The U.S. Department of Justice, the lead executive agency in civil rights enforcement, used its Civil Rights Division to enter on the side of complainants against affirmative action compliance under civil rights statutes! Finally, funding was drastically cut in programs designed to improve the opportunity of disadvantaged workers through grants to localities for education and training. Programs were also shifted away from the most disadvantaged in the labor force, the long-term unemployed and minorities, toward the interests of local private industry.[26]

THE EMERGING FEMALE JOB SUBCULTURE

It is difficult to describe the new work subculture emerging with the growth of services and a mainly women's work force in dry statistics. The new low wage work diverges further and further from the traditional model of the white male worker, or even traditional "women's work." More and more, the new workplace resembles the Kafkaesque world of the machine-dominated human workers of the Fritz Lang films of the 1920s, or perhaps the woolen mills of the turn of the century, with their long lines of spindles and looms that more often than not dictated the paces, the hours, and the rhythm of work for the hundreds passively attending them. While some women's work is notable for its personal and psychic rewards derived from interacting with and helping people, much is unrewarding and drudgery. Much of the work content is boring, fatiguing, and routine. Much is also dirty, heavy, and menial. Much is devoid of personal satisfaction that industrial psychologists agree comes from the use of creative capacity, control, and discretion. Firsthand accounts of women at the bottom reveal, despite this, a highly motivated and disciplined work force.

A typical health care worker today is female and nonprofessional. In the fastest growing sectors—nursing homes, outpatient clinics, and home health care—she is highly likely to be black and to lack education in a world highly stratified by professional nuances. Nonetheless, she may have accumulated an impressive technical knowledge of health, along with her commonsense approaches to the needs of the sick, disabled, infirm, and even the dying. She is also likely to function in an occupational capacity that is the basic building block on which the health care system operates or to substitute frequently for the professional. Whether she is trained as a paraprofessional or lacks formal training, her work load, the quality of her work, and her flexibility at working long hours permit those at the top to "sell" a $600 billion industry as safe, reliable, high-quality, and cost-effective. Her dedication and reliability permit the quality to remain high, even at a serious cost to her in personal time and working conditions.

But there is a serious contradiction in the prevailing model. The true costs of labor may be understated, as, for example, in the cost gap between the high-cost and the low-cost ends of the system. The bottom worker who fuels cash flow and absorbs calculations of cost-effectiveness may be significantly underpaid and inappropriate to absorb the difference in, say, institutional care in a well-run hospital or nursing home and in home care where she is the principal provider of services. Her compensation is not only low, but her hourly wages frequently exclude a pension or a prepaid health plan—costs that may later be passed on to the public in Medicaid or Social Security, or simply in poverty. Wage rates typically paid rarely reflect mainstream compensation rates and further may hide a set of real benefits distributed to other professional or administrative earners in the form of overhead, profits, state tax, and other allocations. Most importantly, she will work as a nearly "captive worker" in a system that can be viewed as a growing phenomenon, the subculture of women's work.

This women's work subculture not only dominates the health care industry, but also increasingly characterizes retailing, white-collar services such as banking and insurance, and many business and professional services activities such as the hotel industry, building maintenance, janitorial and security services, restaurants, and many social services and welfare organizations. The bulk of employment growth and possibly much of the value-added in the U.S. economy in recent years is fundamentally traceable to the new organization of jobs as "women's labor sectors."

Arrangements to hire and rely on a female labor force are in turn fueled by a growing army of women householders whose wages are necessary to provide basic family necessities. Women such as Anna B., who has worked for 15 years as a hotel maid to support three children and, wherever possible, to help out her aging, disabled mother; of Lucy P., who has worked since age 15 and despite her occasional failing health puts in 50 hours and more per week, including travel back and forth between five home-bound disabled patients as a home care giver; and Martha W., who despite eight years as a loving, dedicated manager of a small church organization, has never obtained a raise, and had to wait five years for health insurance coverage. The dependency of these women and millions of others on their wages for income and their captive status at the bottom of the occupational ladder, despite enthusiasm and dedication to work, spill over into their home lives.

In most cases, these women started work early in life because, as one put it, black women never question the fact that they will work. All of their role models, whether family members or community, were women like themselves whose families depended on their "getting out and bringing in a paycheck." They entered the work force in their teens before completing high school. Most stayed in one job or another, through several pregnancies, with little time out to care for their babies. After a quick return to work, each juggled babysitting arrangements with family, friends, and transient and occasionally uncertain community centers. In their twenties they typically encountered a major personal crisis: a marriage breakup, an unemployed or disabled husband, or a child in trouble. The crisis inevitably resulted in each becoming "on her own" at least temporarily and in the workplace "to support the whole family." For each, the future and life stages until old age are seen as a continuation of the complicated logistics of day-to-day management of life with little flexibility and almost no provision for emergency or old age from marginal work and low pay.[27] What is most suprising in reviewing personal history, however, is acceptance and even love for work. Contrary to popular stereotypes, black women are suprisingly motivated and even ambitious for their work futures. Typical is Sarah H., who has evolved a personal theory of work satisfaction centered on making each "task," no matter how undesirable, count toward "my betterment"; or Anna B., who enrolled in a local college program at age 40 to "be the first in my family to get a college degree."

The disadvantage of spending a work life in the women's work subculture for black women extends beyond the problem of an unrewarding job or even the issue of low pay. What is seriously lacking and acutely perceived by those who work in the system is that the jobs are specifically designed to reduce work to inhuman dimensions. Although such women are not always articulate, it is clear that they understand there is a system operating that is set up to emphasize labor flexibility for employers to respond to changes in business organization and cost constraints, at the expense of the worker as a creative, productive human being who perfers, if asked, a measure of control over her work. The new systems that have replaced the old, more paternalistic, and sometimes harsh supervisory systems are also frequently cold, distant, and technologically oriented. Moreover, they are designed to keep a low-status work force in isolation from the mainstream or other places where they could work where there may be different jobs, superior working conditions, and benefits. Communication may be minimized, in fact, to discourage discussion of pay, hours, and other rewards from work.

FRAMEWORK FOR CHANGE: THEORY, TRENDS, AND ISSUES

Unquestionably public policy on labor problems has been handicapped by recent conservative trends in the political arena, but deeper problems lie in the lack of a theoretical framework and an open tradition in the United States for looking at the state of the national economy in distributive terms, particularly in the redistribution of income and in the allocation of work. The United States has severe problems in facing a future united European Community of over 300 million people, even ignoring the rapid movement of Eastern Europe toward economic integration with the West, along with a rising tide of Pacific Rim economies of which Japan may be only a small warning of things to come. In contrast to European states, however, the United States has not begun to consider national economic planning, which would permit evolution of rational public strategies to cope with such serious crises as the decline in basic industry or the exhaustion of natural resources on which the success of the U.S. economy in the past has so heavily depended. The recent shocks in international and domestic credit markets and the potentially staggering burden of costs of massive mergers, acquisitions, and structural consolidations have shaken and disrupted entire sectors of the economy. As a combination of domestic debt and competitive failure has challenged the U.S. economy, little national response has occurred. National action to encourage productivity and competition, while protecting displaced workers, is practically nonexsistent. High levels of regional unemployment persist, along with serious income declines among segments of population groups, particularly minorities.

Along with the absence of national economic planning to meet a growing crisis in the economy, the United States has a major disadvantage in a weak tradition of organized labor. Although strong trade unionism in other parts of the world, notably in Britain and other parts of Europe and more recently in Poland, has politically stalled the closing of obsolete industrial facilities or prevented the automation of others, the value of organized labor at the national level as a political balance against big economic interests, is invaluable. Labor interest has been responsible for most social insurance and family assistance programs and has outweighed any disadvantages of deficit or inflation pressure. For example, labor has most frequently been responsible for social security, including national health, housing finance, urban redevelopment, and subsidies for mass transportation.[28] By contrast in the United States, the current role and impact of labor is almost nonexistent. A recent evolution has seen labor find its role as a collaborator with management interests, frequently sitting, as in the case of the United Auto Workers, on corporate boards where votes are vastly outnumbered and where membership is uncertain whose interests are represented. Most of all, however, the traditional influence of organized labor on legislative and programmatic thrusts of government has dwindled to near zero. This leaves in the U.S. Congress, for example, most statutory lobbying in the hands of corporate management advocates whose consideration of labor is decreasing as the service industry expands and its interest in labor becomes increasingly narrow. Meanwhile, labor as advocate for consumer purchasing power is nearly forgotten in current policy. An evolving macro policy, in fact, rests mainly on defense spending, deregulation of industry, and reductions in social spending.[29]

In the context of these major deficiencies in public policy, the position of black women as a labor force may seem insignificant. As serious as problems of black women workers may be, compared to the more fundamental labor dilemma, they constitute a minor effect at best. There are two reasons, however, for a detailed examination of black women as a work force. First, as noted earlier, black women may constitute a paradigm of the female labor force, since work force participation patterns established by both married and single black females increasingly characterize white women. Second, black women were the first subgroup in the women's labor force to respond to rising demand for women workers. The size and patterns of demand for women are even less understood than female labor itself: hiring patterns, job characteristics, and hours and wages of black women offer key evidence of how the new service economy operates.

Changes that most characterized the past three decades of the U.S. economy and shaped the new opportunity and status for black women were the decline in the production sector and the rise of services. Total U.S. employment expanded from 60 to 106 million jobs between 1950 and 1984, with 20 million new jobs alone added between 1970 and 1982.[30] During this period, manufacturing, agriculture, and the extractive sectors declined rapidly as a source of new jobs in the economy. While, in 1950, 48 percent of all jobs in the United States were in manufacturing or agriculture, by 1985 manufacturing had added only 4 million new jobs and agricultural employment had declined by half. Over the same period, by contrast, services employment had added 46 million jobs, of which 30 million represented private-sector increases. By 1984 nearly seven in every ten jobs were in services.

These dramatic industry changes sent ripple effects throughout the occupational structure of the workplace and drastically altered the types of jobs available, the content of jobs, and the wage structure. While blue-collar jobs were lost in every area of manufacturing, unskilled jobs were particularly hard hit. Blue-collar losses occurred in low-wage sectors of manufacturing as well, irrespective of skills level, such as apparel, textiles, and food processing.

By contrast, a vast expansion of professional, business, and financial services took place, increasing jobs in all occupational categories from high-wage to low-wage. White-collar clerical and sales, goods handling, and human services jobs were the biggest winners. In industrial growth terms, however, the high-value end of services that benefited from growth included utilities, wholesaling, and transportation. These industries provided generally high-wage employment and unionized contracts for the work force. But the bulk of new job growth occurred in banking and financial services, insurance, business and personal services, health care, and retailing, where the occupational picture and wages were far more mixed. Millions of lower level services and clerical jobs were created and most were nonunion. The boom in services was also accompanied by management reorganizations and consolidations of job strategies designed to reduce the well-known "labor-intensive character" of services and increase productivity. Many jobs were organized on a part-time, limited mobility and skills basis to respond to technological or management innovation change in the future where workers might be eliminated.[31]

Accompanying the services changeover was a managerial revolution that included not only a new strategy about the value of labor, but also major changes in the utilization of the work force and its relationship internally, as well as to the supervisory system. This was visible in the hierarchical organization of jobs and, inevitably, wage systems. Job groups were organized in a horizontal fashion, to eliminate advancement potential from the bottom and middle ranks. Thus, in contrast to skilled factory assembly jobs that provided some mobility, or at least wage gains, services jobs were more likely to be organized as single-purpose/title jobs. In contrast to skilled factory jobs, clerical work was organized into tasks that require limited decisions, judgment, professional attitudes, behavior, or cognitive processes.

The technology that accompanied managerial innovation in services carried very different requirements and impacts on labor than the production technology of the past. Many of the new clerical jobs coming out of the services revolution were oriented toward massive growth of paperwork as operations were consolidated and information generated to be processed, accounted for, filed, and summarized. High-speed data processing and ancillary connecting equipment were integrated into systems where clerical workers became the main instrument for operations. Sales, for example, whether in retailing, wholesaling, or insurance, was organized into vast systems combining customer processing, credit debiting, multiple credit sources, check and financial institutional communications, inventory control, and periodic process changing transactions. The traditional interpersonal contracts and interactions with customers were reduced both in time and skills requirements. In other cases, machine management was introduced for those more geographically distant transactions such as billing and sales transaction processing. Specialized sites designed around computer systems, remote data processing links, and actual transaction sites were invented and staffed with an army of assembly workers managed by specially designed programs, frequently located in suburban, rural, and even offshore sites, or wherever cheap marginal labor pools, usually women, were available. In the case of professional and unprofessional services such as health care, very large specialized equipment and technology was frequently the basis or organization of jobs. Even maids, cleaning personnel, and maintenance jobs in hotels and office buildings became increasingly programmed through time management computer analysis. The impact on labor of the new technology occasionally called for "higher computational skills." However, for the most part, the opposite occurred with even middle-management programmers eliminated through prepackaged specialized programs for hotels, insurance, and sales, or contracted jobbers such as computer services firms for one-time tailoring to a particular firm.

The new services industry carried with its expansion a mix of contradictory expectations and risks for employees that relate directly to the evolving subculture of women's work. Many of the new jobs require a high-quality, educated work force, including reading and math skills. But the organization of work and the technologically oriented systems pose severe limits on worker discretion, skills, and productivity normally associated with occupations requiring literacy skills in the past.

Because wages are set low, mobility is nearly absent as are other compensations and benefits (including the psychic reward of creative and meaningful work), and much of the new work seems no more appropriate for an educated work force than the old routine production jobs of a turn-of-the-century mill. This contradiction in requiring education for hiring but providing little in the way of intellectual challenge or rewards explains in part the heavy recruitment of women. Women were considered a more easily manipulated or passive work force than men, and, further, women lacked forceful advocates, including organized labor and other worker's rights advocates. Corporate managements and services entrepreneurs such as part-time agencies were able to maintain marginal work and working conditions and avoid the longer-term commitments and the social contract established in blue-collar industrial workplaces half a century before. Women provided the ideal "high quality" work force eager to take and follow directions, disciplined in producing quality work, but also more easily accepting of irregular or part-time work scheduling, low benefits, and marginality in mobility than a similarly qualified male work force.

BLACK WOMEN AND THE WOMEN'S WORK SUBCULTURE

As noted, the new services employment revolution helped black women gain access to higher status jobs and wages compared to the past, but also forced them into a "women's work subculture." The subculture is characterized by general limitations of "women's jobs," and is segmented and restricted to the lower end of this market. Discrimination still plays an important role in this pattern. Black women, for example, have made the best gains in those workplaces where black males, black women, or white women were traditionally hired, such as the U.S. Postal Service and hospitals where work forces were protected by civil service or integrated unions. But following the tradition of black women's employment, they have continued to be restricted to those jobs that more closely resemble those traditionally performed by black women: blue-collar services jobs such as maintenance, janitorial, and cleaning; restaurant workers including cooks, counter workers, and cashiers; and in personal services such as orderlies, aides, baby sitters, and housekeepers—jobs that are clustered in nursing homes, child-care facilities, and residential facilities for the handicapped. Thus, there is risk that educational gains that have rapidly grown for black women may not be reflected in the kinds of jobs that are most accessible.

Moreover, job growth and hiring trends are not promising for black women. While the 1970s marked a watershed for improving job opportunities for black women, the decade also marked the greatest job growth in half a century. Black women benefited by being in the labor force prior to the massive entry of white women and, moreover, had distinct advantages in proximity to the geographic location of much of the expansion of white-collar and retailing jobs in downtown core cities. During the 1960s and 1970s, prior to suburbanization of much employment, job growth occured in department stores, mail-order houses, government offices, banking and insurance, utilities and hospitals—close to ghettos where most black women lived.

For the future, several problems pose risks to continuation of improvements for black women. In addition to the decentralization of much employment out of cities, a slowdown is predicted in services job growth as industries consolidate activities, streamline management, and downsize labor forces in efforts to increase productivity and output. Low-end jobs will be particularly affected by the introduction of new technology and mechanization. Black women as a labor force are handicapped because of discrimination and because they lack requisite skills to compete for technical work and in services at higher mobility levels of the job system. Black women suffer more unemployment and are restricted or crowded disproportionately in certain classes of women's work, compared to white women. In the future, despite improvements, black women's educational and skills levels are likely to continue to lag behind. Thus, while the irregular job systems of domestic work no longer dominate work opportunity for black women, without intervention stratified jobs and pay systems are likely to leave black women behind. Already the economic slowdowns of the late 1980s indicated problems in rising unemployment and part-time work as well as reduced median earnings for black women compared to their white counterparts.

The key question that remains, and which the remainder of this volume addresses, is whether the recent change in the economy represents long-term hope and progress for black women as self-sufficient contributors to the economy, or whether the case merely underscores the complex political issue of mediation between public and private sectors to assure a reasonable standard of living and full employment for black women and their families. We focus less on black women's efforts as individuals to alter behavior and achieve progress in the work world than how the institutional system of work responds to their presence and effort. It is this focus that we hypothesize will shed light on the potential and constraints of both black women and other segments of the labor force for research and policy.

NOTES

1. See William Julius Wilson and Kathryn Neckerman, "Poverty and Family Structure: The Widening Gap Between Evidence and Public Policy," in Sheldon H. Danzinger and Daniel H. Weinberg (eds.), *Fighting Poverty* (Cambridge, MA: Harvard University Press, 1986), p. 252. Wilson in this and other writings puts strong emphasisis on the "disfunctional" side of black family life. He uses indicators of social disorganization, such as crime and delinquency, as dominant descriptors, in preference to externally caused economic factors such as unemployment or reduced hours of work and wages. To do this, would mean acknowledging the migration of job opportunity for ghetto residents. It would also mean examining whether or not societal structural factors are at the root of reghettoization of poverty in the 1980s and 1990s. In part, the concept of "underclass" used by Wilson is a restatement of the earlier thesis of "culture of poverty" of the 1960s by leading analysts, including Kenneth B. Clark, *Dark Ghetto* (New York: Harper and Row, 1965); Lee Rainwater, "Crucible of Identity: The Negro Lower Class Family," *Daedalus*, 95, pp. 172–216; and Daniel Patrick Moynihan, *The Negro Family: A Case for National Action*, (Washington DC: U.S. Department of Labor, 1965). These earlier studies remain to be updated to incorporate new evidence on the impact of racial stratification in the workplace and how this, in turn, relates to employment migration.

2. Phyllis Wallace, *Black Women in the Labor Force*, (Cambridge, MA: MIT Press, 1982), pp. 10–15.

3. Julianne Malveaux, "Recent Trends in Occupational Segregation by Race and Sex," paper presented to the Committee on Women's Employment and Related Social Issues, National Academy of Sciences, Washington, DC, May 25, 1982.

4. Barry Bluestone and Bennett Harrison, "The Great American Jobs Machine: Proliferation of Low Wage Employment in the U.S. Economy" (Washington, DC: Joint Economic Committee, U.S. Congress, 1986), p. 23. For a response, see Janet L. Norwood, "A Cyclical Rebound: The Job Machine Has Not Broken," *New York Times*, February 22, 1987; also see Ellen Barlett, "Minimum-Wage Jobs Enable Survival, But Little Else," *Boston Globe*, March 29, 1987.

5. Only limited attention has been paid to examining the parallel between blue-collar and white-collar productivity and related work processes. For one study of parallels, see Evelyn Nakano Glenn and Roslyn Feldberg, "Degraded and Deskilled: The Proletarianization of Clerical Work," in Rachael Kahn-Hut, Arlene Daniels, and Richard Colvard (eds.), *Women and Work* (New York: Oxford University Press, 1982); and for an excellent journalistic account of new female work ghettos, see Barbara Garson, *The Electronic*

Sweatshop: How Computers are Transforming the Office of the Future into the Factory of the Past (New York: Penguin, 1988).

6. For a summary of the U.S. tradition in social programs, see Margaret Weir, ''The Federal Government and Unemployment: The Frustration of Policy Innovation from the New Deal to the Great Society,'' in Margaret Weir, Ann Orloff, and Theda Skocpol (eds.), *The Politics of Social Policy in the United States* (Princeton, NJ: Princeton University Press, 1988). For a more recent appraisal of legislative failures in welfare reform, see Bette Woody, ''Welfare Reform: A Summary and Analysis of Current U.S. Congressional Debate over the Family Security Act of 1988,'' *Trotter Review* (William M. Trotter Institute, University of Massachusetts, Boston), 3, no. 2 (Spring 1989), pp. 9–14.

7. Weir, ''The Federal Government,'' p. 149.

8. For an appreciation of the impacts of deregulation in a key sector, the airline industry, for example, see Paul Stephen Dempsey, ''The Disaster of Airline Deregulation,'' *Wall Street Journal*, May 9, 1991, p. A–14 (Dempsey is director of the Transportation Law Program at the University of Denver); and Suzy Hagstrom, ''Tax Breaks Offered UAL,'' *San Francisco Examiner*, May 7, 1991.

9. Wallace, *Black Women in the Labor Force*, pp. 10–22. In Professor Wallace's seminal work, a review of labor theory literature on married women interestingly focuses strongly on black married women. It is clear that the earliest interest of mainstream economists in black women in paid employment was for the model to shed light on the behavior of white female labor, which until the 1960s, as Wallace points out, was relegated to a ''consumer'' model. See also Glen Cain, *Married Women in the Labor Force: An Economic Analysis* (Chicago: University of Chicago Press, 1966).

10. U.S. Department of Labor, U.S. Bureau of Labor Statistics, *Current Population Survey, 1982* (data tapes compiled for the present study) (Washington, DC: U.S. Department of Labor, 1982); U.S. Bureau of Census, ''Money Income and Poverty Status of Families and Persons in the United States, 1982,'' *Current Population Reports*, Series P–60, No. 140 (Washington, DC: 1982).

11. U.S. Department of Labor, U.S. Bureau of Labor Statistics, ''Linking Employment Problems and Economic Status,'' *Bulletin 2169*, Tables 3–8 (Washington, DC, June 1983), pp. 9–10.

12. Bette Woody, ''Executive Women: Models of Corporate Success'' (Wellesley, MA: Wellesley College, Center for Research on Women, 1986). This report summarizes case studies and interviews with 36 corporate human resources managers on new low-end work systems. See also Myra Strober and Carolyn Arnold, ''Occupational Segregation Among Bank Tellers,'' in Clair Brown and Joseph A. Pechman (eds.), *Gender in the Workplace* (Washington, DC: Brookings Institution, 1987), p. 113.

13. See Bennett Harrison, *Education, Training and the Urban Ghetto* (Baltimore: Johns Hopkins University Press, 1972) for an early analysis of employment turnover and secondary labor markets.

14. Julianne Malveaux, ''From Domestic Worker to Household Technician: Black Women in a Changing Occupation,'' in Phyllis Wallace, *Women in the Workplace* (Boston: Auburn House, 1982), p. 85; and Debra Lynn Newman, ''Black Women Workers in the Twentieth Century,'' *Sage*, 3, no. 1 (Spring 1986), pp. 2–14.

15. See William Julius Williams, *The Declining Significance of Race* (Chicago: University of Chicago Press, 1980), particularly Chapter 4. For a view that focuses more on regional growth and residential dispersal patterns and impacts on black economic status, see Phillip Clay, ''Housing, Neighborhoods and Development,'' in Phillip Clay (ed.),

The Emerging Black Community of Boston (Boston: Institute for the Study of Black Culture, University of Massachusetts, n.d. [c. 1988]), pp. 115–144.

16. See James Jennings, "Race and Political Change in Boston," in Clay, *The Emerging Black Community*, pp. 314–337, for an excellent analysis of how local politics interfaced with job creation and employment to produce devastating results on minority and particularly black communities during the 1970s at a time of economic boom. See also Hubie Jones, "Introduction," in James Jennings and Mel King (eds.), *From Access to Power* (Cambridge, MA: Schenkman Books, 1986), which notes that "the cruelest form of racism experienced by the black community . . . has been the failure of white office holders to reward black voters adequately for making their political successes possible"(p. 4).

17. Weir, "The Federal Government and Unemployment."

18. See Peter Flora and Arnold Heidenheimer (eds.), *The Development of Welfare States in Europe and America* (New Brunswick, NJ: Transaction Books, 1987); and Richard L. Rowan, Kenneth Pitterle, and Philip Misciamarra, *Multinational Union Organizations in the White Collar, Services and Communications Industry* (Philadelphia: Industrial Research Unit, The Wharton School, University of Pennsylvania, 1983) for review of government labor policies in OECD (Organization for Economic Cooperation and Development) countries and Asia.

19. Bluestone and Harrison, "The Great American Jobs Machine," p. 23.

20. Wallace, *Black Women in the Labor Force.*

21. William A. Darity, Jr. and Samuel L. Myers, Jr., "Public Policy and the Black Family," *Review of the Black Political Economy*, 13, nos. 1–2 (Summer–Fall 1985), pp. 165–187.

22. U.S. Bureau of Census, *Bulletin 2169*, pp. 9–10.

23. A number of analysts have disputed the simplicity of the "culture of poverty" thesis. Sociologist Robert Dentler, for example, defines social problems as not only the outcome of social behavior, but a combination of cultural values and rules and institutions that can have varying performances in meeting standards. He suggests that standards themselves may become a "social problem" if expectations go unmet. Poverty, he suggests, is thus rooted in the relation between national economy, political culture, and the family system. See Robert Dentler, *American Community Problems* (New York: McGraw-Hill, 1968), pp. 4–7.

24. Oscar Lewis, *The Children of Sanchez* (New York: Random House, 1961).

25. For a critique of neoconservative analysis of poverty and current policy impacts, see William A. Darity, Jr. and Samuel Myers, Jr. Book Review: "Losing Ground: American Social Policy, 1950–1980, by Charles Murray," in Margaret C. Simms and Julienne Malveaux (eds.), *Slipping Through the Cracks: The Status of Black Women* (New Brunswick, NJ: Transaction Books, 1987). Martin Kilson, "Paradoxes of American Acculturation," paper delivered at the International Symposium on Cultural Pluralism, University of Toronto, October 19, 1985, traces much of neoconservative tendencies to the tension between dominant Anglo-Saxon culture and partly acculturated ethnic classes. A combination of political-social structure and institutions has maintained enough tension to provide periodic recurrence of more aggressive hostility toward "outside" or "new" population groups, including occasional paranoia such as extreme "fear" of loss of prestige status.

26. Lynn Burbridge, "Black Women in Employment and Training Programs," in Simms and Malveaux, *Slipping Through the Cracks*, p. 98.

27. For example, see Diane R. Brown, "Socio-Demographic v. Domain Predictors of Perceived Stress: Racial Differences Among American Women," *Social Indicators Research*, 20 (1988), pp. 517–532.

28. Ann Orloff, "The Political Origins of America's Belated Welfare State," in Weir et al., *Social Policy*, pp. 37–38.

29. Robert Reich, *Tales of a New America* (New York: Vintage Books, 1987).

30. U.S. Census data.

31. For discussion and review of job groups, restructuring, and deskilling in the work force and their relation to gender and race, see Heidi Hartman, "Internal Labor Markets and Gender: A Case Study of Promotion," in Brown and Pechman, *Gender in the Workplace*, pp. 59–87; Francine D. Blau, *Equal Pay in the Office* (Lexington, MA: Lexington Books, 1977), pp. 65–69; and Rosabeth M. Kanter, "The Impact of Hierarchical Structures on the Work Behavior of Women and Men," in Kahn-Hut et al., *Women and Work*, pp. 237–238.

CHAPTER 2

Black Women in Paid Employment

To date, only limited attention has been given in labor theory to the role of black women in the paid economy. The absence of historical data handicaps analysis and documentation of the changing position of black women in the workplace. Traditional labor statistics also submerged black women with black men and white women workers, complicating the task of identifying black women as wage earners. One result is a continuing bias that views black women exclusively in terms of social, reproductive, and family roles. Such limited views of black women, however, ignore evidence of the historical role of black women as wage earners and significant contributors to the economic well-being of black families. In some cases, black women provided the principal work force for entire sectors in the economy. What helps define the historical role of black women as workers and at the same time limits analysis, is segregation and discrimination. As recently as the mid-1960s when legal discrimination in employment ended, black women were severely restricted in the workplace to a few occupational categories and industrial sectors in the economy. This restriction is partly the basis for the broad judgment about spectacular recent improvements made by black women in the work economy. A closer examination of progress, however, is more sobering. Black women have endured a very long history in the workplace with exceptional efforts, high labor force participation, strong work force attachment, and motivation for more than a century, despite extraordinary constraints.[1]

Traditional labor theory is both helpful and limited in understanding the behavior and position of black women as a labor force. Neoclassical theory, with its emphasis on labor market equilibrium and wages resulting from an open competitive bid process between worker and employer, offers little to explain either the attachment of black women to the labor force or their limited mobility and wages. In fact, theory largely ignores discrimination barriers as a variable.

Traditional labor market theory thus relies heavily on the concept of "human capital" characteristics, particularly education, to explain differences in individual capacities and wages of workers. Improvements in the educational attainment of black women has occurred, but differences in wages and occupations between black women and other workers remain. Newer theories challenging traditional equilibrium models have improved the framework for analysis of black women, but they still leave important questions unanswered.

Challenges to traditional labor theory in the form of institutional or segmentation analysis have grown recently. In a focus on the general limitations of classical equilibrium models, particular emphasis has been placed on discrimination. Greatly simplified, newer theory hypothesizes that the labor market consists of a complex set of discrete submarkets, each governed by different rules for entry, upward mobility, ultimate status, and security. There are rigid boundaries between each market, with the result that the different labor pools are manipulated to meet particular needs and are characterized by different reward patterns. While most of the initial work on segmentated labor markets centered on black men, more recently women have received increased attention. The particularly unique position of black women as characteristic of a "dual trait" means that the interface between gender and race in labor markets must be more fully acknowledged.

The rapid change in the position of women in the labor force has raised important questions not posed in the case of black men. The issue of labor force attachment of women, for example, has been subject to a lot of analysis. Much of traditional analysis of white female labor was subsumed in a model built on a kind of "sociology of women's work." Women, particularly white women, were either "adjunct family earners" with behavior and wages related to a household consumption model, or unpaid contributors to family income as in the case of agricultural or family business workers.[2] More important, underlying the stress on women as adjunct earners was a strong behavioral model that characterized women as choosing between family and work, or subordinating work to family. In the latter case, women would adjust both wage demands and occupational status downward to account for "intermittent" or "part-time" employment.[3] The rapid expansion of women in full-time employment during the 1970s, however, shifted analysis to entirely new questions about wages. Observed concentrations of women in entirely different occupations than men were seen as explaining long-standing differences in access, wages, mobility, and stability in the workplace. The result was yet another conception of segmentation as gender-defined as well as limited by industrial group and other internal market parameters, including levels of capital investment, unionization, and productivity characteristics.

In the case of black women, new attention to institutional barriers and to women has helped enlighten the problems of occupational and workplace status. On the one hand, segmentation analysis raised the question of whether human capital characteristics or barriers to entry account most for a historically marginal status. Research on gender helped explain somewhat the severe concentration of black women in a very limited range of occupations. But at the same time, questions remained about the historical differences between black and white women in labor force participation as dual earners, in patterns of effort, and in how black women fit the "family" model of women's choice between home and market work. These considerations give rise to a set of investigations focused specifically on the interface between gender and race in labor markets.[4] Black women are increasingly viewed as constituting a separate submarket within a highly stratified market, both as a labor pool and as a deployment model.

There is little question that the status of black women has improved dramatically over the recent past, at least in part because of visible gains in educational attainment and other pre-employment training. But most change is probably caused by changes in the demand side of the labor market. Broad trends in economic expansion and structural alterations in the industry mix are important factors that transformed the occupational structure and mix and produced massive new opportunities for new labor pools. Massive job expansions of the mid-1960s through the 1970s were particularly important to black women. While it is difficult to speculate on the impact of the end to legal employment discrimination, the timing undoubtedly helped black women as a new labor pool who were already in the work force prior to the massive entry of white women into the labor force.

This chapter explores the current framework for assessing the changing labor market position of black women. It first examines current theory and then looks at trends in labor force participation and occupational status changes for black women.

LABOR THEORY AND BLACK WOMEN: DISCRIMINATION AND STRATIFICATION

Traditional economic theory has long viewed labor as one of three main inputs into economic production along with capital and know-how. Labor, however, contrasts with other commodities in several respects. First, there is considerable control exercised by the owner or "renter" of human resources in qualitative content and in hours offered in the market. Second, because of the complex characteristics and differences among individuals, the contributions of labor to productivity are difficult to measure and assign. Third, in the short run it is harder to adjust labor inputs for different production levels than capital or know-how.

Labor theory has traditionally been concerned mainly with the supply side of the labor equation and particularly with the behavior and decisions of the individual to enter the labor force, at what level, when to retire, and to make or not make particular self-investments. For example, workers are presumed to influence the supply of labor available ultimately through individual decisions to participate in or withdraw from the work force. Individual decisions control the level of intensity or hours or willingness to work, as well as motivation and performance on the job. Characteristic differences among worker categories that underscore differences in human capital also justify differences in pay and mobility. The worker, however, controls these through decisions to "self-invest" in preemployment education and training and geographic relocation. Finally, much of the choice individuals make is influenced by household budgets, other income available, and life-style. A key theory, for example, hypothesizes a balance between income derived from market work and value placed on leisure. Women were also long theorized to balance noneconomic benefits of family against earnings in paid employment. Ultimately, the labor market model rests on a strong assumption that individual taste and preference may overrule economic decisions.

On the employer or demand side, the traditional labor market model hypothesizes that producers calculate labor requirements partly from aggregate costs of inputs into production, including labor, and partly on external market conditions such as competitor prices. To set production inputs, efficiencies and trade-offs are then calculated by individual producers between separate costs of labor, capital, and know-how, which must be balanced. This gives rise to substitutions as between capital and labor. As far as the recruitment of labor is concerned, traditional theory offers a complex bidding process wherein workers are hired at specific skill levels and quantity (i.e., hours) at wage levels determined by aggregate (i.e., external) markets. The model assumes that market conditions are "competitive": there are many producers and many workers such that there is no collusion by either side in setting wages, and labor is perfectly mobile among different producers. While there are many labor markets in the traditional model, these markets reflect objective qualitative differences among workers, such as scarcity, education, and skills. Thus, a core of the classical equilibrium model is that human capital is the most important determinant of the individual worker's value in contributing to production and this in turn is reflected in wages offered.

Challenges to the traditional labor model in recent years have centered on several grounds. The assumptions about competitiveness of the labor market and its efficiency in allocating work and wages across labor groups are at the center of the challenge. Institutional analysts argue that labor markets are far from the competitive free market model. Evidence is offered that large oligopolist producers increasingly dominate the marketplace. These producers can internalize capital and labor markets, thus ignoring external cost and wage pressures. Moreover, they can absorb most labor inefficiencies and ignore human capital characteristics through internal training, education, application of technology and equipment, and managerial innovation. Second, because human capital characteristics required by employers are mainly gained not prior to employment, but on the job, larger employers tend to hire "generic workers" for all but the most skilled specializations. In the case of smaller employers, very different calculations result. These production activities in more competitive markets may be reduced to limiting "skilled specializations" to very low levels and, in fact, limiting production to mainly that requiring minimum skills. Low-wage, low-skilled, high-turnover markets are the result. Finally, changes in the labor market may reflect very real restructuring of production activities as the result of shifts in the mix of large and small producers. Thus, many larger producers may resort to internal "cheap labor" activities, to contracting out to smaller marginal producers, or to generally "shrinking" those workers that have traditionally benefited from commitment, high wages, and protection.

A second broad challenge to neoclassical theory posed by institutional analysts is on how internal markets and wage schedules are set. While traditional theory argues that external market demand sets wages, new evidence argues that wages may be mainly the result of internal markets that are defined by job clusters and job groups by dominant producers. Thus, several internal organizations of jobs and wages have evolved to constitute internal wage policy that may or may not correspond to a market-characterized occupational and wage system. In effect, such internal markets permit maximum flexibility in hiring and deploying workers, in commitment to workers over time, and in the amount of mobility assumed in occupational categories. Many larger services employers—such as banking, insurance, retailing, and goods handling—have been subject to such new hiring and wage policy directions. This is related ostensively to organizational change and productivity goals.[5]

Alternatives to classical theories most often focus on how institutional factors operate to restrict the match occurring between workers and jobs. From these institutional factors, differentials in wages and status among subgroups in the work force arise.[6] While institutional theories are less systematic and elegant than traditional market models, the arguments nonetheless tackle important questions related to the existence of marginal work forces such as blacks and women in an otherwise "efficient" labor market. With the proportion of the labor force of these special groups now approaching half, a new theory becomes increasingly imperative.

Institutional arguments center on the notion that the economy has evolved into discrete production units that shape labor demand less in terms of human capital available and an open bidding process adjusted to the needs of production than a marketplace consisting of very limited access points for different labor groups. Dividing the economy into at least two tiers, institutional analysts find one level consists of stable, capital-rich producers who recruit, hire, train, and deploy workers under favorable wage and working conditions, ignoring competitive open market conditions. A second, increasingly significant, part of the production market, however, consists of marginal producers operating in highly competitive open markets, with very unfavorable conditions for labor. The firms in this second competitive group are forced to operate under the realities of low profit margins, lack capital resources, and have little capacity to withstand the effects of business cycle downswings or other external market pressures. These firms are forced to use high turnover in the labor market, layoffs, reduced training, and other commitments to labor over time, as well as lower compensation in obtaining and utilizing their labor forces. Meanwhile, major firms that occasionally dominate industry use a labor pool with little interaction with other labor markets; they create internal labor pools, tolerate unions, limit access, and create internal rules that allow improvements in wages and benefits as well as maintain job security in a protected fashion. This alternative model has major implications for the classical labor model. Workers become highly productive and highly paid, not because of higher quality human capital or more intensive contributions to profits, but because they are hired in one market.

A key aspect of the challenge of the institutional to traditional labor theory has come in the form of a more specific attention to discrimination against some workers. Discrimination by definition is a pattern or deliberate preference for hiring, deployment, and compensation of some workers over others, usually based on personal characteristics that can be noneconomic in nature. Traditional market theorists do not deny institutional segregation or the failure of firms to hire workers based on color, ethnic origin, or sex, but rather view the issue less as disrupting the efficiency of the market than more a problem of measuring the exact distribution and impact of such costs.[7] Gary Becker and others hypothesized models of "preferences" for discrimination, then looked for evidence to test whether or not institutional barriers against blacks, for example, might be significant and result in net benefits that make discrimination "economic" to the firm.

Discrimination Theories

A chief failure of labor theory remains to explain the restricted access of some labor groups to certain job markets. Another related problem is the persistence of low wages for some groups over time. In particular, the cases of minority males and women have been increasingly viewed as either demonstrating bias based on noneconomic characteristics in labor markets or of a failure of theory to provide alternative explanations. Traditional arguments explained differential access and wages of minorities and women compared to white males by using human capital theory on the one hand and, on the other, the preferences of individual workers to forgo wages for other gains. An explanation consistent with the market model was evolved to explain how discriminatory wage systems could exist, for example, without disrupting the overall equilibrium and efficiency of the market. To illustrate, lower quality human capital would result in general restrictions of blacks at the lower end of the market, including low-wage jobs and marginal, low-profit industry. In the case of women who clustered in particular occupations and industry, behavior was used as an explanation. Low productivity industries where most women elected to work, paid lower wages. Why women would elect to concentrate in such industries as health care and retailing, however, was not explained.[8]

The lower wages for women are most often explained by a theory of personal choice. Women are hypothesized to choose the kind of work in which they are employed because it is less physically demanding and "cleaner," and because the work may require less work force attachment or intermittent employment. An important theory, for example, postulates that women are willing to discount "clean" work in lower wages. But with the entry of women during World War II into occupations requiring physical exertion in less clean environments and more recently with the opening of "men's" jobs following passage of Title VII of the Equal Employment Opportunity legislation of the mid-1960s, the theory of clean work has eroded. Another theory that received considerable attention is that of "intermittent employment," wherein women work jobs at lower pay to allow interruption to raise families and are willing to accept lower wages for "rusty" skills.[9] Thus, women prefer not to have careers or jobs that require long-term commitments to typical career ladders. Others argue, however, that such theory merely rationalizes biases that continue to operate to exclude women and minorities, which are based on stereotypes of their expected behavior. The anticipation on the part of employers that women will behave as though they will interrupt their careers acts to reinforce past bias and justifies deployment in jobs that lack career stability and promotions upward.[10]

An important question that remains is how market efficiency is maintained under discriminatory rules that favor some workers and hurt others. Economist Gary Becker's model of the labor market suggests that although some costs may be absorbed by producers as the result of exercising preferential hiring, say of white males over women or black men, the longer term benefits will outweigh such costs in the form of wages paid the "preferred" (i.e., white male) worker.[11] In a segregated labor market, while producers may be indifferent to worker characteristics, market conditions and particularly the potential for hiring the most reliable and best-quality work force (i.e., white men), might be contingent on either avoiding the withdrawal of white males altogether or paying very high premiums to such workers to work alongside of others for whom there is distaste. In either case, a producer might be forced to exclude the less desirable worker altogether. And while the producer would pay a somewhat higher cost to reflect the reduced supply of labor in the form of a "labor shortage penalty," such costs would be lower than the high premium paid for an integrated work force.

Segmentation of Industry and Markets

Recent structural change in the U.S. economy, coupled with the rise of overseas competition, has reoriented much of the debate about labor markets. A new focus also has been given to the growth of women workers in the economy. The recent expansion of women in the workplace has raised questions about the utilization and role of women compared to male workers in the economy. Discussions have been dominated by the problem of how labor has become more marginal and how productivity and the relationship between labor and output or production have changed as the U.S. economy has shifted from a goods-

producing to a services economy, as well as multinational dimensions that produce change in organization and labor structure.[12] In part, the discussion has
focused on growth of a dual or two-tiered economy, consisting of primary and
secondary production sectors, mentioned above. A second discussion has looked
more at an economy of the future, where the deployment of labor reflects more
flexible production systems and internal labor market segmentation. Much less
has been written about the services sector, which now dominates the U.S. work
economy.[13]

The theory of the two-tiered economy, as noted earlier, evolved from the
work of economists examining the effects of institutional factors on the labor
market. As a point of departure, analysts such as Gordon, Bluestone and Harrison, and Reich argue that Western capitalism in the post-World War II period
maintained output principally because of a unique historical set of circumstances:[14] the absence of competition from foreign producers as Europe and Japan
were recovering from the war; a highly internalized domestic market for production; a virtual world monopoly on some strategic production, such as agricultural commodities; and finally, an expanding market for a defense industry
fueled by domestic growth taxes and abroad by American credit. With little or
no competition in the post-Korea world economy, U.S. production grew at a
reasonable pace with a minimum of market reorientation, new products or capital,
or research and development (R&D) investment.[15]

Problems, however started to become visible by the mid-1960s. The "green
revolution" in the developing world, particularly in India, reduced the demand
for American agricultural commodities. This was followed by the steady growth
in competitors for U.S. production in agriculture, including Canada and even
parts of the developing world. Second, rising unemployment in the United States
and the exclusion of an increasingly large part of labor was less and less characterized as "normal," or reflecting cyclical downswings, and more and more
structural or permanent. Finally, as obsolescence and disinvestment took place
in the extractive industry and industry processing of basic raw materials, economists begin increasingly to talk of regional industrial decline and a permanent
loss of a manufacturing economy. The predicted evolution of the economy into
a structure comprised of core and periphery sectors was beginning to come true.[16]

To describe the new postindustrial economy, Gordon, Edwards, and Reich
contrasted traditional production and manufacturing sectors with new growth
sectors that combined manufacturing such as electronics with services such as
retailing and telecommunications:

Small peripheral firms have not been the only enterprises maintaining secondary labor
processes during recent decades. . . . Large corporations . . . size permits the flexibility to
operate in both labor markets . . . and many companies have chosen to take advantage of
both markets simultaneously. . . . In some industries that are dominated by large corporations . . . the large corporations have less impetus to transform the structure of the internal
labor market. Both electronics assembly and watch assembly . . . still rely on intensified

operative work and for the most part employ unskilled women. In both these industries both the level and rate of increase of average weekly earnings fall substantially below the average for all core industries.[17]

An important assumption by the analysts of the postindustrial decline is that value added per production worker, which measures the relative productivity in an industry, is really what distinguishes "core" from peripheral industry in job stability and wage terms. The analysts note that whether an industry is manufacturing, such as electronics, or retailing, if the output per worker has grown less than the U.S. average, it can be considered labor-intensive, geographically mobile, and a likely candidate for transfer of a major part of operations to low-wage locations such as the U.S. South or overseas. Thus, the real distinction of growth for these analysts is whether or not an industry is productive when measured against some national standard, and the extent to which labor becomes less and less productive as industry is transformed.

However, a number of problems arise with the thesis that the economy and labor with it are growing into a core-periphery structure. One problem relates to productivity and how a different quality of labor is used and paid. Gordon, for example, notes that firms solve the problem of losses in productivity not through making production more efficient, as in the case of automobile manufacturing, but rather through the device of contracting or "outsourcing" production to smaller, less stable businesses.[18] This practice permits large producers to have flexibility and control over costs that would normally have to be obtained through layoffs in the primary work force. Citing economists Doringer and Piore, Gordon notes that a "decasualization" of work has accompanied unionization of core workers, made by formal recognition of a permanent pool of casual workers with little or no attachment to the industry and only "residual employment rights." This means that two groups of workers are employed in the same industry and frequently in the same firm, on completely different bases; one is protected and works at high wages, while a second, unprotected group works under marginal conditions with few rights.

Segmentation theory introduces a somewhat different concept of how production is organized and how labor is utilized, although the results may be similar. Segmentation more particularly refers to the organization of work and tasks into different job groups or occupational categories, which in turn permits separation of labor forces and differential stability and compensation. One source for segmentation is the introduction of new techniques of corporate planning by business firms to radically alter the content of the average job. Occupational categories are then organized to break up jobs into discrete tasks with little relationship between them. Business repair services, the hospital and health care industry, insurance, and the computer industry are cited as examples of workplaces where segmentation has been introduced in a large way to increase productivity through limited use of labor. Gordon notes that through deliberate job design, firms now structure job content into minute, routine tasks, permitting a reduction in the number of "thinking" jobs and those requiring other cognitive skills:

The rapid growth of administrative functions has led many firms to organize some of their administrative operations along secondary labor market lines. For example, many corporations have relegated much of their standardized typing work into typing pools organized by secondary labor process principals; few opportunities for promotion exist, turnover can be high and virtually no on the job training takes place . . . some of the growth of temporary clerical services has also resulted from the same impetus.[19]

The aims and results of much segmentation are to raise productivity in what has been considered labor-intensive industry, particularly the services sector.

To date, few analysts have examined how the expansion of the services industry in the U.S. economy has reduced productivity overall, and whether the segmentation and managerial innovation and increased control or "deskilling" of many jobs through job redesign have halted this trend. This would be important in determining whether or not the low wages normally associated with low-productivity work are in fact justified. One problem is that economists assume that only traditional manufacturing production has capacity for increased productivity. This is why institutional analysts view the transformation of the U.S. economy into a services economy and the export of manufacturing with alarm.

There are two problems with the alarmist view. One is that manufacturing employment growth, while slower than services, has not resulted in a loss of position of the high-value production sector to the economy. A second problem is that services industries may in fact be undergoing some of the same transformations as manufacturing and, with it, gains in productivity may in fact be occurring. According to U.S. Census data, manufacturing has maintained a constant 30 percent of gross national product (GNP) since 1900, and durable goods production, for example, actually grew 27 percent between 1960 and 1980. Losses in GNP share in fact were almost entirely limited to agriculture and the extractive industry, sectors that did lose employment. In contrast to the growth of manufacturing jobs, employment in agriculture and mining dropped from 7.7 percent of total employment to 4.0 percent or a net loss of nearly a million jobs between 1960 and 1980. Thus, services employment more correctly "replaced" these manufacturing job losses. The second problem related to productivity in the services industry is more difficult. To date, there is no satisfactory measure of productivity in services or trade. It is nonetheless clear that two factors may change output per worker: (1) job consolidation, where multiple tasks and operations are restructured into single jobs, and (2) the introduction of computers or other mechanization or even management techniques to redesign job content. A third element may be the use of low-cost labor under hiring policies. If output per worker has increased in services, however, the question remains: Why don't wages increase corresponding with such gains? A final trend that should be noted is that of restructuring of production jobs into services jobs.

Recent growth of the production industry has shifted to services as between hardware and software in the computer industry or, in the case of telecommunications, in the sale and rental of basic services and away from hardware and systems.

Labor Market Segmentation and Women

At the core of segmentation arguments is a pattern of deployment of labor that results in stratification of certain labor groups and particularly women. In assessing the labor position of women, traditional labor theory focused less on the quality of human capital and more on individual participation decisions to explain women's participation in the paid work economy. Accordingly, women were long viewed as working outside the home to contribute to family income, but were adjusting their labor force participation to requirements of family. The resulting model of women workers hypothesized that women discount their intermittent employment in lower wages and a lower work force attachment.

Current research, however, challenges the theory that women discount their wages and make "noneconomic" choices as trade-offs for domestic responsibilities, or elect "women's work" to avoid dirty or physically demanding tasks. Rather, evidence is increasingly presented that artificial barriers, whether intended or not, exert important constraints on the access of women to certain occupations and industry. Economist Barbara Bergmann, for example, recently noted that the rising contribution of women to total family income, coupled with the increased value placed on time by women, has resulted in rising wages. This contradicts past arguments that women make deliberate choices to take low-wage employment, reduced work weeks, or otherwise engage in noneconomic behavior when options are indeed accessible. Bergman notes:

An important part of the explanation of women's exodus from exclusive domesticity is the substantial increase over the decades in the wage rate—the price paid for the time they might spend on a job. While the benefit from working at a paid job was rising, the benefit of staying home was declining, as women had fewer children. The benefits of going out to work were bound to catch up with and surpass the benefits of staying home for more and more women. . . . the data indicates that women's real wages have more than quadrupled since 1890. . . . The quantity of commodities a woman could buy with her earnings from an hour's work at a job has grown by 1.64 percent per year on average, between 1890 and 1985.[20]

This value of time calculus by women has been reinforced by social changes that have sustained a momentum that, as Bergman points out, was maintained even when real wages fell—as happened between 1973 and 1984.[21]

Despite the fuller response of women to rising wages, however, a key problem remains in the form of a continuing rigid stratification of jobs and wages open to them. Women's labor, despite improvements, still appears overwhelmingly channeled into static occupational categories that limit mobility to higher status and wage earning. This system of rigid boundaries among occupations caused by occupational clusters may heighten competition for some jobs and result in ''crowding'' and depressed wages. At the same time, artificial labor shortages may be maintained in occupations where women are excluded, and they artificially raise wages. Thus the overall system may suffer from inefficiencies in allocation of human resources. Nowhere is this evidence of segmentation more visible than in the gender structuring of jobs in the rapidly expanding services industry.

Most of the evidence of segmentation of the women's labor market is derived from examination of high concentrations, or ''overrepresentation,'' of women in a limited number of occupational categories. Economist Julienne Malveaux, for example, noted that job stratification for women has vastly different implications than in the case of men:

Job segregation is compounded by the fact that fewer occupational opportunities are available to women than men. . . . In 1981, nearly fifty percent of all women worked in just fifty-three occupations (of 429) that were more than eighty percent male, while nearly sixty five percent of all men worked in some two hundred eleven occupations that were more than eighty percent male. The fact that women are crowded into fewer occupations than males, partly explains why men suffer no ill effects from occupational stratification that they also experience.[22]

Much recent analysis of women has focused on the relative concentration and dispersal of women workers across occupations compared to male workers.[23] In a recent review of occupational segregation, Strober and Arnold noted that in 1980, with women making up 42 percent of the work force, of 503 occupational categories in the U.S. Census, 19 percent were female-intensive, 48 percent male-intensive, and 33 percent neutral. According to these calculations, about 65 percent of women were employed in female-intensive occupations; about 6 percent in male-intensive occupations, and about 31 percent in neutral occupations.[24] Most frequently the jobs women get are those that require a high-quality labor force (education and skills), but that are generally in labor-intensive low productivity industry. While aggregate data are lacking on trends in the restructuring of jobs in the economy, case study evidence indicates that in some industries such organization is taking place through the design of jobs specifically targeted to female hiring at the firm level, such as in retailing, health care, and insurance.[25] Many such jobs are restructured tasks from categories that in the past required higher cognitive and thinking skills and implied commitments by employers over time. The new jobs, by contrast, are increasingly compartmentalized into routine, repetitive tasks that lack discretion. The result is growth of industry where new jobs and job groups that are entirely flexible for change by employers as mechanization or other managerial change takes place in the future. A final trend is for jobs structured to allow the shifting of tasks downward to lower status staff from more costly professionals—as in the case of health care, where paraprofessionals have increased responsibilities in patient care and administration, reducing workloads of nurses and other higher paid medical personnel.[26]

Theories about the status and behavior of black women in the paid work force have increasingly used segmentation theory to take into account the dual effects of gender and race. Malveaux examined employment data on black and white women and found that when age, experience, and educational attainment are controlled, black women are the most "crowded" of all labor groups in occupations in the economy.[27]

When the segmentation hypothesis is applied to black women, the results are a more intense version of gender disadvantage. Women's jobs, or the occupations where women are most concentrated, tend to be undifferentiated and lack the specialization of jobs dominated by male workers as well as the range of wages. In the case of black women, concentration is limited to even fewer occupational categories and narrower wage ranges. To test the full extent of stratification and costs impacts, Malveaux examined 1980 U.S. Census data on occupations where black women were considerably more segregated than white women. She found that only 30 percent of all black women work in jobs not stratified by race and sex.[28]

Malveaux's work confirmed the hypothesis that occupational stratification, or the kinds of job categories workers are hired into, constitutes the principal factor behind status differentials between black women and other workers. She found that in occupations where black women were crowded (or exceeded their proportion in the labor force of 5.4 percent, compared to a similar measure of women overall of 48 percent), the crowding was far greater among black women than women as a whole.[29]

Segmentation and stratification occur not only across occupations, but they influence vertical occupational structures as well and are visible from the top status categories of professional-managerial ranks downward through status clerical positions. To illustrate, the fast-growing services occupations show high concentrations of black women at lower status levels, compared to white women.[30]

WHO WORKS? LABOR FORCE PARTICIPATION OF BLACK WOMEN

Black women have historically entered the workforce in larger numbers and stayed longer than white women. This results in higher proportions of adult black women either working or actively seeking work. As Table 2.1 illustrates, black women made up nearly one-third of all black workers in the U.S. work force historically and through the 1950s, then dramatically increased their share of the black work force over the past four decades. By the 1980s, nearly half of all black workers in the U.S. economy were women. Black women's share of women's employment, though historically higher than their proportion in the

Table 2.1
Black Women Workers as a Percentage of Total Black and Total Female Workers

Year	As a % of Black Workers	As a % of Women Workers
1920	32.3	18.9
1940	32.8	14.3
1950	34.3	12.7
1960	39.8	13.1
1970	43.6	12.7
1982	48.8	12.0

Source: Phyllis Wallace, *Black Women in the Labor Force* (Cambridge, MA: MIT Press, 1982),
   p. 7; and U.S. Department of Labor, Bureau of Labor Statistics, *Current Population Survey,*
   1982 (Micro Data Tapes) (Washington, DC, 1982). Hereafter cited as *CPS 1982.*

population of women of working age of about 11 percent, has, however, declined steadily over the past decades as more white women have entered the work force and as unemployment has risen.[31]

Causes behind these patterns in higher labor force participation are complex and still unclear. The growth in black women's share of total black employment undoubtedly reflects several changes, including the massive expansion of the number of jobs available to women in the economy, the growth of women alone heading families, decline in black family income in recent years, and possibly the slowing of growth of black male employment, particularly at the lower skills end of the occupational structure. But it also may reflect a recent, massive retreat of black men out of the paid economy. This is reflected in the decline of black men of working age in the labor force. The decline is especially visible among young black men.

As Table 2.2 on labor force participation of four groups between 1960 and 1980 indicates, the proportion of both black and white males eligible to work declined, reflecting an overall trend. But black male participation rates fell at almost four times the rate of white males. Although black male unemployment rates were double those of white men, this did not account for the drop in labor force participation.

Some clues about the lower rates of labor force participation rates of black men are offered from an examination of age-specific rates for younger age groups. As Table 2.3 indicates, black male teenagers are considerably less likely to be in the labor force than white males, and unemployment is almost two times that of white men of the same age and black males overall. However, when the next cohort of 20- to 24-year olds is examined, and particularly the relation between unemployment and labor force participation rates, higher unemployment does not entirely explain the failure of black men to enter the work force. As Table 2.3 indicates, unemployment is high for all black males. However, the striking

Table 2.2
Labor Force Participation Rates of U.S. Workers by Race and Sex, 1960–80

	White: Male	Female	Black: Male	Female
1960				
% in the Labor Force 16 years, over	78.0	33.6	72.1	41.8
% unemployed	4.6	4.9	8.8	8.5
1980				
% in the Labor Force 16 years, over	76.1	49.4	66.7	55.3
% unemployed	5.9	5.7	12.3	11.3
Change 1960-1980				
% in the Labor Force	-2.5	47.0	-8.1	32.3

Source: U.S. Department of Commerce, Bureau of the Census, *Census of the Population*, Table 287: "Industry of Employed Persons by Sex, Race and Spanish Origin," pp. 1–372–377 (for 1980 data) [hereafter cited as *Census of the Population*, Table 287]; and Table 213: "Industry of the Experienced Civilian Labor Force and of the Employed and Unemployment Rate, by Color and Sex for the United States," pp. 5–6 (for 1960 data) [hereafter cited as *Census of the Population*, Table 213].

Table 2.3
Labor Force Participation Rates for U.S. Workers by Race, Sex, and Age, 1980

	% in the Labor Force	Unemployed	Not in the Labor Force	% in Institutions
White		Total (000')		
Males 16+ yrs	76.1	5.9	16,650 826	5.0
16-19 yrs	55.1	14.0		
20-24 yrs	84.3	10.2		
Females				
16 yrs, over	49.4	5.7	58,540 48,540	1.9
Black				
Males 16+ yrs	66.7	12.3	2,791 277	9.9
16-19 yrs	36.5	27.6		
20-24 yrs	73.5	20.3		
Females				
16 yrs, over	55.3	11.3	4,637 90	1.9
16-19 yrs	30.3	27.9		
20-24 yrs	61.4	18.7		

Source: *Census of the Population*, Table 287.

difference in the proportion of teen-age black males in the labor force and the older group is not commensurate with the difference in unemployment. Various explanations have been offered for trends in low labor force participation of young black men, including incarceration rates, disability, and lack of information about available work. These causes, however, still need to be verified through empirical research.

A reduction in labor force participation among older black men has also taken place over the past decades, which may have different causes than that affecting young men. Several explanations have been offered, but none have been confirmed by evidence. One explanation to account for the withdrawal of older men is the increased availability of disability insurance. The increased level of benefits, coupled with the higher likelihood that older black males may be in poor health, has given rise to this thesis.[32] Another popular explanation centers on the underground employment thesis. According to this, black men have expectations of earnings that are based on some income level that exceeds market wages but is derived from illegal, irregular, or underground employment, which constitutes a kind of "reserve wage" floor. In this case, the reserve wage may constitute a barrier to the group in accepting low-wage jobs.[33] Finally, data examined in this analysis suggested some causes related to the absolute loss of some kinds of employment formerly held by black men. In addition to laborer's jobs in the construction industry, a number of low-wage, low-skills services jobs appear to have been lost to the economy over the past two decades. For older men, at least, these job options might account for some labor force withdrawal.

The principal outcome of the reduction of employment among black males appears to have been to transfer work responsibilities to black women. While labor force participation rates among black women grew by about one-third between 1960 and 1980, black women heading families increased from about one-third to over half during the same period. At the same time, black male labor force participation decreased by 8 percent of the eligible work force.

Labor force participation by black women, compared to white counterparts, however, declined over the past two decades. Between 1960 and 1980, this gap narrowed from 11.7 percentage points to 3.8. The chief explanation was the growth in the number of white women entering the labor force. The proportion of white women of working age in the labor force increased by 13.6 percent. Causes for the slowing of growth of black women's participation in the work force by the mid-1980s, despite the growth in headship rates, are unclear. One recent analysis of declines in work force participation rates by black women finds that unemployment may be the chief cause.[34] Other causes may relate to a reduction of older black women in the work force. With the expansion of Social Security and other programs to support older Americans, black women, who constitute a larger proportion of the work force than black men and who tend to work in very low-paid, low-status jobs such as domestics, may have been able to retire at higher rates than previously.

By far the largest group of nonparticipants among black women is very young women, particularly teenagers. In 1980, for example, less than one-third of black women between 14 and 20 years old were in the work force, compared to nearly half of all white teenage women. Causes for this difference are not entirely clear. The gap does narrow and becomes negligible by age 20, however. One explana-

Table 2.4

Labor Force Participation Rates for Women by Marital Status, 1978

	Black	White
Single	43.0	61.9
Married		
husband present	56.7	45.8
husband absent	53.1	56.3
Widowed	26.6	21.9
Divorced	67.5	74.4
Total	49.3	47.8

Source: Wallace, *Black Women in the Labor Force* p. 108.

tion offered is the higher fertility rates among black teenage women compared to white counterparts, which could postpone entry of black women into the labor force. Another explanation may be in the form of ''discouraged workers.'' Since unemployment among black teenage women in 1980 stood at nearly twice the rate of white counterparts, it is possible that an even larger number had simply given up trying to find work. Studies on teenage unemployment, as well as programs to help, have been almost exclusively oriented toward black males and thus there is little documentation on how black girls approach the job search, the kind of information they have about employment opportunity, and their attitudes. Since a large proportion of black teenage women drop out of high school before receiving high school diplomas, this could compound the problem of obtaining jobs. Many jobs that are available to teenagers require minimum typing and office work skills. There is some evidence that there are important relationships between low school achievement and dropout rates among black girls.[35]

A key factor influencing the labor force participation rate of black women is marital status. While marital patterns and family formation patterns differ greatly between black and white women, the influence on decisions to work are in some sense parallel. As the data in Table 2.4 for 1978 indicate, marital status acts in quite contrasting ways between the races. While single status tends to increase the participation rates of white women, black women tend to participate at lower rates overall. This is particularly true of those women who have never married. By contrast, marriage still acts to reduce the rate of labor force participation among white women, but increases participation among black women. The very striking difference in participation between black single women and white counterparts, however, is not entirely clear. It may result from the low participation rates of black teenage women just mentioned.

Labor force participation by black women also reflects patterns, as noted earlier, related to age and life cycle.[36] Data provided by economist Phyllis Wallace examining age cohorts and participation rates indicated that between 1960 and 1978, white women between ages 16 and 19, or entry-level ages, increased their participation in the work force rapidly, effectively widening an initial gap with black teenagers. Among young working-age groups aged 20 to 34, similar work force participation differentials characterized the two groups over the period. But among older or prime working-age years of 35 to 54, black women substantially exceeded white women in participation in the work force, although the rate of growth was slightly less even among this group than that of white women. The lower growth rates of the prime working-age group of black women, however, is clearly a reflection of the accelerated entry of white married women into the work force as noted above. Finally, for women aged 55 and over, the participation rates of the two races are similar, with similar declines after age 65.[37]

CONCLUSIONS

Traditional labor theory has neglected discussions about the position and problems associated with black women in the paid economy. Nonetheless, there is strong evidence that the roles and contributions of black women have been significant both in certain parts of the work economy and to black family income. Recent changes in the status of black women have resulted not only in a stronger economic role, but increased interest in the problems of the group in policy. Growth in the dependency of black families on the wages of black women workers has also called attention to the need for new thinking and theory.

Classical labor theory argues that a key determinant of work status and wages is the different human capital or skills that workers bring to the marketplace. Because black women were traditionally poorly educated, their restriction to low-paid work could be explained. With improvements in educational attainment and with the acknowledgement that discrimination was widespread and limited the kinds of work black women could obtain until the mid-1960s, analysts turned to other causes to explain the persistent gap between their wages and those of other labor groups. Some explanations under investigation are stratified labor markets. These can be divided either following a ''primary-peripheral'' dichotomy or according to gender-specific or ''male-female'' jobs. While such theses help to understand forces that contribute to the problems black women face in proving their work status and wages, questions remain, including why segregation of black women continues in newer, nontraditional work and why work force participation of younger black women is so low. In the latter case, it is not clear whether this is a prediction of the future and a decline in the long tradition of work force participation by black women, or if it reflects problems that are unique to this age group. A final problem with current theory is that it has never adequately examined the relationship between the work behavior of black men and that of black women, to define whether patterns are related. This has critical implications for the future of the black family.

NOTES

1. Phyllis Wallace, *Black Women in the Labor Force* (Cambridge, MA: MIT Press, 1982); Barbara Jones, ''Black Women and Labor Force Participation: An Analysis of Sluggish Growth Rates,'' in Margaret Simms and Julianne Malveaux (eds.), *Slipping*

Through the Cracks: The Status of Black Women (New Brunswick, NJ: Transaction Books, 1987), p.11.

2. Wallace, ibid.

3. For a discussion of work-family wages trade-offs, intermittent employment, and women's behavior, see Barbara Bergmann, *The Economic Emergence of Women*, (New York: Basic Books), 1986, p. 137; Patricia Gwartney-Gibbs, "Women's Work Experience and the 'Rusty Skills' Hypothesis" in B. Gutek et al (eds.) *Women and Work*, Vol 3 (Beverly Hills, CA. Sage Publications, 1988), pp. 169–188.

4. For example, Rhonda M. Williams, "Beyond Human Capital: Black Women, Work and Wages," Working Paper No. 183. (Wellesley, MA: Wellesley College, Center for Research on Women, 1988); and William A. Darity, Jr., "The Human Capital Approach to Black-White Earnings Inequality: Some Unsettled Questions," *Journal of Human Resources*, 17, no. 1 (1982), pp. 72–93, are important theoretical explorations of the limits of labor force characteristics in equilibrium theory.

5. For discussions of internal labor markets and wage policy, see Heidi Hartman, "Internal Labor Markets and Gender: A Case Study of Promotion," pp. 59–91; Paul Osterman, "Comments on Hartman," pp. 92–98; and Myra Strober and Carolyn Arnold, "Occupational Segregation Among Bank Tellers," pp. 107–148, all in Clair Brown and Joseph A. Pechman (eds.) *Gender in the Workplace* (Washington, DC: Brookings Institution, 1987).

6. David Gordon, *Theories of Poverty and Underemployment* (Lexington, MA: Lexington Books, 1972); Peter B. Doeringer and Michael J. Piore, *Internal Labor Markets and Manpower Analysis* (Lexington, MA: Lexington Books, 1971); and Bennett Harrison, *Education, Training and the Urban Ghetto* (Baltimore: Johns Hopkins University Press, 1972).

7. Gary Becker, *The Economics of Discrimination*, 2nd ed. (Chicago: University of Chicago Press, 1980).

8. David Gordon, Richard Edwards, and Michael Reich, *Segmented Work, Divided Workers* (Cambridge: Cambridge University Press, 1982).

9. Solomon Polacheck, "Occupational Self-Selection: A Human Capital Approach to Sex Differences in Occupational Status," *Review of Economics*, 58, no. 1 (February 1981), pp. 60–69.

10. See Bergmann, *The Economic Emergence of Women*, for arguments against "capitalization" of work in her "work interruption" and "rusty skills" thesis, p. 123.

11. Becker, *Economics of Discrimination*.

12. Gordon et al., *Segmented Work*, pp. 200–202; Barry Bluestone and Bennett Harrison, *The Deindustrialization of America*, (New York: *Basic Books*, 1982). Bennett Harrison, "Regional Restructuring and 'Good Business Climates': The Economic Transformation of New England Since World War II," in Larry Sawyers and William K. Tabb (eds.), *Sunbelt/Snowbelt; Urban Development and Regional Restructuring* (New York: Oxford University Press, 1984), pp. 48–96. In fact there is some question as to whether in value-added as a proportion of the GNP, this has happened, particularly in the manufacturing sector, which appears to have held its own, slowing only after a surge over 30 percent since World War II. Rather, the services industry has replaced agriculture and the extractive industry's share of the GNP, a very different issue.

13. Frank Hern, "Beyond the Management Model of Industrialized Organization," in Frank Hern (ed.), *The Transformation of Industrial Organization* (Belmont, CA:

Wadsworth, 1988), pp. 194–204. See also Lester Thurow "Building a World-Class Economy," pp. 284–300, in Hern.

14. Gordon et al., *Segmented Work*. See also Carolyn C. Perucci, Robert Perucci, Dena B. Targ, and Harry R. Targ, *Plant Closings: International Context and Social Costs* (Hawthorne, NY: Aldine de Gruyter, 1988), pp. 13–24.

15. Barry Bluestone, "The Characteristics of Marginal Industries," in David Gordon (ed.), *Problems in Political Economy* (Lexington, MA: D.C. Heath, 1971), pp. 102–107; Thomas Peters and Robert Waterman, *In Search of Excellence* (New York: Harper and Row, 1982); Ira Magaziner and Robert Reich, *Minding America's Business* (New York: Harcourt, Brace, Jovanovich, 1982).

16. Bluestone and Harrison, *The Deindustrialization of America*.

17. Gordon et al., *Segmented Work*, p. 200.

18. Ibid., p. 201.

19. Ibid. See also Henry Levin and Russell Rumberger, "The Low-Skill Future of High Tech," *Technology Review*, August–September 1983.

20. Bergmann, *The Economic Emergence of Women*, p. 27.

21. Ibid.

22. Julienne Malveaux, "Recent Trends in Occupational Segregation by Race and Sex," paper, presented to the Committee on Women's Employment and Related Social Issues, National Academy of Sciences, Washington, DC, May 25, 1982.

23. New research on "internal labor markets" is frequently utilized to define occupational segregation of women related to wage and mobility outcomes. As examples, see Strober and Arnold, "Occupational Segregation Among Bank Tellers," pp. 107–157, and Hartman, "Internal Labor Markets and Gender," pp. 59–105, both in Brown and Pechman, *Gender in the Workplace*.

24. Strober and Arnold, ibid., p 108. The authors define degree of segregation according to a 20-percentage-point spread around the female proportion of the work force, where an occupation can be termed female-dominated or female-intensive if 60 percent or more of the workers were female in 1980, male-intensive or male-dominated if less than 20 percent of the incumbents were female, and neutral if it was 21–59 percent female. They note further that among men, 8 percent were employed in female-intensive occupations, 53 percent in male-intensive occupations, and 39 percent in neutral occupations in 1980.

25. Hartman, "Internal Labor Markets and Gender." See also Bette Woody, "Executive Women: Models of Corporate Success" (Wellesley MA: Wellesley College, Center for Research on Women, 1986).

26. Bette Woody, "Black Women in the Emerging Services Economy," *Sex Roles*, 21, nos. 1 & 2 (July 1989).

27. Malveaux, "Recent Trends," p. 23.

28. Ibid.

29. Ibid.

30. Ibid. See also Hartman, "Internal Labor Markets and Gender," p. 75, for findings on internal labor market segregation of black women in an insurance firm.

31. Jones, "Black Women and Labor Force Participation," p. 12.

32. Bruce Kaufman, *The Economics of Labor Markets and Labor Relations* (Chicago: Dryden Press, 1986), p. 115.

33. Ibid.

34. Jones, "Black Women and Labor Force Participation," p. 12.

35. Margaret Simms, "The Choices That Young Black Women Make: Education, Employment and Family Formation," Working Paper No. 190 (Wellesley, MA: Wellesley College, Center for Research on Women, 1988).

36. Wallace, *Black Women in the Labor Force*. See also Jones, "Black Women and Labor Force Participation," pp. 11–31. Jones provides evidence that a combination of inadequate employment opportunity, visible in unemployment rates and low wages, illustrates different returns on investment of education and effort for black women. This explains the slowing of labor force participation rates of black female workers compared to white females.

37. See Diane R. Brown, "Employment and Health Among Older Black Women: Implications for Their Economic Status," Working Paper no. 177 (Wellesley, MA: Wellesley College, Center for Research on Women, 1988) for an excellent summary of a 1984 National Health Interview Survey, Supplement on Aging. Brown finds health and disability, when coupled with lower educational attainment, accounts for lower participation in the work force. A decline in lower status jobs among women 60 and older in 1980 may thus explain reduced labor force participation rates.

CHAPTER 3

Work and Occupational Status of Black Women

Much of the body of work analyzing the employment of black women has centered on their occupational status, or the kinds of jobs they would normally obtain, given education, training, and experience.[1] This implies that workers classified as having a certain occupational status possess the kinds of skills most often associated with the specific job requirements as defined by the marketplace. Occupational status also is frequently divorced from definitions of work settings to better isolate the workers' individual capacity for effort along with their earning power.[2] Another factor associated with occupational status is an assumed connection between the skills and educational attainment of the individual worker and the job held.[3] A characterization as a "service worker," for example, implies comparatively limited education. Occupational status thus can also infer higher or lower rates of unemployment, as well as the number of hours of work obtained. Low-paid, low-level occupational status is usually seen as an explanation for higher rates of unemployment and in some cases for seasonal work, as in the case of cannery workers or agricultural labor. Occupational status may also infer part-time work or reduced and variable hours as in the case of domestic household work. Although a full discussion of both human resources questions such as those related to education and skills and occupational status is beyond the scope of this chapter, we have briefly acknowledged the strong tradition of defining labor by occupational status.[4]

This chapter examines the changing occupational status of black women workers by first looking at some traditional explanations, including educational attainment, unemployment, and hours of work. Because rates of both voluntary and involuntary part-time work are high for black women, and impact negatively in reducing family income, we note some of the special considerations of the

Table 3.1
Educational Attainment and Work Weeks for Women by Race

Labor Category	Black Women Median Yrs. School	Med Hrs. Wk. Worked	White Women Med Yrs. School	Med Hrs. Wk. Worked
Female Heads Household	10.80	31.88	11.26	32.0
No Spouse Present	10.83	32.22	11.28	32.0
Children under 18 yrs	11.20	34.24	11.34	32.3
Children under 5 yrs	11.95	37.34	11.44	30.4

Source: *CPS 1982*.

trends that characterized the economy of the early 1990s toward creating more part-time than full-time jobs.[5]

EDUCATIONAL ATTAINMENT AND EXPERIENCE

Improvements in the quality of the black women's work force are most apparent in the rapid progress in educational attainment. The median years of overall school attained by black women increased from 9.4 years in 1959 to 12.4 years by 1980, nearly closing the gap with white women of 12.6 years of school. Educational gains by black women reflected rapid increases in higher education, as well as accelerated retirements of older less-educated women from the labor force during the 1970s. Black women made dramatic gains in college enrollments during the 1960s and 1970s and improved overall education rates. This also helped increase the proportion of black women in higher status jobs. The second factor—the rapid exit of older, less-well-educated black women from the labor force—was helped mainly by changes in coverage and levels of social security insurance programs.

As Table 3.1, compiled from 1982 Current Population Census data on the educational attainment of women workers, indicates, the differential between black and white women has narrowed most among younger women (i.e., those with children under five years of age). One important influence of higher educational attainment visible in this table is in the number of hours worked weekly.

Gains by black women were also made in skills and experience over the past two decades. Measured by the rate of experienced workers and the distribution of women working full-time workweeks, annually black women made gains. In 1978, for example, black women were more likely than white women to be employed in a workyear constituting less than 26 weeks; 15 percent of all black women worked less than 26 weeks, compared to 15 percent for white women. But black women were also more likely to exceed 50 weeks of employment annually than white women. They were also more likely to work full time. While just over one-quarter of black women worked part time in 1978, well over one-third of white women were so employed. At the same time, they were also more likely to be unemployed or underemployed.

UNEMPLOYMENT, DISCOURAGED WORKERS, AND SUBEMPLOYMENT

Unemployment is an extremely serious problem among black women and has reached particularly high, even crisis, levels among teenagers and young adults. While the unemployment problem and the problem of underemployment among black women have taken a backseat to those problems of males, the accelerated rate of women heading black families indicates that a far more serious look is appropriate. The very low participation rate of younger black women in the labor force, coupled with high unemployment or twice the rates of white teenagers, also suggests that a high number of "discouraged workers," or those who have either given up searching for work or failed to seek work because of perceptions of failure, may be a hidden dimension to the problem of work. Another problem for black women is subemployment rates, or the number of workers who must accept a reduced workweek or -year because full-time work is unavailable. Both unemployment and subemployment are extremely high among both white and black women, compared to white men. But the problem plagues black women more than white counterparts. Since unemployment is more acute among younger age groups of black women, particularly first-time inexperienced workers, it may be that a combination of lack of skills, experience, and information poses problems. In addition, education, family status, geographic location relative to available work, and discrimination may play varying roles.

Unemployment rates among black women averaged twice that of white women and four to five times that of white men in 1980. Unemployment also followed patterns of marital status. As noted, unemployment rates are highest among black single women. In 1980, one in four single black women was unemployed, compared to only one in eight single white women. The lowest unemployment among both groups was among married women with a husband present, while rates for divorced and separated women fell in between the extremes. The link between marriage, high labor force participation, and low unemployment is most apparent in the case of women between the ages of 20 and 44. Wallace and others have noted that higher participation in the work force by black married women, as well as lower unemployment, results from the tradition and norm of two-earner households among black families.[6] Two-earner families among blacks were widely assumed to "keep black families in the middle class," because of the lower earning power of husbands. For white women, similar income pressures may be growing with the economic recessions of the 1970s and mid-1980s. What is less clear, however, is why unemployment rates are so much higher among divorced and separated women of both races. One reason may be the need for these women to hold out for full time jobs. Another may be that statistically married women who have never entered the work force tend to be included in a different category of labor force status. A final factor, at least among those with young children, may be public assistance, or Social Security benefits. By 1980, in many states women receiving Aid to Families with Dependent Children (AFDC) were required to register for work whether or not they were immediately able to take jobs.

Subemployment, which includes employment at less than full time and full year where workers desire and are willing to assume full-time year-around work, is another work problem area for black women that has received inadequate attention in analysis or policy.[7] Part-time work has long characterized women workers, both black and white. While common wisdom suggests that women exercise a "clear preference" for part-time work in order to take care of family responsibilities, this hypothesis may cloud an important reality of the need and requirement for women to work full time to support families. Only recently, for example, has the U.S. Census provided a category of "part-time involuntary work" to account for those workers who are forced into less-than-full workweeks and workyears because of the absence of full-time work available to them. Even these statistics may understate the sub-employment problem among black women, however. A very substantial proportion of single women who work part time and support families may be considered subemployed because their earnings and benefits fall drastically below federally defined poverty levels. Black women on average are more likely than white women to work full time, year around. But as 1982 CPS data indicate, black women who work part time are more likely than white women to work part time on an "involuntary" basis.

RECENT GAINS IN THE OCCUPATIONAL STATUS OF BLACK WOMEN

Occupational status is a frequently cited measure of economic and employment status gains that black women have made over the past two decades. As noted earlier, throughout a long and painful work history, black women were openly excluded from working in most jobs, even including the restricted number of jobs available to white women. Even in the northern United States, employers did not stop widespread segregated hiring until the mid-1960s, when federal equal opportunity legislation outlawed open bias in advertising, hiring, and promotion. Labor shortages during World War II did open some occupations to black women and they responded eagerly to openings in skilled blue-collar work and clerical jobs. Immediately following the end of the war, however, most of these jobs were closed off to women. By the mid-1960s, when black women were not able to enter a broad array of occupations, an economic slowdown acted to reduce the number of jobs in the economy. Particularly hard hit were certain blue-collar jobs, notably in manufacturing.

The 1970s was probably the period of greatest gains for black women, the result of accelerated growth in services and white-collar work spurred by growth of personal and business services and such professional services as health care.

Table 3.2
Occupational Status of Women by Race, 1960 and 1980

Occupation	% Total Female Labor Force in Occupation:			
	1960		1980	
	Black	White	Black	White
Professional, Technical	6.7	13.2	11.8	14.6
Managerial, Administrative	1.0	3.9	4.7	7.8
Clerical	9.9	40.7	25.7	40.8
Services	56.3	16.6	26.3	15.9
Production Workers	13.3	16.6	6.9	2.1
Retail Sales	1.4	8.7	5.5	11.8
Other, Misc. and not reported	11.3	0.2	23.5	6.9

Source: U.S. Department of Commerce, Bureau of Census, Table 1, "Selected Characteristics of Employed Persons," 1980, pp. 2, 3; and "Occupational Characteristics," 1960, pp. 21–30.

Black women were beneficiaries of massive growth in clerical and sales jobs. For the first time, black women made inroads into the middle ranks in such occupational ladders as health care professionals, administration, and even blue-collar supervisory jobs. Most of the gains, however, were made against the yardstick and standard of white women's employment. Women overall remained remarkably disadvantaged over the growth period when compared to men, particularly in the range and depth of occupations. Black women thus made both gains and losses in the occupational structure. A range of new jobs was available to them. At the same time, black women found themselves becoming more rigidly segregated, particularly at the low end of the occupational status scale.

Two changes have characterized the occupational structure of black women over the past two decades. First, an increasing diversity of occupational choices has occurred. Second, there is a trend toward increased segregation in a limited range of "women's jobs." Current U.S. Census data of selected occupations illustrate how shifts have occurred in black women's occupational status (see Table 3.2). Although the total share by black women of women's jobs has declined as more white women have entered the workplace, black women have made gains. Particularly visible are increased shares in higher status areas such as professional, managerial, and crafts jobs. Despite these gains, only in crafts and social work professional categories have black women reached full parity with their proportion in the work force. In fact, the number of occupational categories where black women held between 10 and 14 percent of total occupations remained stable at 8 between 1962 and 1980. At the same time, the number of job categories that were "crowded" for black women (exceeded 15 percent or more) grew from 7 in 1960 to 14 by 1980.

Patterns of occupational crowding for women by race for 1982 are displayed in the Appendix. In the middle occupational ranks where black women gained most, clerical workers showed the "best distribution" compared to their proportion in the work force. In both blue-collar manufacturing jobs and in services (except for restaurant workers such as cooks and counter operators, where employment for black women declined), black women remained disproportionately concentrated.

NEW JOBS AND OLD JOBS: SELECTED SERVICES AND PRODUCTION OCCUPATIONS

The expansion of black women into a broad diversity of occupations was spurred primarily by economic factors. In particular, the growth of administrative functions throughout the economy, as services grew in all industries, gave rise to an accelerated total job gain, as well as differentiation within what was formally a quite generic clerical work force of the past. Another trend was organizational in nature and occurred at the firm level. This is the restructuring and consolidation of managerial functions, particularly into lower status, routine clerical job groups. A third large trend in the economy was the growth of nonadministrative services, particularly in personal and professional care and in business services. Related to this industry expansion were jobs in human services and hospital patient care; janitorial and maintenance categories; employment related to food services; most categories of retail sales; and, finally, jobs associated with goods handling such as packing and shipping, communications and transportation. A final expansion category was actually a shift in the traditional production sector (manufacturing, construction, utilities) from jobs that formerly were production in nature and employed male workers, to jobs that mixed production and services/administration and were now associated with the hiring of women. The computerization, data processing, and mechanization of many industrial processes were associated with this transformation.

As we have indicated earlier, clerical occupation gains by black women are one of the success stories of the past decade. Black women gained diversity in clerical occupations as well, and this is visible in the distribution of black women across several clerical occupational categories. While some of these gains can be attributed to public-sector protection against discrimination, such as in the case of postal service clerks, jobs such as cashiers, bookkeepers, clerical supervisors, library assistants, computer peripheral operators, keypunch operators, statistical and shipping clerks, and telephone operators reflect the growth of new administrative functions in the economy.

When occupations are examined at a more detailed U.S. Census three-digit code level and black and white women are compared in the 1982 CPS data, the tendency for crowding and higher concentrations of black women in lower status occupations is visible. This suggests that black women are more segregated than white women, that segregation is weighted on the lower end of the status scale, and that therefore gains are somewhat more limited. For example, in jobs where the highest proportion of women work, such as receptionists, typists, and secretaries among clerical workers, and as waitresses, nursing aides, and maids among blue-collar service categories, black women work in the most routine, heavy, and dirty jobs. Thus, secretarial jobs that require judgment and decision-making and constitute the high status and earnings end of clerical work constitute less than 7 percent black women; while in the more routine typist category, nearly 16 percent of jobs are held by black women. Among food service workers, black women hold 20 percent of total employment, while only about 5 percent of waitresses are black women. In the lowest status services jobs that require the most heavy work, nearly 30 percent of nurse's aides, about 50 percent of all private household workers, and 37 percent of dry cleaning workers are black women. In blue-collar jobs employing women, black women are closer to their proportion in the women's population. These are mainly in manufacturing jobs and include such categories as assemblers, checkers, and examiners; and sewers and stitchers. Black women are more likely to work in somewhat lower concentrations.

Clerical Jobs

The expansion of administrative functions where clerical work dominates cuts across industrial sectors as well as public and private sectors. Thus, the massive growth that occurred in clerical jobs reflected expansion of both white-collar services sectors and administrative functions in nonservices sectors. Since one of the key themes of this book is the impact that industrial growth exerts on hiring and wages of black women, we examine industrial-sector influences in detail in Chapters 4 and 5. In addition to industry, however, clerical jobs have undergone other influences that shape the status of black women. One evolution has taken place at the firm level—the finer differentiation of clerical work categories.

In theory, differentiation of jobs suggests specializations and higher pay. The opposite appears to have occurred in recent times with clerical positions, particularly as they have increasingly become "women's jobs." Unlike male job diversification, which creates more salary steps within job groups, the growth of clerical jobs now held mainly by women has increased the number of low-status jobs. The increase in entry jobs results from the design of jobs where content is restricted; tasks are divided into minute, routine operations that are clearly separated from decision-making and any creative process that might be employed by the individual worker. As illustrations, the occupational categories of billing clerk and payroll clerk have been redesigned to be highly routine, involve few decisions, and are developed in association with computerized systems. This allows the introduction of "machine management" of the work load for the clerical worker. The cumulative effect is initially to expand the number of jobs at entry level (serving to reduce costs and a need for investment and training workers), after which, in a second stage, reductions occur in the number of workers. Examples of this process include the payroll and billing clerical positions, keypunch operators and data entry clerks, peripheral terminal operators, and statistical and medical clerks. More of these patterns can be expected in the future as administrative functions become consolidated, segmented, and finally mechanized out.

A final trend that can be observed is that toward "downgrading" higher status, high-paid occupations into lower status "support" categories. Such jobs as teachers and librarians, clerical supervisors, and other lower to mid-level management personnel are increasingly supported by lower status personnel to reduce their work load. Black women have tended to be hired into the professional support positions and into lower status managerial jobs. Black women, for example, made up about 9 percent of clerical supervisor jobs and only about 7 percent of manager's jobs in 1982. This occurred at a time when women overall increased managerial employment between 1960 and 1986 from less than 25 percent of all manager's jobs to nearly 40 percent.

As the detailed occupational distribution of black women indicates, gains have occurred in the diversification of clerical occupations. However, black women remain crowded compared to white women at the lower and more routine end of work or in public-supported work such as education and health categories and the U.S. Postal Service.

Blue-Collar Production Jobs

Although the expansion of blue-collar production jobs has leveled off in the economy, the growth of women's jobs has taken place mainly in smaller, diversified industries where jobs are nonunionized and the status and pay are low. Large manufacturers also have increased their contracting to firms that are flexible as an alternative to expanding jobs within. The electronics and electrical equipment industry, consumer durables, and even the automotive and transportation equipment industry have expanded women's employment, along with traditional women-intensive industries such as apparel and food. Black women have particularly benefited from this job expansion as operatives and in the goods-handling and inspection end of the production sector. To the extent that women may be preferred as workers in some of the heavier jobs in the production industry (i.e., laborer jobs), black women may also have an edge on employment over other workers.

Services Jobs

The growth of nonadministrative services jobs has provided the bulk of new employment opportunity for black women. These jobs comprise a wide range of internal content, but can be divided for discussion purposes between (1) personal needs or people-oriented services such as health, education, and child care; (2) maintenance, such as cleaning of buildings, maids, janitors, and house-keepers; (3) services associated with some kind of production such as laundry and dry cleaning machine operators and food preparation workers. Black women have made their greatest status gains in professional jobs such as teachers and nurses, but the bulk of employment is in the lowest status jobs. Such occupations as professional support and paraprofessionals have grown most rapidly. Jobs available as nurses aides, library assistants, teacher's aides, and child care workers increasingly reflect efforts to increase productivity in labor-intensive service functions by off-loading part of the work content of professional jobs into lower status categories where lower education and salary are required. To illustrate, a new job called "welfare assistant" was created to replace part of the work load of professional social workers. Library assistants, essentially entry-level clerks, are employed to perform routine cataloging and data entry work, to reshelve books, and to handle checkout and book returns. This frees the higher paid professional librarians to perform system management work and to supervise clerical staff. Health care subprofessional jobs have expanded for two reasons: first to increase productivity of the professional staff by performing routine patient care chores, and second to play a key function in the radical restructuring of the health care industry, the decentralization of health care from high-cost hospitals to lower cost outpatient and home-based care. The rapid growth of such flexible job categories as nurse's aides, health aides, home care workers, homemakers, and the like in the health care industry submerges the job content related to what was formerly the exclusive domain of the physician or registered nurse.

OCCUPATIONAL STATUS AND WAGES

Improvements in the occupational status of black women were reflected in wage gains. At the same time, however, a persistent downward pressure on annual income was continuing the high rate of part-time work, particularly as the result of growth in services and the retailing industry.

Black women's wages grew dramatically over the past two decades. For full-time, year-around workers, gains of 72 percent were made between 1960 and 1976 alone, compared to 52 percent for white women. At the same time, the earnings gap between black and white women narrowed from 53 percent in 1970 to 83 percent by 1976. Moreover, in 1976 the median income for black women working year-around was about $7,000, compared to $8,300 for white women, $10,500 for black men, and $14,000 for white men.[8] Some 64 percent of wage gains for black women alone took place over the decade of the 1970s.

The 1980s marked a slowing of earnings growth for black women, particularly when compared to white women. Bluestone and Harrison analyzed CPS data on earnings growth for four labor groups and found that, overall, white women were the biggest winners, with the other groups—black males, black females, and white males—falling considerably behind.[9] A key explanation given by these analysts was the accelerated growth of white women in higher paid managerial jobs.

One reason black women lost ground in annual earnings in the 1980s was the shortened workweek. In 1982 about 43 percent of black women worked part time, only slightly less than the 46 percent rate for white women. In addition to higher weekly earnings, white women are less likely to be sole family bread-winners. The impact of part-time work on the earnings of black women was dramatic. While the median earnings of black women who worked full time in 1982 were $6,179, the earnings of part-time workers dropped to less than half or only $3,000 annually. In addition, part-time workers benefit far less on noncash compensation, such as pensions, prepaid health, and paid holidays, than is the rule for full-time workers.

Trends in and causes for the growth in part-time work in the economy overall have only begun to be analyzed.[10] As more part-time than full-time jobs are created, and as part-time jobs become the source of income for family bread-winners, particularly men, questions have been raised about the extent to which business firms may ignore traditional occupational groups and deliberately or-ganize work on a part-time basis.[11] While in the past, such work frequently was assumed to be scheduled to accommodate women who preferred shorter work-weeks to take care of family responsibilities, current trends suggest that business firms may seek to reduce obligations and costs such as long-term commitments to workers and the costs of group health, life insurance, pension contributions, sick and vacation days, overtime rates, and other costs that typically add up to 20 percent on salaries of full-time workers.[12] The temptation to reduce overall labor costs by replacing full-time employees and thereby cutting nonwage fringe benefits may increase with more pressures for raising wages and benefits for full-time employees in specific occupational categories.

NOTES

1. Much labor research, whether directly examining the question of gender or race, has traditionally used occupational status to describe labor characteristics. On the one hand, this reflects hierarchical job groupings and skills long used by government censuses and other sources of statistics. It also may reflect the traditional "human capital" approach to considerations of wage distribution and skills attainment. A main disadvantage of the use of occupational status to describe labor is the lack of a clear connection between an occupational category, the actual tasks to be accomplished, and the skills required to do the job successfully or meet stated performance standards. For a discussion of some of these issues, see Bruce Kaufman, *The Economics of Labor Markets and Labor Relations* (Chicago: Dryden Press, 1986), pp. 212–216; and Sally T. Hillsman and Bernard Lev-enson, "Job Opportunities for Black and White Working-Class Women," in Rachel Kahn-Hut, Arlene Daniels, and Richard Colvard (eds.), *Women and Work* (New York: Oxford University Press, 1982), pp. 218–233, which links occupational status with skills training and formal schooling.

2. The U.S. Department of Labor reporting and analysis is typical in its reliance on occupational categories and characterization of worker work and earnings capacity. See Diane Nilsen, "Blacks in the 1970's, Did They Scale the Job Ladder?" in Richard L. Rowan (ed.) *Readings in Labor Economics and Labor Relations* (Homewood, IL: Irwin, 1985, pp. 32–43.

3. In part, efforts to develop "comparable worth" programs in government have accepted the occupational status systems as reflecting work content and skills and have argued for better pay, rather than a restructuring of the occupational system altogether. For a recent discussion of comparable worth, see George T. Milkowich, "Comparable Worth, the Emerging Debate," in Rowan, *Readings in Labor Economics*, pp. 324–338; and *Pay Equity in the Public Sector* (Washington, DC: National Committee on Pay Equity, October 1989).

4. Milkovich, "Comparable Worth," pp. 329–338, illustrates some of the current efforts to separate "occupational" status from actual tasks performed and to reclassify many task-occupational categories in ways that more closely resemble actual performance standards or skills. The movement of government merit systems generally toward generic rather than specialized job categories also reflects efforts to remove the "stigma" of occupational classifications from definitions of the individual worker's capacity to perform in an organizational or work environment.

5. Thomas J. Nardone, "Part Time Workers: Who are They?" *Monthly Labor Review*, February 1986; Carol Leon and Robert Bednarzik, "A Profile of Women on Part-Time Schedules," *Monthly Labor Review*, October 1978, pp. 3–12; and William Deutermann, Jr. and Scott Campbell Brown, "Voluntary Part Time Workers: A Growing Part of the Labor Force," *Monthly Labor Review*, June 1978, pp. 3–10. (Although the emphasis in much Department of Labor analysis is placed on the "voluntary nature" of part-time work decisions, U.S. Census data show a persistent and continuing trend in the composition of new jobs of less than 35 hours weekly. See Barry Bluestone and Bennett Harrison, "The Great American Jobs Machine: Proliferation of Low Wage Employment in the U.S. Economy" (Washington, DC: Joint Economic Committee, U.S. Congress, 1986).

6. Phyllis Wallace, *Black Women in the Labor Force* (Cambridge, MA: MIT Press, 1982), p. 10.

7. A literature search as part of the current research project revealed almost no work devoted to the problem of black female unemployment, or shortened workweeks. One recent analysis of structural change impacts on labor does find much higher rates of unemployment among black women and men than whites, as well as longer waits for reemployment. See Francis W. Horwath, "The Pulse of Economic Change: Displaced Workers of 1981–85," *Monthly Labor Review*, June 1987, pp. 3–12.

8. Wallace, *Black Women in the Labor Force*, p. 60.

9. Bluestone and Harrison, "The Great American Job Machine."

10. Nardone, "Part Time Workers." According to U.S. Census data reported by Nardone, the part-time work force in the economy grew by over 75 percent between 1968 and 1985, compared to the growth of full-time workers of only about 35 percent over the same period (p. 18). Nardone also indicated that, in contrast to traditional "voluntary" part-time work, the greatest new growth results from retail trade and services industry expansion, or those industries that are likely to recruit part-time workers exclusively to satisfy growth needs.

11. For a discussion of the relationship between occupational status, segregation and

part time work, see Karen C. Holden and W. Lee Hansen, "Part-Time Work, Full-Time Work and Occupational Segregation," in Clair Brown and Joseph A. Pechman (eds.), *Gender in the Workplace* (Washington, DC: The Brookings Institution, 1987).

    12. For a discussion of the economics of fringe benefits and trends, see Kaufman, *The Economics of Labor Markets*, pp. 344–352.

CHAPTER 4

Trends in Job Expansion in U.S. Industry

Massive postwar changes in U.S. industry transformed the economy and in the process pushed labor out of jobs dominated by the production industry and into new services occupational structures. The principal forces underlying these industry, production, and job changes also spurred a changeover of the labor force from male to at least equally male and female mix and, in the process, dramatically altered the status of black women. Industrial sectoral changes transformed black women from the most marginal end of the labor force to a mainstream work force. At the same time, by the dawn of the 1990s the direction of the economy and industrial growth predicted a leveling, if not erosion, of gains and growth of poverty in a work force now providing main support of families.

Industrial trends that were most influential in shaping the postwar U.S. economy and jobs were rooted in a series of events that evolved during the three decades following the end of World War II. Manufacturing declines, which are most-cited as symbolizing trends, resulted from a combination of complex problems, including failure of U.S. producers to retool production facilities, develop and market new product lines, and adopt management strategies geared to long-range stability goals. The long existence of a virtually protected domestic market crumbled from the rise of European and Asian producers, which challenged American production successfully in both international and domestic marketplaces with highly competitive products and prices. The initial toehold into U.S. markets was aided by lower labor costs, but also by very different deployment of labor and, above all, very innovative marketing techniques. Thus, while both foreign and U.S. producers pursued protectionist and domestic production subsidy policies to promote international competitiveness, U.S. producers contrasted to foreign counterparts in ignoring the long-range perspective. This was visible in policies on capital investment and in research and new product development. The rise of the services industry in the recent past and currently is now threatened and may follow some of the same patterns, with an added disadvantage of relatively low productivity and a far less optimistic labor picture.

An important corollary to change caused by economic restructuring was the evolution of new divisions of labor within the American labor force. This is nowhere more visible than in changes in female-male work force distribution across industrial sectors. Women remained concentrated in a few female-intensive industries, but services growth, coupled with the emergence of new internal labor markets and job systems, produced new concentrations of women workers in sectors previously dominated by male workers.

The emergence of black women as a legitimate labor force working in the mainstream workplace reflected both broader economic change and industrial restructuring. It also resulted from specific labor-related social changes. The rapid rise of the services industry helped spur a dispersal of black women in the economy, as the initial demand for massive numbers of entry-level clerical, sales, and support workers provided vast new work opportunities. The strong history of black women in the work force forecast changes that were to follow as white women entered the labor force. Thus the women's work force grew from less than one-quarter of all U.S. workers in 1950 to about half by the late 1980s. Equal opportunity legislation and educational gains helped move black women from domestic work at the end of World War II to a mainstream women's work force and nearly closed the gap with white women in status and pay. Demographic and social forces were also at work in the form of escalating dependency rates for black women. The massive contraction in production sectors, particularly agriculture and heavy manufacturing, resulted in losses of millions of jobs. The most dramatic impact was to increase unemployment rates among black men. Black women were pushed into the workplace as principal breadwinners for black families. As similar unemployment has grown among white males, white women have also entered the workplace as primary family earners.

This chapter reviews how changes in key industrial sectors transformed the economy and, with it, the role and economic position of black women in the workplace. We examine first overall industry sectoral trends shaping employment growth, then look more closely at the transition of black women into specific occupations and industrial sectors.

POSTWAR ECONOMIC CHANGES AND JOBS

General U.S. economic growth slowed toward the end of the post-World War II period, accelerating its downward spiral by the 1980s, as agriculture and manufacturing declined and the service industry and trade grew rapidly. These changes in the composition of the economy reflected a general leveling of domestic economic growth. The U.S. gross national product rose from the end of World War II through the 1960s at an average annual rate of 4.1 percent, then fell to just over 2.0 percent by the 1970s. Declines were visible in domestic sales and export trade. Corporate profits fell from an annual return on investment of 15.5 percent in the 1960s to less than 10 percent by 1980. Meanwhile, the U.S. share of world manufacturing dropped from about one-quarter to under one-fifth between 1960 and 1980. Investment abroad also eroded, as the U.S. share of direct investment in 13 OECD countries fell from 61 percent in the 1971–77 period to 30 percent by the 1974–78 period. Even more telling, the U.S. share of world trade declined by 16 percent between 1960 and 1970.[1]

The erosion of the U.S. economic position at home and internationally has been attributed mainly to declines in the production sector. Agriculture, manufacturing, and, to a lesser extent, extractive activities and construction all suffered a leveling of growth, if not actual declines. These trends were caused in part by the new competition from European and Asian producers in domestic markets. But in agriculture a decline in export sales also hurt U.S. trade contributing to a growing trade deficit. Losses of agricultural sales reflected a new element: shrinking world demand for U.S. agricultural production.[2] Demand fell off dramatically from traditional Third World consumers such as India and other parts of Asia over the decades 1950 to 1980. As Third World consumers became principal beneficiaries of the biogenetic and technological revolution in agricultural production, they not only became self-sufficient, but indeed found new positions as exporters of their own surpluses. Meanwhile, U.S. domestic agricultural policy exacerbated a growing problem. Agricultural policies born in the 1930s, in the form of government floors and surplus to assure price stabilization for small farmers, constituted a massive subsidy to a dwindling number of producers by the 1970s.[3] Policies accelerated consolidation of land, mechanization of production, and promoted vast monocultures of unmarketable surplus commodities such as grain, tobacco, sugar, cotton, and dairy products. A side effect was the loss of thousands of smaller family farms and more than a million agricultural jobs between 1960 and 1980.[4] Losses fell hardest of all on black males, as between 1960 and 1980 the number of black man employed in agriculture dropped from 460,000 to 132,000.[5]

Declines in U.S. manufacturing are widely considered to be the most serious threat to the competitive position of the United States in the world marketplace, as well as to domestic economic well-being and employment.[6] Growth in U.S. manufacturing sales and employment leveled dramatically over the past three decades. Even before the oil shocks of the 1970s, output declines were visible in basic steel, machinery, and other durables. For some sectors such as steel, problems have been traced to a trend of capital disinvestment, a management failure to reinvest or replace aging plant and equipment. Reduced rates of capital investment resulted in declines in efficiencies and added costs to production for U.S. makers of such products as rolled steel, which became far less costly when manufactured in newer European and Japanese mills. Other manufactured products suffered additional problems, however. One widely identified problem was poor product design, or failure of manufacturers to address changing consumer tastes and preferences with appropriate product lines and design, including products that reduce service and maintenance costs. Markets for consumer durables such as electronics and television were quickly lost to Japanese producers because of superior maintenance-free designs.[7] The automotive industry also may have lost market shares even before the energy crisis escalated consumer demand for smaller vehicles, because of service-free product design superiority of European and Japanese products. In any case, by the 1970s, at the start of the Organization of Petroleum Exporting Countries (OPEC) oil boycott, U.S. manufacturers were faced with two additional competitive cost disadvantages: one was the cost of goods production caused by obsolescent, high-energy-consuming manufacturing facilities. A second cost occurred in products designed with little attention to energy costs and efficiency, such as refrigeration equipment and buildings. Faced with cheaper, more efficient imports, U.S. sales in products from production equipment to automobiles slipped further.[8]

The reaction of producers to the escalation of crises and decline in economic position was late, and may have served to reinforce, rather than resolve, problems.[9] Managements focused mainly on short-term actions to shore up sales and profits, using a variety of techniques known collectively as "restructuring." These ranged from accounting and financial reorganizations to actual buying and selling of specific assets in the interest of showing favorable balance sheets. Restructuring, however, had dramatic consequences for production units and for labor in the longer run.[10]

One widely used technique, for example, was to buy and sell capital assets of acquired firms that permitted profits to be gained from special accounting of tax treatments in the parent firm, without growth in production output or sales. Another technique was to acquire product markets, sometimes in production and markets related to a parent business, to give the impression of market expansion. In many cases, large firms would buy out the market distribution network of a firm, then shut down the production. Consolidations of the food industry, including brewing, meatpacking, and other processing of the 1970s, are examples. By the 1970s, acquisition trends had reached a frenzied pace as thousands of firms changed hands and larger firms swallowed smaller ones.[11] By the 1980s yet another trend occurred that coincided with the election of the Reagan administration and massive deregulation of industry. Larger and larger companies became targets of takeovers under new rules. The reasoning behind the takeover mania was frequently ambiguous in business growth terms. In some cases, takeovers and buyouts were justified through calculations of undervalued assets or stock prices failing to reflect the true value of assets, inventory, or sales.[12] The petroleum industry was an example. Petroleum reserves and the book value of equipment were widely reported to be frequently recalculated by takeover specialists such as T. Boone Pickens, who then charged that management was deliberately cheating stockholders, or was simply incompetent, as in the highly publicized case of the Marathon Oil Company. Managements were accused by takeover specialists of working merely to keep their jobs, rather than for the company's best interest. Statistics were generated to demonstrate "new" market values on which financing of acquisitions were to be based. With the explosion of financial specialists and banks probing new areas of activity, highly leveraged aquisitions followed: debt paper was floated (so-called junk bonds), which in turn was backed by the assets of the company targeted for takeover; however, the asset value was established.[13] The debt would then be paid, once the new management took control. If a company management chose to fight a takeover, it would be in a similar position of selling assets and "indebting" the company by diluting stock to pay off a hostile suitor. The side effects included closing of facilities, erosion of jobs, and frequently transformation of the company into a "cash cow" to meet short-term needs.[14]

Growth of the services industry was spurred by the reverse of trends affecting the production industry. A large part of services expansion through the 1980s occurred in protected marketplaces, shielded from both international and domestic competitors through a tangle of regulatory systems at state and national levels. Banking, insurance, and professional and business services were examples of growth in a protected environment based on a captive domestic market of expanding populations and rising incomes. Added to this was the growth of the welfare state—public expenditure increases to support the aged, veterans, and the disadvantaged. Government and regulation stimulated growth of major industries such as health services, health insurance, education, and transportation, along with trade.[15] As a result, nonmanufacturing activities were responsible for 74 percent of all nonmanufacturing jobs and 69 percent of all national income by 1984.[16]

IMPACTS OF INDUSTRY CHANGES ON LABOR

Sectoral changes had major implications for labor overall but affected different labor subgroups differently. Distinctions were most visible in a new division of labor between gender and racial groups and among skilled and less-skilled workers. As the Appendix illustrates, employment changes by sector between 1960 and 1980 produced a range of job growth patterns.

The position of white men, the segment with the highest participation rates in the labor force, eroded between 1960 and 1990, mainly as the result of job declines in durables manufacturing, though expansion slowed in construction and mining as well. White male jobholders continued to dominate the production sector overall, but lost ground with white women in white-collar work and trade, and with black men in production work. For example, in the automobile industry, despite the more serious declines, black men increased their employment by over 50 percent between 1960 and 1980, compared to less than 15 percent by white men. But white male workers made gains in white-collar and sales employment, more than offsetting blue-collar industry job losses.

Table 4.1

Male Employment by Race for Selected Production Sectors, 1960–80

	%Gain 1960-80	
	White Men	Black Men
Construction	41.0	17.0
Mining	40.0	79.0
Manufacturing	7.0	45.0
Durable Goods	15.0	40.0
Fabricated Metals	-4.0	57.0
Transport Vehicles	15.0	87.0

Source: *Census of the Population*, Tables 213 and 287.

Wages also slipped for white men, particularly for hourly workers. While white men maintained their lead as the highest paid workers in all industrial sectors, the earnings gap closed with other groups, particularly white women. This reflected changes in the industrial job mix as well as wage gains by women. Relatively high-wage blue-collar manufacturing employment, traditionally dominated by white men, declined and may have been replaced by somewhat lower paid hourly sectors. A second change is the trend in collective bargaining agreements that in the 1980s in particular saw major "givebacks" and other wage concessions.[17]

In contrast to white men, white women made the biggest gains in sectoral dispersion and in earnings. Of the 52 million jobs added to the economy between 1960 and 1980, 16 million went to white women, compared to a 10 million gain by white men. Moreover, increases were made in such nontraditional sectors as mining, construction, and durables manufacturing. Occupational improvements also occurred in such untraditional jobs as management and technical-professional work. Although full-time year-around employment and high unemployment still place white women behind white male counterparts, the wage gap was closed somewhat, as women moved from roughly 60 percent of male earnings in 1980 to around 68 percent by 1986.[18]

The black male labor group may have suffered the most job losses, if not wage problems, as a result of sectoral changes over the past two decades. Black men were particularly concentrated in production work and in subsectors that declined most rapidly. Black men lost most in the contraction of the agriculture sector. In 1960, for example, nearly half a million black men, or nearly 10 percent of the black male labor force, worked as agricultural workers. By 1980 nearly 65 percent of black men had been displaced in the sector, despite growth in the black male work force by 28 percent. Black men did make some important gains, compared to white counterparts, in durable goods overall and in such industries as mining and motor vehicle manufacturing, where wages are generally high as the U.S. Census data in Table 4.1 indicate. Black men, however, were more concentrated than white male workers in the services industry which underwent a massive decline in male employment in the 1960s. In personal services, for example, nearly 6 percent of employed black men worked as private household workers or in hotels and laundry and dry cleaning establishments in 1960. By 1980 the number of black men was reduced by half and fewer than 2.5 percent of the black male work force remained in these activities. One reason for losses particularly affecting black men compared to whites was the occupational stratification of black men into low-skilled jobs. Agricultural employment, personal services jobs, and many jobs in construction, for example, were unskilled laborer jobs or services jobs requiring little or no training. With organizational changes, such work was the first to be mechanized or phased out. The higher unemployment rates of black men, compared to white males, may be explained by this displacement trend.

The lower skills, concentration in marginal sectors, and higher proportion of part-time work among black male workers explain the continuing earnings gap between black and white men, as well as the generally lower pay structure across industries. Black male wages continued to lag and constituted about 73 percent of white male earnings in 1986, nearly unchanged over the prior decade. The exodus of black men out of such low-paid work as personal services did not result in much improvement, since new jobs were concentrated in low-paid nondurable manufacturing or retailing (particularly restaurants) or in such professional services as health care.

Impacts of sector change were more striking for black women than any other labor segment. Black women were key beneficiaries of the accelerated growth of white-collar and retailing jobs in this way, and also gained in some low-end production sectors, principally nondurable manufacturing such as food processing. The rapid expansion of a third category of professional services, principally health care and education, however, opened low-status personal care and blue-collar services jobs to black women, providing them with their most important new source of employment.

HISTORICAL TRENDS IN HIRING BLACK WOMEN IN U.S. INDUSTRY

The most striking reality about the industrial status of black women prior to 1960 was the extent to which segregation out of mainstream workplaces was maintained. Prior to World War II, so segregated was the status of black women that market forces had little or no influence on their status. Until the eve of the war, black women were systematically barred from most work and overwhelmingly employed in agriculture and domestic work. A handful of educated black women who managed to obtain employment outside these two settings worked almost exclusively in segregated organizations such as black school systems, hospitals, or black-owned businesses. In the South, where most black women were located, segregation was strictly enforced, including the use of police power.[19] In the North, though less direct, similar patterns persisted, with segregation enforced in the workplace through occupational designations in white-dominated workplaces. Domestic household work thus provided the overwhelming source of employment for black women throughout the United States until the eve of passage of the Civil Rights Acts in the mid-1960s.

Domestic household work has recently been documented for both its severe restrictions on mobility of black women and the internal disadvantage compared to almost all other work in the labor economy. Domestic work above all contrasted in its organization, which permitted enforcement of very low standards of pay, work content, and a tradition of intimidation and exploitation of the worker. The system was and remains extremely fragmented, consisting of individual employers who set rules on job content, work hours, pay, and benefits. Because there is no central clearinghouse, and the work is essentially unregulated, ad hoc rules, discretion of individual employers, and other variations dominate. Recent documentation of domestic work has shown that it was generally the heaviest and dirtiest (i.e., that refused by white householders) and the hours and pay were at the mercy of employer-dominated negotiations. Resulting work arrangements might be capricious and generally were exploitive in an essentially class-race based system.[20]

Despite the disadvantage to the work, particularly in the availability of hours and pay, domestic work continued to be a key source of paid employment for black women until recently. As recently as 1950, for example, domestic work constituted about 33 percent of all black women's employment and, as late as 1970, 14 percent. Not until 1980, in fact, did domestic household workers fall below 10 percent of total black women's employment.

World War II mobilization and migration out of the U.S. South provided an initial phase for expansion of black women into mainstream industrial workplaces for the first time. A second important expansion took place with rapid growth of jobs and the passage of Civil Rights legislation in the mid-1960s. Both these trends provided means for the opening of new industries—first blue-collar production work during labor shortages of wartime, and then in the 1960s in white-collar and retail industries.

The wholesale expansion of black women into mainstream work was underscored by a combination of three forces: job growth in several new sectors, the ending of barriers to employment, and the geographic dispersion of employment with suburbanization. The massive growth of jobs in the 1960s and 1970s took place almost entirely in white-collar services, retailing, and professional services. Jobs, moreover, were overwhelmingly in entry-level clerical, sales, and services categories—occupations traditionally held by women. With the end to legal discrimination, black women were able to capture large numbers of these jobs. In contrast to manufacturing, which decentralized to suburban locations, growth of banking, insurance, retailing, hotels, and health care took place in core locations accessible to black women.

INDUSTRIAL EXPANSION, WOMEN'S JOBS, AND BLACK WOMEN

Sectoral growth and hiring trends and particularly the accelerated growth of women's employment,[21] are key to understanding how the status of black women

Table 4.2
Female Employment by Industrial Sector, 1980

Sector	Females as % of Total Work force	% of Total Female Work force	% of Total Male Work force
1.Male-Intensive Goods Producing			
Agriculture, Fish, Forest	17.9	1.2	4.3
Mining	13.7	0.3	1.6
Construction	8.4	1.1	9.4
Manufacturing	31.9	16.8	26.6
2.Male-Intensive Services			
Transportation	20.7	2.1	6.1
Communications	47.2	1.6	1.3
Utilities	16.6	0.6	1.3
Public Administration	40.0	5.0	5.4
3.Transitional			
Finance, Banking, Insurance, Real Estate	58.0	8.2	4.4
4.Female-Intensive Services			
Personal Services	70.4	5.2	1.6
Professional Services	66.3	31.4	11.9
Retail Trade	50.9	19.2	13.8
Other Industries		7.3	12.3
5. TOTAL WORK FORCE	42.6	100.0	100.0

Source: Census of the Population, Table 287.

was radically changed in the economy in a few short decades. Black women benefited less from the great job explosion than white women. Nonetheless, employment for black women grew 78 percent compared to a near doubling of employment for white women between 1960 and 1980.[22] The current status of women can be viewed in terms of changes in the distribution of labor by industrial sector between male and female workforces. In part these changes were driven by general sectoral growth trends, but also by internal labor market changes, reviewed below in more detail. While much analysis of women workers has focused on the concentration of female-dominated occupations, industrial sectoral concentrations hold the key to changes in the status of women workers in the economy. This is in part because industry change tends to drive internal market factors such as job organization, mobility, and wages. Thus as Table 4.2, based

Table 4.3
Female Employment by Race for Industrial Sectors, 1960 and 1980

| | % Total Women's Work force by Race | | | | % Change | |
Sector	1960 White	Black	1980 White	Black	White	Black
1. Male-Intensive						
Goods Producing					-26	38
Agr/For/Fish.	1.9	3.8	1.3	0.6		
Mining	--	--	0.3	--		
Construction	0.8	--	1.2	0.5		
Manufacturing	23.5	9.6	16.5	17.4		
Non-Durables	19.1	6.6	8.1	9.4		
Durables	9.4	2.9	8.2	7.6		
2. Male-Intensive: Services					6	181
Trans/Comm/Utilit.	4.2	1.1	4.1	5.2		
Utilities	0.6	--	0.6	0.6		
Transportation	1.3	0.5	2.0	2.4		
Communications	2.3	0.5	1.5	2.2		
Public Administration	4.3	3.6	4.6	8.0		
Federal	2.2	2.2	1.6	3.5		
Federal Postal Serv.	0.3	0.3	0.3	1.0		
State/Local	2.1	1.3	2.7	3.5		
Wholesale Trade	2.4	0.7	2.9	1.5		
3. Transitional					6	313
Finance/Insurance/Real Est.	6.7	1.5	8.6	6.2		
Banking/Financial Serv.	3.0	0.3	2.9	2.5		
Insurance	3.7	1.2	2.7	2.2		
4. Female-Intensive: Services					8	-24
Personal Services	9.3	49.1	4.5	9.8		
Private Households	4.6	39.7	1.0	5.5		
Hotels, Lodging	1.4	2.8	1.4	2.2		
Professional Services	23.2	19.0	31.0	36.2		
Health	8.9	9.4	12.8	17.4		
Education	11.0	8.1	13.2	13.7		
Social Services	3.6	1.5	1.8	3.5		
Business Services	1.8	0.6	3.4	2.8		
Retail Trade	20.9	10.1	20.5	11.2		

Note: Subcategories may not add up, since only selected industries are examined.
Source: *Census of the Population*, Tables 213 and 287.

on 1980 data, illustrates, women were concentrated in a few sectors. Further, dividing the economy into male-intensive, female-intensive, and transitional, based roughly on the representation of the work force of each sex in each hiring sector, women work mainly in female-intensive professional services and re-tailing, as over half of the women's work force is concentrated in these two sectors. Moreover, while 17 percent of women worked in manufacturing (the third highest hiring category for women), less than 33 percent of the total work force was female.

Changes that took place for women of both races in the 1970s with the rapid growth of women in the work force are illustrated in Table 4.3 in 1960–1980 Census data. Women of both races increased their share of employment in traditional male-intensive services and transitional sectors (i.e., those that became female-intensive over the period). But women also increased their share of traditional female services (professional services, retailing) and percentage declines took place only in personal services (mainly private households). Overall dispersion out of female-intensive sectors was most spectacular for black women. Black women gained shares both in manufacturing and traditional male-intensive services such as communications, transportation, and government. This occurred mainly, however, because of a deployment of black women from segregated household work.

Black women made their most important gains in durable goods manufacturing, white-collar services (including government), and professional services. Patterns of gains differed among employing sectors. Key factors underlying the improvements of black women were the radical transformation of workplaces and particularly change in the organization of work, occupational categories, and job content associated with them, as well as the relevant system of entry requirements, job and work rules, and compensation. These internal market changes were key to most gains by black women during the 1970s and 1980s.

NOTES

1. Barry Bluestone and Bennett Harrison, *The Deindustrialization of America* (New York: Basic Books, 1982), pp. 17, 29–31, 42.

2. See Lester Thurow, *The Zero-Sum Society* (New York: Penguin Books, 1981), pp. 91–92.

3. Ira C. Magaziner and Robert B. Reich, *Minding America's Business* (New York: Harcourt, Brace, Jovanovich, 1982), pp. 246–249.

4. Thurow, *The Zero-Sum Society,* pp. 123–125.

5. Bette Woody, "Recent Employment Experience of Black Women Workers in the Services Economy: Implications for Policy and Practice," *Sociological Practice Review,* 2: 3, July 1991, pp. 188–200.

6. Bluestone and Harrison, *The Deindustrialization of America.* See also Thurow, *The Zero-Sum Society*; David Gordon et al., *Segmented Work, Divided Workers* (Cambridge: Cambridge University Press, 1982).

7. Magaziner and Reich, *Minding America's Business*, pp. 12–13.

8. Ibid., p. 34.

9. For some perspectives on the impacts of industrial and corporate restructuring, as well as causes, see Lynn E. Browne and Eric S. Rosengren (eds.), *The Merger Boom* (Boston: Federal Reserve Bank, 1987), which comprises papers and discussion presented at a conference on mergers, March 1987; and Larry Sawyers and William K. Tabb (eds.), *Sunbelt/Snowbelt: Urban Development and Regional Restructuring* (New York: Oxford University Press, 1984), comprising papers presented at a conference on urban political economy, Washington D.C., 1981; and Thurow, *The Zero Sum Society.*

10. Gregory Squires, "Capital Mobility Versus Upward Mobility: The Racially Discriminatory Consequences of Plant Closings and Corporate Relocations," in Sawyers and Tabb *Sunbelt/Snowbelt*, pp. 152–161.

11. See Dean LeBaron and Lawrence S. Speidel, "Why Are the Parts Worth More Than the Sum? 'Chop Shop' A Corporate Valuation Model," in Browne and Rosengren, *The Merger Boom*, pp. 78–95.

12. Ibid.

13. For a perspective on the role of "junk bond" financing, see David Ravenschraft, "The 1980s Merger Wave: An Industrial Organization Perspective," pp. 17–37, and John D. Paulus and Stephen Waite, "Discussion," pp. 38–47, both in Brown and Rosengren, *The Merger Boom.*

14. Ravenschraft, "The 1980s Merger Wave."

15. Anne Kahl and Donald Clark, "Employment in Health Services: Long-Term Trends and Projections," *Monthly Labor Review*, August 1986, p. 14; Milt Freudenham, "Volleyball on Health Care Costs," *New York Times*, December 7, 1989, p. D1, reports estimates by the Congressional Budget Office and the administration where the nation's total health care bill is expected to exceed $600 billion in 1989, up about 11 percent from 1988.

16. James L. Heskett, *Managing in the Services Economy* (Boston, Harvard Business School Press, 1986), p. 3.

17. Robert B. McKersie and Peter Cappelli, "Concession Bargaining," in Richard Rowan (ed.), *Readings in Labor Economics and Labor Relations* (Homewood, IL:, Richard D. Irwin, 1985), pp. 243–253.

18. U.S. Department of Labor, Bureau of Labor Statistics, "Linking Employment Problems to Economic Status, *Bulletin 2169*, Tables 5, B–1 (Washington, DC, June 1983); U.S. Bureau of the Census, *Census of the Population*, Table 287, 1980.

19. Debra Lynn Newman, "Black Women Workers in the Twentieth Century," *Sage*, 3, no. 1 (Spring 1986), pp. 10–15.

20. Ibid. See also Sharlene Hesse-Huber, "The Black Woman Worker: A Minority Perspective on Women at Work," pp. 26–35, and Julianne Malveaux and Susan Englander, "Race and Class in Nursing Occupations," pp. 41–45, both in ibid.

21. See Gordon et al., *Segmented Work*, p. 198.

22. Phyllis Wallace, "Increased Labor Force Participation of Women and Affirmative Action," in Phyllis Wallace, *Women in the Workplace* (Boston: Auburn House, 1982), pp. 1–24.

CHAPTER 5

Internal Markets in Key
Industrial Sectors

We have noted that industrial sectoral growth trends opened workplaces to black women that had been closed prior to 1960. The types of jobs created were the main mechanisms by which this change took place. Industrial groups that dominated expansion spurred growth of specific occupational categories. White-collar industry such as banking, insurance, and government services, for example, underwrote growth in paper processing jobs such as clerical and secretarial work. But a second factor was the organization of jobs into functions and tasks. This included specific occupational clusters and groups and work scheduling and division of work into part-time and full-time jobs. Although there are variations at the firm level, and even among work sites of a particular company, the impacts of industry sector growth on labor is most visible in occupational structures within sectors and the stratification that occurs among job categories. For the remainder of this chapter, we examine how occupational patterns in industrial sectors work differently for black and white women workers.

In general black women have different industrial-sector concentration patterns than white women and, within sectors, the races also contrast in occupational distribution. Black women are more likely than white women to work in heavy manufacturing, in mail-order retailing, and in food processing. Also within manufacturing, higher proportions of black women than white work in blue-collar production work and as operatives and laborers. By contrast, white women are likely to work in less-dirty jobs and in the retail specialty trade, grocery stores, and drugstores. Another pattern is in employment of black women in heavy work, which explains their presence in sectors dominated by industries such as dry cleaners and laundries. These personal service sectors include substantial amounts of unskilled and heavy work, as is visible in the hotel industry (maids) or hospitals (maintenance, laundry workers, food service workers, and the like). Thus, while black women now have more diversified employment (e.g., telecommunications, transportation), they continue to dominate low-status traditional job groups in most business establishments. In the workplace, moreover, black women may have the lowest status clerical jobs or those that are routine back-office work, while white women are more likely to work as secretaries and even in entry-level administrative and managerial positions.

Key questions that may be asked are: To what extent do industry and the dominant firms influence the evolution of particular occupational structures and the differentiation among job groups? How does this shape the hiring of different labor forces? The following section examines how the organization of work and job characteristics, skills and task content, influence the relative status of black women.

MANUFACTURING AND OTHER PRODUCTION SECTORS

Historical distinctions between durable and nondurable manufacturing have blurred increasingly, as occupational categories and job content have changed. For example, nondurables have traditionally been considered less labor intensive and thus less subject to mechanization and productivity gains. But continuous processing industries, such as chemicals, pharmaceuticals, tobacco, textiles, and even food manufacture, have been transformed and become far more capital intensive. Moreover, the content of manufacturing itself has been transformed from a "craft" requiring skills to more routine operations with limited cognitive and manual skills, as in the case of electronics and computer assembly. A second large distinction may be with industrial relations and collective bargaining. Traditional durables manufacturing (basic steel, paper, chemicals, petroleum, electrical equipment, automotive assembly) were historically characterized by strong collective bargaining agreements. Nondurables were, by contrast, subject to weaker labor agreements. This was true of such industries as apparel and food processing. Coincidentally, nondurables also tended to be more fragmented in organization and more likely to hire women and nonwhites as principal work forces.

Durable and Nondurable Manufacturing

Trend data indicate that black women made their best gains in durable manufacturing, though nondurables continued to be more important as employers. Most gains in durable manufacturing were in transportation (motor vehicles and aircraft in particular), in electrical and electronics assembly, and in fabricated metals. The characterization of these sectors, however, may be misleading. While they maintain a large core work force, automotive manufacturers have recently shifted much production to peripheral manufacturers where work is performed on a contracting basis known as "outsourcing."[1] Many nondurable parts of the automotive assembly are produced under such arrangements, including interiors,

Table 5.1
Selected Durable Goods Manufacturing Employment

% Total Workforce Employed:

	Total employ-ment in sector		Managerial		Prof/Tech		Cler-ical		Operat-ives	
	B	W	B	W	B	W	B	W	B	W
Elec. Comp. Equipment	1.33	1.55	.04	.02	.04	.11	.17	.19	.08	.18
Radio/TV	.62	.59	--	.06	.10	.06	.04	.16	.42	.27
Elec. Equip.	1.30	1.72	.05	.04	.16	--	.41	--	.96	1.02

Source: CPS 1982.

plastic parts, and other small accessories. Outsourcing has also recently included more durable parts to permit more flexibility in production, to adjust scheduling of delivery, and to reduce inventories.[2] But lower pay generally results from these nonunion shops, or operations outside the United Auto Workers (UAW) main workplace agreements.[3] Another manufacturing category, electronics and electrical assembly and computers, is a relatively new industry with traditions of employing women as a main labor source under depressed wage conditions.[4] Black, Hispanic, and Asian women have particularly important employment in these groups. Work is frequently nonunionized and many manufacturers are small job shops producing parts for larger computer or electrical equipment manufacturers under contract.[5]

The employment of black women in durable manufacturing is generally at the lower status end of the sector, with the exception of some categories such as transportation equipment noted above. In Table 5.1, the internal job structure compares the proportion of total black and white women in electronics/computer equipment and electrical equipment. The distribution shows high concentrations in assembly categories for both black and white women, while few women of either race are employed in technical or managerial work.

The nondurable manufacturing industry still dominates blue-collar production work for black women. Trends indicate that a visible slowing of growth took place between 1960 and 1980.[6] In 1960 food processing was the second largest blue-collar employer of black women, but by 1980 the sector had slipped to fourth place behind apparel, electrical equipment, and textiles. The slowing of growth of the sectors that hire black women are caused by two trends: mechanization in the industry, and consolidation (mainly through acquisitions) of groups that formerly were traditionally small employers.[7] Particularly affected by these trends were meatpacking, seafood and poultry processing, and canning. Textile employment increases for black women did occur, probably reflecting the geographic shift of textile mills and jobs to the U.S. South between 1960 and 1980.[8]

Most black women are employed in three nondurable subsectors: food processing, where black women account for 12 percent of women workers; textile industry categories of yarns and finished fabrics, where 50 percent of the women are black; and the apparel industry, where 15.25 percent of women workers are black. By contrast, black women are underrepresented in the women's work force in some significant employers of women, such as the newspaper industry and printing and publishing. Black women tend to be hired in publishing overwhelmingly in operatives categories and are underrepresented in the higher status crafts and managerial, technical, and professional jobs. Finally, at the upper status and more heavily unionized end of the non-durable sector scale, in more mechanized high-tech industries such as tobacco, chemicals, drugs, rubber, and plastics, both black and white women have only a negligible employment presence.

Industrial Services: Transportation, Communications and Utilities

The industrial services group probably represents the most important gains for black women in both job status and wages. Wages are discussed in Chapter 6, but in at least one subsector, communications, in 1982 black women had nearly reached wage parity with white women. Earnings were the highest of all industrial sectors, including government. The gains for black women coincided with spectacular job growth. Expansion in relatively high-status blue-collar crafts employment and higher skilled operatives and clerical activities such as telephone operators helped black women workers. Institutional factors undoubtedly also played a role in opening job opportunities in all occupational categories. Strong collective bargaining and highly visible government regulation and oversight in several parts of the industry helped push wages up.

Both black and white women have made only limited employment break-throughs in utilities, transportation, and telecommunications services. In utilities, which consists principally of natural gas, electric, and water utilities, most jobs are in blue-collar maintenance work where women have failed to penetrate to date. Gains were more important in transportation and telecommunications. Government influence in public transit may have played a role in facilitating integration. In telecommunications an additional impetus may be successful affirmative action litigation such as the influential AT&T case of the 1970's.[9]

Industrial services such as transportation and telecommunications represent a new employer of black women, with the bulk of hiring having taken place after 1960. In 1982 the group constituted 6 percent of total women's employment, but it was far more important for black women than white counterparts. Black women's employment more than doubled in the transportation sector from .65 percent to 1.49 percent between 1972 and 1982, while employment in the communications industry grew from 2.0 to 2.92 percent over the period.

PERSONAL AND BUSINESS SERVICES AND TRADE

Overall trends in personal and business services reflect three separate economic changes: (1) consolidation and expansion, particularly of a national corporate

Table 5.2
Distribution of Female Personal Services Employment by Race, 1982

	% Total Women's Employment	% Total Women's Employment: Black Women	White Women
Private Households	1.89	33.29	66.71
Hotel/Motels	.97	23.40	76.60
Lodging	.94	16.08	83.92
Laundries, Dry Cleaning Estab.	.50	33.51	66.49

Source: CPS 1982.

industry; (2) reduction in the number of jobs associated with highly individualized personal services; and (3) growth of a new range of temporary help businesses, based on needs of larger businesses to subcontract out specialized needs on a temporary basis for flexibility and efficiencies.[10] Personal services, which includes hotels, laundries, and dry cleaners in the industrial category and private households, have undergone radical transformation in recent years. The hotel industry is increasingly managed through highly consolidated corporate organizations.[11] It employs large numbers of low-skilled maintenance workers, maids, and housekeepers, as well as clerical staff. In large new corporations the bulk of employment is organized around high-efficiency principles and thus job expansion has occurred at a moderate pace. As Table 5.2 shows, current employment for black women is mainly in low-skilled maintenance categories. Laundries and dry cleaners also remain an employers of black women at the low skilled end although some consolidation has taken place with a resulting leveling of job growth. Rapid declines in domestic employment are reflected in modest current levels. As mentioned, the decline in domestic jobs overall between 1960 and 1980 was precipitous. Change in the nature of much domestic household work has come about less through corporate consolidation of maid services by employers such as hotels than through subcontracting of the more lucrative jobs on a specialized basis such as floor and carpet cleaning, window washing, and, above all, building janitorial and maintenance services (categorized under the business services industry).

Personal Services

Personal services still represents an important employment source for black women. Slightly over 7 percent of black women are employed in the sector, compared to 5.27 percent of total women's employment. Black women are also more likely to work in laundry and dry cleaning and in the hotel industry than white women, as well as in domestic employment.

Table 5.3
Occupational Distribution of Women by Race in Personal and Business Services Sectors, 1982

	Total		Management		Clerical		Operatives		Services	
	B	W	B	W	B	W	B	W	B	W
Private households	5.37	1.43	–	–	–	.04	–	–	5.08	1.25
Hotels/ motels	2.03	.79	–	.10	.18	.22	–	–	1.84	.41
Laundries/ dry cleaning	1.42	.37	.05	.02	.20	.16	.99	.17	.05	.01
Building services	1.20	.29	–	.01	–	.06	–	–	1.46	.21
Employment, temp help agen.	.61	.41	–	.04	.35	.25	–	–	.23	.02
Entertainment	.11	.54	.03	.04	–	.14	–	–	.09	.17
Beauty shops	.44	.75	–	–	–	.02	–	–	.44	.73

Source: CPS 1982.

Business Services

The business services group includes a complex of activities and is one of the fastest growing parts of the services sector.[12] In the main, growth is related to the expansion of contracting specialized services of a wide range, from maintenance and unskilled to skilled professional categories such as nurses, technical draftsmen, and computer services professionals. The bulk of employment, however, is in white-collar clerical work (particularly temporary help agencies) and blue-collar service work, such as building maintenance. As a result, these employers have become an important employment resource for black women. In 1982, for example, black women constituted 17 percent of all women employed in temporary employment agencies and 35 percent of women in the building services sector.

The occupational structure for both personal and business services industries as illustrated in Table 5.3 shows similar patterns. Most black women are employed in lower status categories of blue collar services or as clerical help.

Retail and Wholesale Trade

Retail and wholesale trade gains for black women followed established patterns set by white women, although within subsectors hiring patterns differed considerably as Table 5.4 shows.[13] Occupational distribution indicates that important stratification between the races persists. Black women are far more restricted within female intensive retailing than white women. For example, few black women work in drug and grocery retailers or in specialty retailing compared to white women. But black women continue to work in restaurants and have been integrated in mail order and department stores since the 1960s.

Table 5.4
Occupational Distribution of Women by Race in Retail Trade, 1982

	Total		Mgmt		Sales		Clerical		Other	Services
	B	W	B	W	B	W	B	W	B	W
Grocery	1.14	2.24	.07	.18	.12	.29	.69	1.25	.07	.09
Apparel, acc.	.34	1.04	.01	.23	.13	.57	.14	.14	--	.01
Drugs	.28	.71	.03	.06	.04	.22	.16	.27	.04	.09
Dept, mail	2.57	3.20	.13	.41	.77	1.34	1.29	.07	.13	.07
Eating, drin.	4.10	5.42	.24	.50	--	.02	.51	.41	3.23	4.37

Source: CPS 1982.

In general, wages in retailing are among the lowest in the economy. This reflects a continuing concentration of low-end jobs, but also some recent changes in management and technology. Restaurant and food retailing offer examples. Fast food chains have produced new jobs characterized by the introduction of highly mechanized, high productivity production systems. Most food is prepared in assembly operations in factories, then transported in prepared form to chain outlets. Staffing in the restaurant is at minimum or low wages, requires little judgment or personal service, and is highly routine. Combinations of cashier, service, and kitchen staff are incorporated into typical jobs, and part time work and high turnover are built into the job system. Similar innovation has driven discount stores and department store expansion to aim at very high productivity (increasing sales per square foot) while reducing customer service. The boom in mail-order business reflects an even greater automation of retailing. Customers themselves perform much of the service, leaving a staff comprised almost wholly of routine clerical workers processing orders. Conversion of these parts of the trade sector to new forms has involved identification and recruitment of a very different kind of worker from the past, an entry-level, relatively low-skilled labor force with almost no face-to-face service skills required.

Within the trade sectors, black women tend to have different occupations than white women. They are likely to work in services and clerical work as well as in sales in department and specialty stores, and they are rarely employed selling big-ticket items such as furniture and appliances. Black women have made considerable gains since the 1960s in department store sales jobs, although the high proportion in mail-order establishments reflects a high concentration of routine clerical work. In the case of restaurants, black women most often work as cooks, kitchen help, dishwashers, and in maintenance work.

Wholesale trade remains a male-dominated sector with few gains made by women in the past two decades. Retail trade, by contrast, is female-dominated although subsectors may differ considerably. In retailing, large-ticket items such as furniture, home appliances, automobiles, hardware, and lumber are dominated by men, while department stores, mail-order establishments, and restaurants are considered female-intensive workplaces. Black women's gains in the trade sector,

Table 5.5
White-Collar Employment of Women by Race

	Total		Prof./Tech.		Management		Sales		Clerical		Other Services	
	B	W	B	W	B	W	B	W	B	W	B	W
Banking	2.52	3.16	.28	.21	.01	.49	.05	.01	2.08	2.42	.10	.03
Insurance	2.12	3.00	.34	.22	.09	.26	.29	.44	1.28	2.06	.11	.02
Credit Agency	.38	1.02	--	.05	.09	.20	--	.01	.28	.76	--	--
Real Estate	.79	1.43	.01	.01	.05	.35	.06	.50	.51	.48	.11	.08
Federal Postal Service	1.10	.41	--	--	--	--	--	--	--	--	--	--
Other Federal	3.56	1.59	.57	--	.28	--	--	--	2.49	--	.17	--
State Government	1.20	1.09	.28	--	.01	--	--	--	.80	--	.10	--
Local Government	1.92	1.60	.17	--	.14	--	--	--	.95	--	.59	--

Source: CPS 1982.

therefore, were made almost exclusively in the retail trade specializations dominated by women.

WHITE-COLLAR SERVICES INDUSTRY

The impressive gains made by black women in white collar services industries reflect both the growth of the services industries in the postwar economy and the transformation of employment categories and work content by management innovation.[14] Work force improvements, however, were uneven. The public sector registered the strongest gains in both total employment and status.[15] In nongovernment employment, some sectors proved more favorable for black women than others. For example, black women in public administration underwent the only employment increase of the four labor groups from 1960 to 1980 and while the ratio of public- to private-sector white-collar jobs for white women was 63 percent in 1980, this ratio for black women was 133 percent. While gains were made by black women in private white-collar sectors such as banking and insurance (the so-called FIRE group [finance, insurance, and real estate]), the record is somewhat mixed compared to public-sector employment. Between 1972 and 1980, the proportion of black women working in banking increased from less than 2 percent to over 3.5 percent. But insurance employment over the same period fell by a full percentage point from 4.11 to 3.10 percent.

The distribution of black women within white-collar employment, as well as occupational groupings illustrated in Table 5.5, contrasts with white women and reflects both stratification of occupations and industry growth. In this, the subsectors have responded differently.

Government

Government employment overall is more important than private white-collar employers to black women. Public employment gains have been higher in the federal sectors (federal administration and the U.S. Postal Service) than at state and local levels. Interestingly, black women are also more likely than white women to seek careers in the military services.[16] Part of this difference may be attributed to a traditionally open hiring policy toward blacks by the U.S. Postal Service (integrated in pre-World War II times), and to the stronger Civil Rights actions at the executive level in the U.S. government. Executive orders promoted ends to racial barriers as early as the Roosevelt administration and continued through the Kennedy years. Only in the mid-1960s did state and local governments become subject to U.S. statutes forbidding discrimination based on race. A final reason may be the more systematic application of civil service testing for entry and promotions than at state and local levels. Thus black women have benefited from the rapid expansion of local government jobs, and from promotions up the ladder in professional and managerial work in federal employment.

Private-Sector Employers

The most significant employers of black women in private-sector white-collar industries are banking and insurance. Employment in these sectors, as well as in credit agencies and real estate, are far more important for white women, however, as Table 5.5 indicates. In all cases, jobs are stratified somewhat by race. Although both black and white women are employed overwhelmingly in clerical jobs, white women are more likely than blacks to work in management and sales in insurance and real estate, and less likely to work in professional and technical work. The key driving force helping black women in white-collar jobs was the rapid postwar growth of white-collar services industries. Between 1960 and 1980, white-collar services expanded by 87 percent, compared to 51 percent of total jobs in the economy. The transformation of work content and organization within occupational categories, however, was another key factor.[17] In banking and insurance industries in particular, the spread of automation and replacement of manual transactions with computerized data processing in accounting and other paper processing tasks created an entirely new array of occupations to replace the old.[18] These new clerical jobs, however, effectively downgraded many of the jobs they replaced, which were characterized as technical or managerial jobs and generally held by men.[19]

PROFESSIONAL SERVICES: HEALTH, EDUCATION, AND SOCIAL SERVICES

The professional services sector is dominated by health and education, both in the number of establishments, and in the size of budgets and employment.[20] The group is also the most significant employer of women, though black women are far more dependent on health and welfare as a source of employment than white women. The health care industry hires over one-fifth of all women workers and accounts for nearly one-fifth of all black women in the work force. Educational services employ roughly 17 percent of all women and a similar proportion of black women. Finally, social welfare organizations comprise less than 2 percent of total women's employment but around 2 percent of the black women's work force.

All three subcategories of professional services have undergone massive expansion of jobs during the recent past, far outstripping overall employment growth by substantial margins. Health services employment alone grew by 55 percent, compared to 23 percent for total employment during the 1970s. Behind this spectacular expansion was the escalation in public spending, underscored by demographic changes and rising family incomes. In the case of health services, the growth in elderly populations, legislation, insurance, and subsidy programs spurred expansion of hospitals and long term care institutions. At the same time, consumer spending growth helped by workplace health insurance coverage underwrote the rise in private physicians and outpatient and other specialized health care.[21] In the case of education, while elementary and secondary school populations declined somewhat, little leveling in expenditure in these sectors occurred. Growth also occurred in the postsecondary and adult training segments of the market.

Growth patterns in expenditures, sales, and employment in professional services also reflect relatively low productivity or generally high ratios of personnel per client or output unit. A possible related factor is the high level of government licensing and standard setting. In contrast to other white-collar services, health, education, and most human services such as counseling and social work are relatively labor-intensive and difficult to automate or apply managerial efficiency techniques to. Although isolated gains have been made in some areas such as adult training, through the use of audiovisual technology and computer applications, traditional methods overwhelmingly characterize service delivery techniques whether medicine, psychological counseling, or teaching at all levels. The complex licensing practices frequently interface with labor force standard-setting on the job. In the case of education, for example, government standards restrict staffing of elementary and secondary school systems, which reduces the supply of teachers. At the same time, local governments negotiate and set standards of pupil/teacher ratios, which may further reduce productivity. In education, as in health care and human services, much of the assumption about staffing assumes a qualitative dimension to services that could decline if client or services caseloads were pushed up without restraint.[22]

Growth in employment may slow and level in the future, owing to a combination of institutional and internal market efforts to reduce costs.[23] Health care has been particularly targeted for cost reduction by national Medicare and Medicaid program managers. Employers have also lobbied private insurers for reduction in cost-sharing burdens.[24] These cost containment efforts may alter job content drastically, increase work loads, and reduce employment and wage growth. Because of past employment patterns, these trends will have important impacts on the anticipated level of black women's employment in the future. In education, demographic shifts will curtail employment for black women more than others. Black women are heavily employed in elementary and secondary education, where employment will decline most.[25]

The Health Care Industry

The health care industry comprises four principal U.S. Census categories defined by the type of facilities and care offered: hospitals, convalescent homes, private practitioner offices, and "other" health care. The latter category comprises mainly outpatient facilities, community health centers, health maintenance organizations (HMOs), and laboratories. Distinctions have blurred somewhat recently, particularly between physicians' offices and more institutionalized forms, with the growth of group practices. Health care constituted one of the fastest growing employment sectors in the economy in the recent past, although signs of slowing occurred during the mid-1980s. For example, between 1960 and 1980 employment in health care doubled. By 1984 nearly 7.2 million individuals were employed in the sector. A slowing of growth is predicted for the next ten years, as well as a shift of growth from hospitals and convalescent homes to outpatient care facilities and physicians' offices.

Public and private spending on health from federal Medicare, Medicaid, and third-party private insurers was an important factor behind the dramatic increase in employment in health. These insurance programs supported spending growth and permitted massive expansion in the number of hospital beds, as well as the proliferation of new, high-cost, specialized technologies and equally specialized personnel to operate them.[26] The biggest expansions took place during the 1970s. In 1970 about 4.3 million people worked in hospitals, convalescent institutions, physicians' offices, and other health care facilities. By the end of the decade, the number had grown to more than 6.7 million, or an increase of 55 percent, compared to an expansion of the total work force by 23 percent. For black women, expansion of both the hospital industry and the $18 billion nursing home industry was critical to employment growth. By 1980, over 11 percent of all black women in the labor force were employed in either of these two sectors. Black women were key beneficiaries with the shifts from higher cost institutions to outpatient care, decentralized care, community-based care, and HMOs. One reason was that the shifting of care from higher cost hospitals and residential facilities to cheaper outpatient care was accompanied by growth in less-skilled care workers and lower cost administrative and clerical workers. Black women benefited from this downgrade process. As Table 5.6 indicates, expansion of the health industry is forecast to continue, though at reduced rates.

Hospitals dominated the health care industry both in revenue and employment, constituting more than 40 percent of the 2.8 million new jobs created between 1972 and 1984. In part, the growth of hospitals was spurred by the evolution of medicine itself, and particularly the expansion of specializations. Increasingly

Table 5.6
Health Industry Employment Growth Forecasts

Industry	Actual	1984	Projected	1995
Physician's Office	1,363.0	1,778	1,908	2,061
Other Health Practitioners	148.1	227	290	356
Nursing Homes	1,144.6	1,271	1,650	2,057
Hospitals	4,078.1	3,401	4,366	5,045
Medical, Dental Labs	113.2	126	135	140
Outpatient Care Facilities	190.7	284	390	450
Health and allied Services not elsewhere classified	151.0	238	315	426
Total Health Services Industry	7,188.7	7,325	9,054	10,535

Source: A. Kahl and D. Clark, ''Employment in Health Services: Long Term Trends and Projections,'' *Monthly Labor Review* 109, no. 8 (August 1986), p. 19.

sophisticated technology grew with specialized medical procedures in both diagnosis and treatment. A second force, related more to the health care financing system and particularly the growth in government-subsidized Medicare insurance for older patients, is cost control caps and decentralized and contracted services.[27] While elderly patients were more likely to require the highly sophisticated approaches to care, as well as higher rates of surgery and hospitalization, the method of payment worked to encourage more costly hospital-oriented medicine. Recently, federal policy has aimed at controlling facility expansion and treatment costs within typical hospital settings by a system of regulatory permissions for bed expansion and prospective diagnostic and procedure cost limits. These will probably level cost expansion and reduce employment growth as well. Similar trends may take place in the convalescent home industry.[28] Both elderly and nonelderly patients are being shifted to other kinds of facilities, particularly outpatient care, group practice, and HMOs. This change represents a unit cost reduction and a change to less labor intensive care. Coincidental with the change, decentralized and outpatient care require increased responsibility on the part of patients, lower per patient professional time, and, finally, more reliance on preventive strategies to avoid more costly treatment.[29]

Deployment of labor within the health care industry traditionally emphasized a woman's work force, including a high proportion of black women providers. Some 15 percent of all women workers are employed in the health care field, with nearly 9 percent alone employed in hospitals. In the case of black women, approximately 30 percent were reported by the Current Population Survey to be employed in health care in 1982, with around 12 percent in hospitals. In subsectors, however, the races contrast somewhat. Black women are more concentrated in convalescent homes and outpatient clinics, while white women are slightly more likely to work in physicians' offices and hospitals.

Internal job structuring and occupational stratification unique to health care also influenced past employment growth and wage trends in the industry, and may contribute to racial stratification patterns.[30] One source of influence on stratification of health jobs and wages was the institutional effect of strict, professional rules that separated jobs vertically and horizontally into groups defined by specializations. Licensed specializations define job groups to reduce overlap or flexible assignments among jobs. Professional work categories dominate the industry, with physicians at the top of the hierarchy, and subprofessional categories such as licensed practical nurses, health aides, orderlies, and other assistants at the bottom. While the 1970s saw revival of older categories (midwives, for example, to supplement obstetricians), and new categories, such as nurse practitioners to extend the range of responsibilities of registered nurses and health aides to supplement and extend the caseload of professional technicians, the effect of licencing largely offset intended productivity gains. Many support and helper roles ended up being narrowly defined and subject to strict rules and tasks, particularly in the case of patient care.

A second kind of internal managerial change was the deployment of workers for maintenance activities. Hospitals have long used large numbers of maintenance workers for janitorial, cleaning, building maintenance, grounds keeping, laundries, and food services, as well as patient-related maintenance chores (bed-making, personal hygiene, housekeeping). Growth of these jobs was spurred mainly by the addition of new facilities, as each institution was, by definition, self-contained. A third category of jobs that expanded was that associated with administration of the institutions themselves. These were essentially white-collar clerical jobs related to patient intake and scheduling, extensive medical record-keeping, financial and billing activities, and general administrative work such as payroll. Jobs in most of these three categories were organized quite separately, with little overlap. Typically, hospital job expansions were greatest at the lower end of the status, pay, and responsibility scales. While, in principle, subprofessional categories of jobs were designed to increase productivity of higher cost physicians, technicians, and managers, in fact, productivity changes were unclear. In the case of administrative clerical work, while mechanization expanded rapidly for record-keeping, new work was generated as more sophisticated medical information systems were introduced, and in contrast to, say, lawyers (to name another professional job), physicians rarely became directly involved with inputting and retrieving data from patient data banks. Instead, physicians now required a new class of support workers. The proliferation of low-end jobs in clerical, direct care, and maintenance work thus ended by extending the problem of labor-intensive low-productivity themes that historically characterized health care services.

The need for millions of new low-status and low-skilled workers provided an important resource for women workers, particularly black women. Black women had long been employed in nursing, despite strong barriers in access to nursing education and the fact that most employment was in racially segregated health

Table 5.7

Occupational Distribution of Women by Race in the Health Care Industry, 1982

	Total		Prof/Tech		Clerical		Operatives		Services	
	B	W	B	W	B	W	B	W	B	W
Health Care										
Physicians'										
offices	.44	1.76	.22	.40	.10	.91	.03	--	.09	.34
Dentists'										
offices	.27	.74	--	.15	.11	.20	--	--	.16	.32
Hospitals	11.87	8.30	3.28	3.95	1.93	1.83	.24	.06	6.27	2.05
Convalescent										
homes	4.09	2.39	.24	.34	.05	.14	.27	.09	3.52	1.72
*Other	2.70	--	.85	.72	.58	.35	--	--	1.06	.24

Source: CPS 1982.

facilities.[31] Both black women and men were employed in large numbers in unskilled jobs at hospitals as laundry, janitorial, maintenance, and kitchen workers. The massive expansion of subprofessional jobs during the 1970s provided new occupational opportunities, making health care one of the most important employers of blacks and other minorities. But while white women continued to constitute a large part of second-tier professional and technical jobs, owing to hiring patterns in nursing and lab technician jobs, black women were three times as likely as white women to work in low-status services categories.

As Table 5.7 indicates, black women continue to be far more dependent on employment in the health industry than white women. They also work in different sectors and jobs within the industry. Black women are nearly two times as likely to work in convalescent homes as white women and three times as likely to work in outpatient clinics, HMOs, and community health care. Occupational differences between the races are visible in the fact that black women are three times as likely to work in nonprofessional services and maintenance work where skill requirements are low. Higher proportions of black women than white women also work as licensed practical nurses (LPN's) or nurse's aides than as registered nurses (RN's). Future job growth for the industry as a whole in employment terms, as well as for particular occupational categories, is currently forecast to decline. Various federal and state efforts to reduce or contain costs may result in the leveling of jobs at the lower end of the scale, as the losses in nursing home jobs (mainly unskilled) between 1972 and 1982 illustrate.

Education

The education sector both resembles and contrasts with health. Employment for women of both races has traditionally been high. Elementary and secondary education, like nursing, provided one of the few professional occupations historically open to women. Other similarities with health are the professional stratification of occupations and work through licensing, which limits mobility. High levels of institutionally defined access are also the rule. But there are major differences in the financing and organization of education. These differ vastly

Table 5.8
Occupational Distribution of Women by Race in Education and Social Services, 1982

	Total		Prof/Tech		Admin		Clerical		Other Serv	
	B	W	B	W	B	W	B	W	B	W
Elementary/										
Secondary	10.36	10.72	5.27	6.87	.60	.30	1.93	2.03	2.45	1.40
Colleges/										
Univ.	2.58	2.63	.70	1.05	.12	.12	.76	1.15	.88	.27
Welfare										
Services	3.27	1.37	1.16	.49	.15	.15	.82	.43	1.14	.29
Religious	.22	.64	.06	.18	--	.01	.06	.35	.10	.10
Other	.35	.66	.07	.10	.14	.12	.14	.31	--	.12

Source: CPS 1982.

among the three principal education categories of elementary-secondary, colleges and universities, and proprietary schools. Local school districts dominate financing and hiring in elementary and secondary education, with a growing influence of states in regulation and cost-sharing since the 1960s. But unlike health, federal financing is limited. A large part of elementary-secondary education is also privately financed and managed in the form of state-regulated parochial and tuition-based schools. In some communities, more than half of all enrollments are in the private parochial sector. Higher education is also similarly split between public (financed primarily through states) and private institutions. About two-thirds of employment in postsecondary education currently is in private institutions, which are largely unregulated except for voluntary standard setting and accreditation through various college and university associations and programs. Proprietary institutions constitute a miscellaneous group of nondegree postsecondary education institutions, dominated by vocational training activities.

The strong gender-specific hiring traditions in education have continued to dominate the industry, despite a decade of federal intervention under Civil Rights directives.[32] Affirmative action has been managed by the U.S. Department of Education Office of Civil Rights. Women dominate professional jobs (mainly teachers and librarians) in elementary schools, while secondary and postsecondary education faculties and professional ranks are dominated by men.[33] The administrative and managerial ranks at all levels are also male-dominated, as are most of the oversight boards responsible for policy and top appointments, whether elected (local school boards) or appointed (trustees, regents, state education commissions, etc.). This governance problem, coupled with other factors such as lack of regulation at the state level, may be responsible for the lags in hiring and promotion of women and minorities in public higher education.[34]

Elementary and secondary education employ the most women in the education sector, with black and white women employed at about equal levels of 11 percent. As Table 5.8, showing employment in the education sector, indicates, within elementary and secondary education black women are slightly more likely to be employed than white women in services and administrative work, and slightly less likely to work in professional or clerical work.

Postsecondary education of all categories also provides limited employment for white or black women, or only 2.63 percent of the women's work force. White women are somewhat more likely than black women to work in colleges and universities, and more likely to work in professional and technical categories and less likely to work in other services jobs than black women. Low rates of hiring in teaching and administrative jobs, many of which are associated with teaching careers traditionally closed to women, explain much of the underrepresentation of women in general and black women in particular.

Factors that influenced past growth of education and the patterns of black women's employment may, as in the case of health, shift in the future.[35] Institutional rules are likely to maintain high degrees of stratification among jobs and a strict hierarchy that will continue to dominate mobility. In fact, the fragmentation of oversight mechanisms in education may result in more stability than in the case of health care, where state and national standard setting have been influential in broadening occupational classifications, as well as increasing the numbers in paraprofessional and services employment. A second factor is productivity. Even more than health, education has been very slow to adopt technology and new approaches to substituting high-cost labor, or extending the decentralization of services to the household or workplace setting. Under employment arrangements, training has grown considerably. Employer training covers a range of in-house educational services, from short-term to advanced degrees. This training uses a variety of technology, from computer interactive systems to satellite down links, thereby increasing the productivity of labor investments. But traditional education, whether elementary-secondary or at the postsecondary level, has gained little from new approaches. This is reflected in the spiraling tuition rates and public subsidies. Deficits have mainly been covered by the introduction of new enterprises into higher education systems, such as research laboratories, contracted services, and adult education programs that operate with high levels of efficiency and increasingly support traditional teaching and degree systems. Demographic changes and shifting demand for educational services may act to reduce institutional expansion in the future and, with them, the numbers of lower status jobs in clerical, paraprofessional, and service workers.

Social Services and Religious Organizations

Welfare, social services, and religious organizations employed collectively somewhat more than 2 percent of the women's work force but black women are more dependent on the sector than white women. Around 4 percent of black women work in social-services-related activities, principally in institutions and service organizations associated with social welfare, compared to just above 2 percent of white women overall. The bulk of employment is in human services activities, divided between clinical and counseling services to families, individuals, and residential institutions serving the mentally and physically disabled.

The sector is generally driven strongly by public subsidies. Traditionally state spending dominated in the mental health and child welfare areas. From the 1960s onward, however, massive expansions took place in federal grants for a variety of social welfare and human services needs. Among primary federal programs are Aid to Families with Dependent Children, a federal-state matched cash grant program administered by states; Supplemental Social Security and Disability Insurance; and a miscellany of grants for the economically and socially disadvantaged (job training, disabled, youth, corrections, child care, mentally retarded, and families). Two trends spurred expansion of employment in the sector: the Office of Economic Opportunity (OEO) during the 1960s, and the current trend toward deinstitutionalization of institutionalized populations, particularly the mentally ill.

Black women are disproportionately employed in social services compared to white women. They are three times as likely to work in welfare services, for example, as white women. One reason may be the domination of the sector by black professional women. Social work and management of social services agencies were a few of the traditional professional and managerial occupations open to black women and they continue to provide leadership and professional staffing for much of the sector. A second reason may be that higher proportions of black than white families constitute the clientele of such organizations and programs. A third reason is that in the case of health institutions, residential welfare facilities (mental hospitals, for example), employ large numbers of unskilled care workers, as well as constituting somewhat less desirable clientele and work.

IMPACT OF INDUSTRY SECTORAL CHANGE ON BLACK WOMEN WORKERS

Industry growth and change patterns play a crucial role in the employment of black women. With the massive expansion of jobs in services beginning in the 1960s, black women were provided with a strategic opportunity to gain both more employment for those wishing to work as well as occupational diversity within the black women's job economy. As an example, black women went from a high concentration outside the mainstream employment economy in domestic household work to near total deployment in mainstream workplaces within three decades. Job expansion has provided striking status gains in blue-collar production work and in professional, technical and clerical jobs. But a negative trend is a higher-than-average concentration of black female labor in declining industries, such as low productivity manufacturing or sectors where large numbers of unskilled and clerical workers may disappear as a result of mechanization. Typical of potential declines at the low status end of the employment ladder are human services and the maintenance-based industries such as hotels, restaurants, and retailing. The other kinds of jobs likely to disappear are clerical support jobs in white-collar-dominated industries such as banking, insurance, and communications, where black women have made substantial gains over the past two decades. But because many jobs are likely to be transformed, phased out, or exported overseas, it is not clear based on current industry forecasts that industry expansions will necessarily result in the same rates of growth of employment for black women in the future.

Another problem is represented by sectors dependent on public subsidies and regulatory mandates. Included are some of the workplaces where black women have made their "best" gains: health, education, public administration, and transportation. With downswings and retrenchment in the general economy, pressures tend to increase to reduce public spending, which results in cutbacks in employment by hiring institutions. Typically, the jobs that are least resistant to manpower reductions are administrative and managerial staff, followed by higher paid professional and technical positions, many of which are tenured through seniority systems. The lower status jobs—including paraprofessionals, low-skilled and nontenured entry-level jobs—are those that tend to be cut first to save costs, as the nursing home industry staff reductions following Medicaid cutbacks demonstrate. To assess the impact on growth and cutbacks resulting from industrial growth and change, it is important to look at compensation and work scheduling of black women workers more closely in the next chapter.

NOTES

1. David M. Gordon, Richard Edwards, and Michael Reich, *Segmented Work, Divided Workers* (Cambridge: Cambridge University Press, 1982), pp. 199–201.

2. Ibid. Also see Barry Bluestone and Bennett Harrison, *The Deindustrialization of America* (New York: Basic Books, 1982), pp. 7, 166–167.

3. Ibid. These analysts refer to "parallel" production systems where major firms in the most powerful industries, such as automobile manufacturing, create duplicate facilities to produce the same equipment. The facilities contrast, however, in the fact that the original is unionized and the new uses nonunion labor (p. 166).

4. Carolyn C. Perucci, Robert Perucci, Dena B. Targ, and Harry R. Targ, in *Plant Closings: International Context and Social Cost* (Hawthorne, NY: Aldine de Gruyter, 1988), provide a summary of employment and wage trends in the domestic electronics industry that resulted from the combination of internationalization of production in a search for cheap labor and technological innovation (pp. 25–29).

5. Ibid. This source builds a detailed case of one large company, RCA, which employed a variety of techniques to build a multinational business wherein electronics were an increasingly limited source of business revenue and the local social consequences of by-products of decisions in the form of plant closings, very high unemployment, and economic stress. See pp. 29–43 and Chapter 3, pp. 44–68.

6. U.S. Department of Commerce, Bureau of the Census, *Census of the Population,* Table 213: "Industry of the Experienced Civilian Labor Force," (for 1960), pp. 5–6; and Table 287: "Industry of Employed Persons By Sex, Race and Spanish Origin," (for 1980), pp. 1–372–377.

7. Perucci, et al., *Plant Closings*, p. 28. Bluestone and Harrison, in *The Deindustrialization of America*, provide interesting evidence of consolidations and ownership transfers during the 1970s (Appendix Table A.4, pp. 277–278) and one postwar case

study of the Textron Company's "acquisitions and known divestures" between 1943 and 1980 (Appendix Table A.5, pp. 278–282).

8. The textile industry is widely regarded as having moved South to escape unionization. For a recent review of efforts at unionization in the South, and wage differences between textile work and other industrial work forces such as the automotive industry in the South, see Terry W. Mullins and Paul Luebke, "Symbolic Victory and Political Reality in the Southern Textile Industry: The Meaning of the J.P. Stevens Settlement for Southern Labor Relations," in Richard Rowan (ed.), *Readings in Labor Economics and Labor Relations* (Homewood, IL: Irwin, 1985), pp. 196–200.

9. See Phyllis Wallace (ed.), *Equal Employment Opportunity and the AT&T Case* (Cambridge, MA: MIT Press, 1976), which includes detailed evidence on white-collar job restructuring and labor stratification by race and sex as part of the famous AT&T Court Challenge during the 1970s.

10. Perucci, et al., *Plant Closings*, p. 23. This source quotes Audrey Freedman, a labor economist at the Conference Board, as suggesting a 25 percent increase in the number of part-time and temporary workers in the U.S. work force between 1975 and 1985 (p. 23). See also Barry Bluestone and Bennett Harrison, "The Great American Jobs Machine: Proliferation of Low Wage Employment in the U.S. Economy" (Washington, DC: Joint Economic Committee, U.S. Congress, 1986). For an excellent analysis of the interaction between part-time job and occupational segregation, see Karen C. Holden and W. Lee Hansen, "Part-Time Work, Full-Time Work and Occupational Segregation," in Clair Brown and Joseph A. Pechman (eds.), *Gender in the Workplace* (Washington, DC: Brookings Institution, 1987), pp. 217–237.

11. For a review of the hotel-motel industry growth in recent years, see James A. Urisko, "Productivity in Hotels and Motels, 1958–73, *Monthly Labor Review*, May 1975, pp. 24–28. Productivity gains have been modest but growing in a relatively labor-intensive industry according to this analysis, reflecting technological development, organizational change, and increased demand. See also Lois M. Plunkert, "The 1980's: A Decade of Job Growth and Industry Shifts," *Monthly Labor Review*, September 1980, pp. 3–16, which points out that the hotel industry grew by another 50 percent between 1979 and 1989, compared to total nonagricultural employment of 20.9 percent over the period. For a general appraisal of the strength of services growth related to business cycles, see Michael Urquhart, "The Services Industry: Is it Recession-Proof?" *Monthly Labor Review*, October 1981, pp. 12, 13.

12. Wayne J. Howe, "The Business Services Industry Sets the Pace in Employment Growth," *Monthly Labor Review*, April 1986, pp. 29–37, describes the recent spectacular growth of services provided to business on fee and contractual bases; this analysis particularly cites the personnel supply business and temporary help as the second fastest employment growth area within business services between 1974 and 1984 at 221 percent. This may understate the growth of temporary employment, however, because the fastest growth in business services was experienced by computer programming and data processing services, which represented contracted manpower indirectly, since much of the labor hired by contracted organizations is, in fact, hired on a temporary, free-lance, or consulting basis. For a more detailed look at the temporary help industry, see Max L. Cary and Kim Hazelbaker, "Employment Growth in the Temporary Help Industry," *Monthly Labor Review*, April 1986, pp. 37–44.

13. Steven Haugen, "The Employment Expansion in Retail Trade, 1973–85," *Monthly Labor Review*, August 1986, pp. 9–11. According to this analyst, retailing was one of

the fastest growing industries in employment, adding 5 million jobs between the mid-1970s and mid-1980s; a major recession at the end of the two-decade period, however, resulted in massive consolidations, restructuring, and inevitable layoffs.

14. See Urquhart, "The Services Industry," which details the longer term services sector growth since 1948, particularly as related to growth sustained through business cycles and larger recession downturns; and Michael Urquhart, "The Employment Shift to Services: Where Did It Come From?" *Monthly Labor Review*, April 1984, p. 15–21, which indicates that, in part, growth in white-collar services relates to the increased participation of women in the labor force.

15. Charles Betsey, "Wage Gap by Race and Sex in Public Sector Jobs," *Policy and Research Report* (The Urban Institute), 15, no. 1 (July 1985), reports that of the 91 million jobs, government employment accounted for only 17 percent, but nearly 22 percent of employed minorities held government jobs; the pay gap by race and sex has declined by about 5 percentage points from 1973–82 but remains significant. In 1982, black men in the federal government on average earned only 76 percent of white male earnings and black women earned only about 55 percent of white males, levels close to the total labor force (p. 17).

16. According to recent analysis, black women have been extremely successful in the U.S. military and in 1984, for example, made up 28.9 percent of the enlisted females in all services. A number of explanations have been offered for this phenomenon, but very little research has documented these trends. For a summary analysis of black women in the military services, see James R. Daugherty, "Black Women in the Military," *Focus*, Joint Center for Political Studies, 13, no. 7 (July 1985), p. 3.

17. Many efforts at what has become known as "job redesign" were aimed at introducing other kinds of managerial innovation (i.e., reducing the number of supervisory personnel) new equipment, mechanization, and thereby increasing productivity in the services industry. See James Heskett, *Managing in the Services Economy* (Boston: Harvard Business School Press, 1986), pp. 100–105.

18. Myra Strober and Carolyn Arnold, "Occupational Segregation Among Bank Tellers," in Brown and Pechman, *Gender in the Workplace*, pp. 107–148, explore causes for occupational segregation patterns developed in the postwar period in one industry, banking.

19. Evelyn Nakano Glenn and Roslyn Feldberg, "Degraded and Deskilled: The Proletarianization of Clerical Work," in Rachael Kahn-Hut, Arlene Daniels, and Richard Colvard (eds.), *Women and Work* (New York: Oxford University Press, 1982), pp. 202–217.

20. Anne Kahl and Donald Clark, "Employment in Health Services: Long-Term Trends and Projections," *Monthly Labor Review*, August 1986, pp. 17–36.

21. Robert Frumkin, "Health Insurance Trends in Cost Control and Coverage," *Monthly Labor Review*, September 1987, pp. 3–8; and "Research Summaries: Pay Relationships Examined for Hospitals and Nursing Homes," *Monthly Labor Review*, January 1981, pp. 58–59.

22. There have been major efforts to measure output of services in order to develop performance standards, particularly in tax-financed services such as social welfare services and public education. The results have not been promising. For examples of approaches in human services and social welfare, see Peter Pecora and Michael Austin, *Managing Human Services Personnel* (Beverly Hills, CA: Sage Publications, 1987), particularly Chapter 4, pp. 56–91.

23. Frumkin, "Health Insurance Trends," p. 7.

24. Ibid. According to this analyst, national health expenditures grew from $215.1 billion to $387.4 billion between 1979 and 1984, or a 9.6 percent annual rate, compared with the Consumer Price Index increase of 7.4 percent over the same period. According to a survey of 209 employer-based health insurance plans reported in this article, employers used a combination of restrictions on type of care and increases in employee cost-sharing to help contain rising costs of insurance.

25. George T. Silvestri and John M. Lukasiewicz, "A Look at Occupational Employment Trends to the Year 2000," *Monthly Labor Review*, September 1986, p. 55.

26. Kahl and Clark, "Employment in Health Services," p. 25.

27. For a review of the trends in health cost containment, and efforts made to reduce hospital stays, inpatient care, decentralized care (nursing and personal care facilities outside of capital intensive facilities), see Plunkert, "The 1980's," pp. 14, 15.

28. Ibid.

29. Ibid.

30. Silvestri and Lukasiewicz, "A Look at Occupational Employment Trends," p. 55, report that two trends may be predicted: one is the shifting in work load to lower occupational status workers to save costs (i.e., more use of physicians' assistants, nurses, etc. instead of physicians); and the second is increased use of decentralized and lower cost care facilities, such as convalescent homes rather than hospitals, HMOs rather than higher cost clinics and private physicians' offices.

31. Darlene Clark Hine, "From Hospital to College: Black Nursing Leaders," *Journal of Negro Euducation*, Summer 1982, pp. 222–237; and Julianne Malveaux and Susan Englander, "Race and Class in Nursing Occupations," *Sage*, 3, no. 1 (Spring 1986), pp. 41–45.

32. For trends on public education employment, see Barbara Cottman Job, "More Public Services Spur Growth in Government Employment," *Monthly Labor Review*, September 1978, pp. 3–7. This analyst pointed out that both women and blacks are overrepresented in government and public education compared to white men. This is particularly true of elementary education, where many school systems in big cities in particular have become resegregated with white flight to suburban locations and, in the case of women, where affirmative action has failed to offset seniority rules and the preference of men for more desirable secondary education jobs.

33. For a recent summary on progress and problems of discrimination in employment in U.S. higher education, see Gerald David Jaynes and Robin M. Williams, Jr. (eds.), *A Common Destiny: Blacks and American Society* (Washington DC: National Research Council/National Academy Press, 1989), pp. 275–277.

34. Ibid.

35. Silvestri and Lukasiewicz, "A Look at Occupational Employment Trends," p. 55.

CHAPTER 6

Wages and Benefits

By far the most widely recognized impact of industry on labor is on wages and other compensation. Analysts have long noted that wages vary substantially among industrial categories and change at different rates over time. Industry wage rate differences have been explained by many causes, including occupational concentration, level of capital investment, strength of unionization, and the average size of individual firms in an industry.[1]

Historically, however, wage theory has centered mainly on distinctions among workers such as skills, work experience, and the behavior and choice of individual workers and less on industry structural and market factors. Only recently has attention been paid to how industry and workplace influence pay. Dual labor theory noted that factors related to the internal structure of industry and firms may result in different productivity and opportunity for contributions of individual workers, thereby resulting in diverse pay and benefit levels.

Other industry-focused analysis has noted other causes for wage variations. Concentration effects, or the relative firm size in particular markets; broad regional characteristics such as those of the U.S. South; and internal job markets have all been noted to contribute to wage differences among industry categories.

FACTORS INFLUENCING WAGES

While wage differences among industrial groups may reflect market-based differences in how wages are related to production, changes in pay rates over time appear to reflect other causes. Included are changes that reflect different growth rates of industry and in the approach firms take in restructuring work and organizing job categories. Services have been important in developing entirely new types of task organization and production systems, as well as wage structures. This contrasts substantially with traditional blue-collar manufacturing on which much wage theory has been based.

Services industries have produced a proliferation of new occupational systems and job groups that reflect the intrinsic nature of services work in both routine and thinking-based activities. Both have in common blurred and clouded relationships between output and wages. Since output values are more difficult to calculate and measure, in services both qualitative and quantitiative values of labor may be set somewhat arbitrarily, compared to those of production-based enterprises.[2]

Other recent influences on wages are business structure trends. Consolidations, aquisitions, mergers, and other internal restructurings are some influences, as has been the phenomenon of a rapid growth in part-time work, which cuts across industry and occupational lines. Consolidations and ''downsizing'' have reduced the size of administrative overhead and management systems which in turn resulted in the establishment of new wage and pay floors in the form of both informal pay systems and formal ''renegotiated'' labor contracts.[3] Another change is in the mix of wage and nonwage components of compensation systems. New definitions of the value of work and changes in its measurement result with the accelerated growth of prepaid health insurance, pensions, paid time off, layoff protection, and employee profit sharing and stock ownership plans. These compensation mix trends have proved very volatile, shifting from year to year and making it more difficult to measure or relate compensation to business production or traditional means of establishing a value for labor as a contribution to firm profits.[4] Job security and layoff provisions have grown in popularity recently in collective bargaining agreements, demonstrating that this benefit is one clearly favored by the work force.[5] But other benefits such as employee stock ownership are less clear. Such compensation may be valuable to labor when it is used as a strategy to control layoffs, but it may also be used as a strategy by management to create a ''poison pill'' effect and abort firm takeovers. In the latter case, it is management's position that is mainly enhanced.[6]

A final trend influencing wages is in massive change in work scheduling for much new employment generated in the economy. The growth of part-time work may reflect the evolution of new work systems that use labor in ways that maximize flexibility in production schedules and reduce costs of labor wage gains over time.[7] The impact on compensation of part-time work, however, runs deep. Hourly rates tend to be lower for part-time work and most social contract benefits such as promotions, health insurance, pensions, and paid time off are eliminated. The recent growth in part-time work has been significant. By the late 1980s, part-time jobs constituted over half of all new employment created in the economy.[8]

The impact of industry-specific wages for black women has not been well studied to date.[9] As noted, analysis of labor market discrimination has centered on race-based occupational differences and those between male and female workers. Occupational skills differences, however, are inadequate to explain wage and compensation variations as, for example, between jobs such as librarians and nurses held mainly by women and jobs such as sanitation work and construction held mainly by men.[10] Occupational crowding, or high concentrations of women in a few undifferentiated occupations, has also been cited as a factor depressing wages for women.[11] By artificially raising the supply of workers relative to the demand in occupations, wages can be depressed. Other causes for wage differences among workers, however, may relate more to internal markets and work and wage systems of specific industrial sectors.[12]

Many newer services sectors have emerged as key employers in the economy and in the process are evolving internal wage and occupational systems that are isolated and distinct from traditional systems. They are frequently no more than internal job pools that limit wage and status growth and are designed to be flexible in long-term commitment of the employer to workers. To the extent that a production industry such as manufacturing is increasingly service product dominated, as employment expands mainly in nonproduction activities such as financial services, marketing, and sales, trends established by services industries work and wage systems are being duplicated throughout the economy.[13]

Wage patterns of industries influencing black women result from two market trends: growth of services sectors and expansion in demand for female labor as a whole. Services growth provided a leap forward for black women from wages long associated with domestic work. New wage levels for black women became associated with prevailing systems of high, middle, and low wages in the marketplace. The new marketplace for black women, however, was mainly in female-intensive industries, or those employing majority female labor forces. The influence of a growth of demand for women in the labor force accelerated during the 1970s and shortages, particularly in white female labor, helped black women make gains, especially in white-collar employment sectors. These trends also spurred rapid wage gains for black women during the first part of the period of services expansion prior to a leveling in the 1980s when white women entered the labor force at more rapid rates. Overall, percentage gains in black women's wages led those of all workers, but the gap between the races in the female labor force remained at the close of the 1980s.[14] Annual earnings, a better measure of the status of black women given a relatively higher contribution to family income, remain a disadvantage. Continuing concentrations in low-paid employment within the services industry and the high rate of part-time work are factors that contribute to a continuing disadvantage for black women earners.

This chapter will examine how industry and sector hiring patterns influence black women's wages. We first examine some theoretical perspectives and evidence on wage variation among industrial sectors in the U.S. economy. Included are interindustry wage variations, as well as trends over the recent past. A second part examines impacts of industry on black women's earnings, particularly related to the extent to which women or men are traditional workers. Finally, we examine a compensation issue that is related to growth of nonwage compensation and part-time work.

Table 6.1

Average Hourly Earnings 1984 and Percent Change in Earnings 1974–84 in Nine Industries

Industry	Average Hourly Earnings 1984	Percent Change in Earnings 1974–1984
Nonagricultural Economy	$8.29	95.6
Gas Stations	5.24	75.8
Leather Footwear	5.40	86.2
Knitting Mills	5.88	89.7
Hospitals	8.51	132.5
Newspapers	9.39	71.6
Trucking	10.60	83.7
Carpentry	11.57	67.7
Basic Steel	13.02	107.6
Coal	14.91	138.2

Source: Bruce E. Kaufman, *The Economics of Labor Markets and Labor Relations*, (Chicago: Dryden Press, 1986), p. 209 (from Bureau of Labor Statistics, *Employment and Earnings*, September 1984 and March 1975, Table C–2).

TRENDS IN WAGE VARIATION AMONG INDUSTRIAL SECTORS

One striking characteristic of wages in the United States is the wide variation across industrial groups, in addition to variations by occupations and regions[15] As Table 6.1 of recent median wages for selected industry groups shows, current wages for broad sectors show a wide variation from the highest in coal mining, to the lowest in gas stations. While average hourly earnings in coal mining in 1984 exceeded the overall U.S. average for the nonagricultural economy by nearly 50 percent, hourly wages in gas stations, a retailing activity, were just 6 percent of the U.S. rate.[16] In addition to the distance between the top hourly rates and those at the bottom, wage growth trends also vary among industrial sectors. In recent years the goods-producing sectors, except for agriculture, have tended on average to fall above the national median, while services and trade fall consistently below. During the past two decades wages have grown faster in services than in manufacturing.[17] This reflects the need for services to compete in the broader labor market as well as recent improvements in productivity. In manufacturing, by contrast, wage gains have flattened with a slowing of growth.

What factors explain these variations among industrial sectors? While causes are complex, there is wide agreement that occupational mix, work organization, collective bargaining, capital investment patterns, and industry concentration effects or the degree of relative fragmentation in an industry are important.

The occupational mix of an industry is most often cited as a cause of low wage structure if predominate jobs require low skills.[18] Retailing and most service sectors are examples of industries that depend on large amounts of unskilled labor, which results in a low overall wage structure for the industry. Retailing also depends on a substantial proportion of part-time work. Part-time work pays lower hourly rates than those of full-time jobs and this contributes to an already depressed wage structure dominated by low-skilled sales and clerical workers. But industry wage rates over time may also reflect changes in the demand and availability of workers at particular skills levels. Labor-short New England in the 1980s, for example, with 3.5 unemployment compared to nearly 6 percent national unemployment, saw hourly wages in retailing and white-collar services rise substantially above national minimum wage floors and national averages. Apparel manufacturing illustrates another effect of occupation/skills labor supply effects on wages. The median wage for stitchers of men's suits and coats for example, paid $3.98 hourly in 1978, while, by contrast, the wage paid for stitchers of men's shirts was $3.29. Stitchers in men's shirt manufacturing, who are mostly women, were in greater supply than mainly male tailors in men's suits and coat manufacturing, showing how wage rates tend to vary despite similar skills.[19]

Collective bargaining has been broadly credited for contributing to wage levels in an industry as well as exerting pressures on nonunionized industry in regions.[20] There is debate, however, about the extent to which unions have raised wages above competitive levels during business downturns, and where foreign labor costs come into play, as in the case of the automotive industry. Higher labor costs in some unionized industries may merely reflect an aging work force where seniority translates into wages. Wage gains also slowed considerably during the recession and economic slowdown years of the 1970s and 1980s. Union concessions and givebacks were the most important trend in collective bargaining during the 1980s and had important impacts in reducing rates of hourly wage gains of the 1970s.[21] It is also possible that one of the main influences during the 1980s was not wage gains at all, but such components of the work package as job tenure, incentive pay, layoff protection, and early retirement severance agreements. By contrast in nonunionized industry, compensations such as health benefits and pensions have grown more rapidly to approach the unionized shop median compensation.[22]

The relative concentration or fragmentation of an industry may be exerting influence on wages in several ways. Concentration generally refers to the number of firms operating in an industry and their relative size. A high level of concentration indicates a few large firms. Concentration has grown through mergers and acquisitions in such sectors as transportation, banking, and manufacturing, and this may raise wage rates if corporations are forced to extend collective bargaining or higher wages to newly acquired firms. Barsky and Personick examined Bureau of Labor Statistics' Industry Wage Survey data and concluded that the more fragmented an industry was (i.e., the more firms operating in an industry), the more wages were dispersed and the more likely a sector was to fall in the "low-wage" category.[23] Using cross-sectional analysis of 43 manufacturing and 6 services industries and controlling for occupational wage structure, two factors were found to explain why fragmentation depressed wages. As expected, low-wage industries lacked companywide collective bargaining. Second, there was an absence of broad occupational staffing patterns and incentive pay systems. In general they found the higher the variation in pay rates and incentive systems, the larger the wage spreads.[24]

The following summarizes some current factors influencing industry wages:

1. *Industry profit margins*: Lower profit industry reflects lower labor costs as a part of total production costs.

2. *Industry production technologies and methods*: Technological innovation tends to reduce labor costs as a part of total production costs, or raises output; higher wages can result if productivity gains are passed to workers.

3. *Capital investment rates*: Capital-intensive industry may infer high levels of equipment and machinery, allowing individual workers to raise individual efficiency; can increase production capacity without increasing labor; and can result in higher profits passed on to workers.

4. *Market competitiveness*: Stable markets and low levels of competition can reduce labor turnover and allow labor costs to be passed on more easily to customers than in highly competitive markets.

5. *Regional Location*: Geographic locations can reflect labor supply conditions; labor surplus regions with high unemployment will tend to have low living standards, a less-educated and less-skilled workforce, and low wages.

6. *Industry hiring tradition and corporate culture*: Industry race and gender hiring traditions may reflect traditional values and attitudes toward each labor group in setting "a social value" of labor in wages, occupations, and compensation components, as well as policy on layoffs, promotion, advancement, raises, commission, and profit sharing.

7. *Unionization and collective bargaining*: There is tradition and effectiveness of labor organization and outcomes.

8. *Public regulatory tradition in industry*: There is an extent of public regulation, including standards, licensing, and price setting.

9. *Occupational mix and job system effects*: There are effects in weighting toward rigid or flexible occupations; extent of fine gradation of hierarchies; extent of skilled, craft, and professional job categories versus general, unskilled, or undifferentiated job systems.

Human Resources Causes for Wage Differences

There is a continuing controversial debate about the extent to which individual work force characteristics influence wage structures within industrial sectors.

Labor theory assumes that wages reflect differences in labor force characteristics. In essence, a widely accepted theory of marginal labor product argues if workers earn less, they deserve less because their contribution to output is worth less.[25] There are many problems with this construct, however. One is that labor input may be very hard to define and connect to particular production. Human resources characteristics are rarely matched with specific job criteria in hiring, and even less in production. Most employees are hired based on generic skills, then trained for specialized jobs as required. On the job, many if not most tasks either cannot be disaggregated and designed to a specific worker, or reflect team or group effort. By the same token, some workers with specialized skills may be under-utilized or undervalued by deployment patterns and internal firm work systems. Also, the promotional system used by most employers is carried out utilizing criteria other than performance on a specific job. Such factors as future potential and even interpersonal relations may dominate promotional systems.[26] A second problem is that output is even more difficult to define with the shift from goods to services. Measures of services output frequently cannot distinguish qualitative differences among services, such as on-time delivery compared to late shipments in a transportation industry, or between patients requiring ten-minute visits compared to those requiring more than one hour in health care.[27]

The case of low-skilled labor working in marginal industry represents another set of problems. As has been noted by dual-labor theorists Bennett Harrison and David Gordon among others, certain industries may deliberately hire work forces at low skills levels because the industry lacks the capacity to become more productive through application of technology, know-how, or better utilization of its labor force. This is the argument made by Bennett Harrison in finding that low-skilled workers may in fact be deliberately maintained at an unskilled, marginal level to permit low-profit-margin producers operating in uncertain and highly competitive markets.[28]

Demographic Mix and Work Force Segregation as Factors

The demographic mix of work forces and worker segregation patterns of black women may also support the argument that there are mechanisms for sustaining low-wage systems that are widespread in some industries. Past segregation of minorities in such industries as textiles, agriculture, and food processing in the U.S. South, as well as the hotel and restaurant industry more generally, created a nearly captive work force at generally depressed wages. With the end of segregation, however, low-status work systems were carried over into workplaces and industry without much change. The high concentration of black workers in the U.S. South provides an ample labor supply for sustaining a traditional low-wage system without much change, particularly if employers elect not to train and deploy workers in other than low-skilled jobs. The impact is to maintain depressed wages for black workers. In 1980, for example, over 17 percent of wage and salaried workers in the U.S. South were black, compared to 10 percent nationwide; and earnings for black southern workers were just 68 percent of the earnings of workers residing outside the South. By contrast, there was an 87 percent difference between wages of white southern workers and those residing outside the South.[29] In fact, the wage gap between southern and nonsouthern whites narrowed considerably over the recent past, even in the absence of unions and collective bargaining, while the black wage differential remained wide.[30]

Women workers of both races may be specifically recruited by certain industrial sectors because of the availability of workers partly caused by traditional barriers to the women's labor force entering other male-dominated industries. It is well known that industries dependent on part-time or flexible and seasonal work forces—such as retailing, restaurants, and the apparel trade in manufacturing—depended on women as a main work force, although explanations usually emphasized a collaborative agreement between workers (usually housewives) and employers favoring part-time and less-skilled work over full-time work.[31] With growth in the demand by women for full-time jobs during the 1960s, however, many traditional employers of part-time women workers faced labor shortages.[32] But the notion of labor shortage is difficult to interpret in traditional labor economics terms when women are involved. A true shortage would be reflected in either reorganization of the work into full-time employment, consistent with the demands of the available work force, or wages would rise to attract those workers who might then consider substituting full-time work for part-time options. The key employers in some parts of the economy, however, have resisted economic responses such as expanding work hours or raising wages. Recent trends in growth of contracted labor services and temporary employment agencies suggest that employers are more likely to stick with part-time labor, even if it means paying a high premium in the form of higher contract rates.[33]

Black women's earnings reflect interindustry wage structures as well as their labor force characteristics as value under competitive market conditions. Higher concentrations of black women in particular sectors appear to result in lower wages overall. The effects of industry crowding on black women's wages is visible in such sectors as personal services and the nursing home industry. Black women appear to earn less because they work in female-intensive industry, or in those sectors that traditionally employ a mainly women's labor force.[34] Analysis of female-intensive industries has demonstrated that wages are depressed for four reasons. First, there is an abundance of low-skilled occupations that depress wages overall. Second, women are more crowded in these industries, serving to increase competition and reduce wages.[35] Third, female-intensive industries may lack the kinds of occupational diversity and specializations that tend to raise wages by providing more steps in the wage ladder.[36] Since black women are overwhelmingly concentrated in female-intensive industries, and work mainly in the low end of the industry scale in such sectors as blue-collar services and nursing homes, they tend to be even more disadvantaged in earnings levels. Further, their occupational classifications are nonspecialized, with few steps in the wage ladder. A final contributing factor may be part-time

Table 6.2
Female- and Male-Intensive Industry

Sector	Percentage Total Female Employment in Industry	Distribution of Employment %Total Female	%Total Male
Agri/Fish/Forestry	17.9	1.2	4.3
Mining	13.7	0.3	1.6
Construction	8.4	1.1	9.4
Manufacturing	31.9	16.8	26.6
Durable Goods			
Non Durable Goods			
Transportation	20.7	2.1	6.1
Communications	47.2	1.6	1.3
Utilities	16.6	0.5	2.1
Wholesale Trade	26.9	2.7	5.5
Retail Trade	50.9	19.2	13.8
Finance/Insurance/			
Real Estate	58.0	8.2	4.4
Personal Services	70.4	5.2	1.6
Professional Services	66.3	31.4	11.9
Public Administration	40.0	5.0	5.4
Unclassified		4.7	6.0
Total	42.6	100.0	100.0

Source: *Census of the Population*, Table 287.

employment. Black women are increasingly employed in industries with large numbers of part-time workers such as retailing, hotels, and temporary agencies. This also depresses hourly wages and annual earnings.[37]

To the extent that there are barriers of access of black women to a full range of workplaces, there may be higher competition within the black women's labor force for those jobs that are close by and known to be available. The larger number of available workers for fewer jobs would tend to depress wages. The limited number of jobs, as well as geographic isolation of black women from a range of sectoral opportunity (i.e., concentration in the South, lack of transportation access to suburban employment in northern cities), reinforces the effects of a higher concentration of black women in some industries.

MALE-INTENSIVE AND FEMALE-INTENSIVE INDUSTRIES

As was noted earlier, men and women are distributed differently across industrial sectors and this pattern has important influences on black women workers. Although the severe concentration of women in a few industrial sectors has declined recently, problems remain and may exert influence on the earnings of women in both races. Table 6.2 of the distribution of male and female workers in main industrial sectors illustrates the principal concentration patterns of women. While women constitute 42 percent of the labor force, for example, they are concentrated at rates higher than their overall work force average in 5 of the total broad groupings of 13 sectors. Moreover, professional and personal services are overwhelmingly dominated by the women's labor force (column 2). Nearly half of the women's labor force is concentrated in retailing and professional services. This relative male- or female-intensiveness of industrial sectors has important consequences for earnings.

Black women earn most at their highest levels and have the smallest wage gap with other workers in industries where male workers predominate. In addition to the relatively higher wage structure, black women may have benefited from more aggressive affirmative action in those firms and industries where women workers had the lowest presence, and from a relatively recent entry, such as telecommunications. Women recently recruited into production work benefited from getting access to a broader range of occupational categories than they had in industry dominated by traditional women's jobs. By contrast, in sectors where women constitute a traditional hiring pool, black women tend to fare much worse. The gap between black and white women, for example, is greatest in sectors where wages are low and where women have historically provided the principal labor force—sectors such as nondurable manufacturing and retail trade. But in some low-wage sectors, notably personal services and private households, the longer hiring tradition has led to a more experienced black female labor force that earns higher wages than white women. In 1982, for example, the median age for "other personal services" was 42.2 for black women compared to 35.0 for white women. In Table 6.3 a more detailed industry breakdown illustrates the wage ratios for black women and white men and women for 1982. While the wage gaps between black women and white men are wide, this narrows considerably in higher wage sectors.

Median Annual Earnings by Sector for Black and White Women Workers

Earnings for black women workers have improved dramatically over the Census periods 1960 and 1980. The performance of industrial sectors, however, shows a wide range in mean earnings for black women, as well as industry-specific differences when black and white women are compared.

As Table 6.4—showing median annual earnings for black and white women in main sectors in the economy—indicates, black women have a very wide range of earnings. In agriculture and domestic employment, for example, where wages are lowest, black women earn approximately one-third of what they earn in public administration, the highest earnings sector. This gap is similar for white women, but black women overall lag more than 10 percent behind annual earnings of white women in ten employment categories, while they earn more than white women in only three. What is further significant is that in the categories that are the most significant for black women—professional services, personal services, retailing, and white-collar FIRE—the widest earnings gap occurs between the races. By contrast, in traditional male-dominated, high-wage industries, the race-wage gap

Table 6.3
Earnings Differences by Sector and Race

	% Male Employment	% Female Black	Employ. White	Ratio/Earnings BF/WM	BF/WF
Industrial Sector					
Agricult./For./Fish	50.0	0.6	1.3	51.7	76.0
Construction	91.3	0.6	1.2	65.0	98.3
Trans/Comm/Util.	73.3	5.2	4.1	63.4	98.3
Wholesale Trade	72.7	3.2	1.5	53.7	95.1
Finance/Insurance/ Real Estate	40.8	6.1	8.5	44.0	90.8
Business Repair	65.9	2.8	3.4	45.1	68.3
Entertainment	59.8	1.0	0.6	47.8	85.2
Manufact./Durables	77.8	7.6	8.1	52.9	89.5
-Electr.	60.2	2.1	2.2	52.7	98.0
Manufact./Non- Durables	67.1	9.4	8.1	50.5	94.3
-Textiles	44.4	1.8	1.0	54.6	95.7
-Apparel	19.9	3.0	2.2	38.0	80.5
Retail					
-Ml.Order/Dpt.St.	30.6	3.7	2.8	49.8	86.8
-Grocery Stores	51.3	2.9	1.4	61.4	106.3
-Eating, Drinking	48.3	4.1	6.2	52.3	92.0
Personal Services					
-Private Households	9.6	5.5	1.0	80.3	130.3
-Other Pers. Serv.	33.9	2.0	2.1	64.2	104.2
Hotels/Motels	34.5	2.2	1.4	45.8	76.6
Health Care					
-Hospitals	23.0	12.4	7.5	51.6	79.5
-Nursing Homes	12.0	3.4	2.1	52.0	79.9
-Other Hlth.Care	24.2	0.9	0.8	46.3	80.9
Education					
-Elementary/Sec.	29.7	10.6	9.7	63.8	95.4
-Other Education.	48.3	3.4	3.1	48.1	93.7
Welfare/Social Services	22.4	3.4	1.8	49.5	81.4
Other Professions	47.9	1.0	0.3	53.4	75.3
Public Administr.					
-Postal Service	63.6	1.0	0.3	63.4	94.8
-State/Local Govt	64.1	1.7	1.2	57.9	90.1

Source: CPS 1982.

Table 6.4

Median Annual Earnings for Black and White Women by Industry

Industry	Full-Time Women Workers		Ratio	Part-Time Women Workers		ratio
	Black	White	B/W	Black	White	B/W
Agricult./fores./fish.	5,432.3	7,151.6	76.0	1,189.7	4,662.0	25.5
Construct.	12,463.5	12,676.0	98.0	6,500.0	6,239.9	104.0
Trans./Comm./Utilities	14,677.6	14,936.8	98.0	4,888.2	7,000.3	69.8
Wholesale-Trade	11,541.0	12,138.4	95.2	4,026.9	6.081.3	69.8
Fin./Insur./Real Estate	10,999.8	12,114.9	90.8	3,936.6	7,197.3	54.7
Busin.Repair	8,108.4	11,866.8	68.3	3,894.0	3,382.6	115.1
Private Household	4,886.6	3,751.4	130.2	2,526.1	1,465.2	172.4
Public Administr.	14,428.6	14,649.4	98.5	5,943.7	7,889.8	75.3
Elect.Mfg.	12,110.7	12,363.4	97.9	6,000.0	9,378.1	64.0
Other Dur.Mfg.	11,449.0	12,785.0	89.6	8,540.0	7,434.3	114.9
Text.Mfg.	8,937.7	9,388.7	---	9,418.2	7,612.7	123.9
Other non-Dur.Mfg.	9,491.8	10,816.6	87.7	5,141.0	7,073.5	72.7
Retail: Mail Order/Dept. Stores	8,973.8	10,840.2	82.7	4,335.5	4,920.7	88.5
Other Retail.	10,618.3	9,989.6	106.1	3,042.0	5,582.8	54.5
Eat/Drink.-Establish.	7,326.3	7,960.3	92.0	3,928.8	4,254.8	92.3
Hot./Motels	6,458.0	8,431.6	76.6	5,236.3	4,301.5	121.7
Pers.Serv.	8,345.0	8,007.0	104.2	5,937.0	4,797.9	123.7
Hospitals	10,969.0	13,727.3	79.9	8,185.0	7,968.2	102.7
Nurs.Homes	6,905.4	8,539.9	80.8	6,068.0	4,128.0	146.9
Other health Care	11,352.9	11,906.1	95.3	2,578.0	7,051.7	36.6
Elemen./Sec. Education	12,588.5	13,426.5	93.9	3,897.9	3,855.6	101.1
Other Educ.	10,929.4	13,085.1	83.5	6,753.3	6,112.0	110.5
Welfare	11,630.1	12,683.3	91.7	3,969.0	3,540.3	112.1
Other Prof.	8,820.7	11,714.0	75.4	4,410.0	5,633.2	78.7

Source: CPS 1982.

tends to close. High-paid construction, transport-utilities, public administration, and higher paid durable manufacturing have very similar earnings patterns.

Part-time work seems to have a very different effect on annual earnings. Black women who are part-time workers earn more annually than whites in about half the sectors shown in Table 6.4. Moreover, no relationship is apparent between the wage rates and whether or not the industry is male- or female-intensive. Annual earnings appear to reflect the number of work hours rather than the hourly wage rate differences or occupational status. Because black women tend to work more hours on average than other labor groups in part-time postitions, their annual earnings are higher. At the same time, while both races work at very high part-time rates, or at about 40 percent of the work force, part-time work for black women is more likely to be involuntary.

Male-Intensive Production and Services Sectors

Although fewer than 20 percent of the women's work force are employed in traditional male-dominated goods-producing sectors, there are important benefits in wages for those who are so employed. In 1982, median wages in goods industries were the highest for full-time women workers of all sectors in the economy. Similar patterns were visible in capital-oriented services such as transportation, utilities, and telecommunications, another traditional male-dominated employment group, and in public administration, also traditionally male-intensive.

For durable goods manufacturing and electrical goods, two significant employers of women, both races have relatively high earnings in all occupational categories. These higher wage levels are attributed to strong unionization among blue-collar work forces, as well as high rates of capital investment in machinery and equipment. The narrowing of the wage gap between black and white women also characterizes occupations within sectors. The internal structure of occupations is stratified for black women, however. In both durable manufacturing as a whole and in electrical goods manufacturing, the higher the skills level generally, the greater the gap in earnings between the races. In administrative jobs, for example, earnings between black and white women are similar in the lower status computer/keypunch and secretaries job categories. The distance in earnings grows between black and white women in higher status professional and managerial jobs. This same problem is visible in the blue-collar occupations. The earnings patterns of black women operatives are close to those of white women but drop considerably in the higher skills crafts jobs. The earnings of construction industry occupations are similar to those of durable goods, except that black women tend to earn somewhat more than white women. The differences in pay at different occupational strata may reflect less experience or time on the job, but they do indicate lower mobility in status and pay for black women workers.

The more industrial services such as utilities, communications, and transpor-

Table 6.5
Annual Earnings for Selected Occupations in Male-Intensive Sectors

Construction	Full-Time Women Workers Median Annual Earnings:		Ratio
	White	Black	B/W
Prof./Technical	18,736	30,400	162.2
Crafts	12,470	10,400	83.4
Computer/Keypunch	15,880	11,900	74.9
Secretary/Typist	11,235	10,176	85.5
Other Clerical	11,898	6,565	58.7
TOTAL	12,696	12,463	98.0
Utilities/Transport			
Prof./Technical	16,707	19,880	119.0
Managerial/Admin.	15,062	NA	NA
Crafts	20,543	19,433	93.0
Operatives	9,739	8,000	82.1
Transportation	10,179	10,865	106.7
Non-Farm	12,314	8,787	71.4
Bookkeeper	16,044	15,226	94.9
Cashier	13,951	13,896	99.6
Computer/Keypunch	16,285	10,520	64.6
Secretary/Typist	13,640	13,486	98.9
Other Clerical	14,961	14,192	94.9
Other Services	13,960	16,114	115.2
TOTAL	14,936	14,678	98.2

tation are distinguished from other services by their capital-intensive features. Such services have generally high levels of investment in plant and equipment, thus coming closer to manufacturing than more labor-intensive services. They may also include production of tangible goods, as in the case of water and gas utilities. Industrial services activities are traditionally male employers and earnings patterns by women workers are similar to those in durable goods production.

As Table 6.5 indicates, the overall earnings gap between the races is virtually closed, and there is more equality between the races than in manufacturing. This is true for most occupations, whether administrative or blue-collar. It is also important to note that the wage structure tends to be higher in industrial services than in durable manufacturing for most occupational categories, with the exception of operatives. A number of explanations might be offered for these wage differences. One reason is the nature of collective bargaining and wage agreements. Public utilities and transportation, as well as the fast-growing telecom-

Table 6.5 (Continued)

Durable Manufacturing	Full-Time Women Workers Median Annual Earnings:		Ratio
Electrical	White	Black	B/W
Prof./Tech.	16,538	13,566	82.0
Managerial/Admin.	16,836	9,000	53.4
Crafts	14,992	8,692	60.0
Operatives	11,073	12,292	111.0
TOTAL	12,343	12,110	98.1
Other Durable			
Manufacturing			
Prof./Technical	16,838	15,200	90.3
Managerial/Admin.	20,488	15,500	75.6
Crafts	15,086	13,826	91.6
Operatives	11,221	11,140	99.3
Computer/Keypunch	13,475	12,840	95.3
Secretary/Typist	11,117	11,785	100.6
Other Clerical	12,607	10,890	86.06
Cleaning/Janitorial	11,706	3,275	23.32
TOTAL	12,785	11,449	89.6

Source: CPS 1982.

munications industry, tend to set national industrywide labor agreements, while negotiations in manufacturing and other production industries have become increasingly fragmented among multiple locals.

Transportation, utilities, and communications sectors have in common the highest wage structures in the economy, which may help raise wages paid to female workers. In part, higher than average median wages reflect strong unionization traditions of large blue-collar work forces, along with higher productivity on average than traditional female-intensive sectors. This permits firms to pass higher revenue through in the form of higher compensations for women. As Table 6.5 illustrates, for median annual earnings for occupations in selected sectors, differences in earnings between black and white women are generally low in construction and utilities. However, the more skilled the occupational category, the less the gap. Wage differentials are lowest in crafts and higher skilled clerical positions, and widest in routine clerical jobs such as keypunch operators.

The telecommunications industry is split between white-collar services and production and mostly blue-collar capital maintenance activities. Black women made strong inroads into the white-collar jobs, which produced wage gains. These improvements can be attributed to collective bargaining traditions of the industry and important equal opportunity court rulings from the federal court consent decrees of the 1970s, brought under the 1964 Civil Rights Act. Wage differentials between the sexes are fairly narrow in the clerical categories as a result, although blue-collar employment for women remains modest.

White-Collar Services

White-collar services can be divided between industries paying relatively high wages and those that are lower wage sectors. Public administration, like the utilities industry, is essentially dominated by male workers and, thus, has a relatively high wage structure. By contrast, earnings in the finance, insurance, and real estate sectors are lower. Public-sector wage levels may also be influenced by collective bargaining. Unionization has a long tradition in public-sector uniformed services and in blue-collar infrastructure maintenance jobs, such as public works occupations. Recent union gains have been made in organizing technical, professional, and clerical workers.[38] In addition, wages may be boosted in the public sector by rules on promotion and wage increases through established civil service systems.

Civil service systems help protect seniority, facilitate tenure and other layoff protection, provide for regular rate increases, and help promotions and pay gains. The domination of the employment base by men as in other sectors may contribute to success of the government labor force in stabilizing promotional ladders as well as higher wages overall. This benefits women workers in the form of higher than average earnings. Black women in public-sector employment are even better off. The gap between black and white women is the lowest of all industries in government. This undoubtedly reflects the perceived "fairness" of government employment as an attraction to black women as well as the reality of a more open hiring and promotional system.[39]

Earnings of black women employed in public administration illustrate striking advantages. Black women working full-time year around in government jobs earned median incomes of $14,429 in 1982 or 98 percent of the median earnings of white women. By contrast, the same earnings gap widens by nearly $3,400 to about 91 percent of white women's earnings in other white-collar industries. Public-sector wages are also uniformly higher across occupational categories, including both high and low ends of the job ladder in government. Explanations for the very close earnings parallel for women of both races may lie in the very different attraction each has for public employment. Because government jobs are perceived by black women to be "more open" in opportunity, it is likely that a ''creaming'' effect occurs and the brightest and best of the black female work force, including those with the most education and skills, enter government jobs. In addition to the reputation for more open hiring, government is also credited with assuring relatively fair and open promotions and assuring job security.[40] Recent studies also indicate that timely successes in affirmative action in state and local government employment on behalf of black women as well as active unionization and political pressures have helped total pay and status gains.[41]

Finally, it is possible that other regulations, such as those governing collective bargaining, may help boost wages and help monitor any subjective bias against hiring and promotions of black women. The strong influence of federal-standard setting in local government in wages and contract compliance such as Davis-Bacon, and in workplace safety and health rules governing work environments, hours of work, and other restrictions, have helped smooth out geographic wage differences and discrimination in hiring that has long characterized some local governments.

The white-collar private industries that employ mainly female work forces currently are dominated by two sectors, banking and insurance. Financial services and real estate are included under the FIRE nomenclature. As Table 6.6 indicates, median earnings for black women in FIRE are extremely low compared to the typical male intensive sectors reviewed previously.

Black women's earnings are also less compared to white women in high-status professional, technical, and managerial work categories. One reason may be that black women have less work experience than white women. Some indication of this is visible in the differences in median age between the races. In 1982, the median age for black women in nongovernmental white-collar services, for example, was 32.0 years, compared to 34.5 years for white women. We noted in Chapter 5 that FIRE sectors are ''transitional'' from mainly male- to female-dominated. Because of this and the internal occupational differences among sectors, wages are somewhat higher in clerical and managerial occupations in FIRE than in retailing and other female-dominated services sectors. Thus, on balance, black women have made important wage gains through expansion into the FIRE sectors.

Retailing and Personal Services

Retailing and personal services earnings for women of both races drop considerably below the overall median for all industries, as can be seen in Table 6.7. This reflects the very low wage structure of these industries and, in the case of retailing, the large amount of part-time work. Black women also earn considerably less than white women in nonfood retailing and in the hotel industry. The generally low pay for black women in personal services and particularly in such blue-collar services as building maintenance and the hotel industry reflects occupational concentration. Earnings for occupations where black women work,

Table 6.6
Annual Earnings for Women in Selected White-Collar Services, 1982

	Full-time women workers		Ratio
	Median Annual Earnings:		B/W
Public Administration			
Prof-Technical	17,202	19,829	115.28
Administrative-Manager	17,437	20,278	111.5
Bookkeeper	14,059	14,459	102.8
Cashier	11,073	10,700	98.6
Computer-Keypunch	11,505	14,160	123.0
Secretary-Typist	12,284	12,366	100.7
Other Clerical	14,477	15,117	104.4
Cleaning-Janitor	12,328	10,048	86.5
Food Services	10,081	6,232	61.8
Other Services	15,540	7,754	50.5
TOTAL	14,649	14,429	98.5
Financial, Insurance, Real Estate			
Prof-Technical	15,757	14,303	90.7
Managerial-Admin.	16,080	14,597	90.8
Crafts	12,051	11,500	95.4
Insurance Agent	14,760	12,168	82.4
Real Estate Agent	14,401	19,200	133.3
Bookkeeper	10,784	10,581	98.1
Computer-Keypunch	10,864	8,405	81.0
Secretary-Typist	10,207	9,815	96.2
Other Clerical	10,825	10,588	97.8
Cleaner-Janitor	10,325	4,201	40.7
TOTAL	12,115	11,000	90.8

Source: CPS 1982.

Table 6.7
Earnings in Retailing and Personal Services

Industry	Median Earnings Black Women	Black–White Differential
Retail (mail order, department stores)	8,974	86.8
Retail (eating, drinking establishments)	7,326	92.0
Hotels–Motels	6,458	76.6
Other personal services	8,345	104.2

Source: *CPS 1982.*

for example, are similar to those of jobs in food services and janitorial services in other industries that generally have higher wage structures, such as government. But this acts to lower wages overall for personal services.

The low earnings for women in the retail trade and personal services sectors echo the low wage structure characteristic of low-productivity, labor-intensive industries, which remain at the lower end of output per worker in U.S. industries.[42] An equally persuasive explanation of low pay in retailing, however, is the high rate of part-time work, which reduces annual earnings per worker and contributes to lower compensation rates overall. The occupational structure of food retailing and personal services is heavily weighted by such low-status, semiskilled occupational categories as maids, janitors, cooks, dishwashers, laundresses, waitresses, cashiers, and general maintenance jobs. These occupations require relatively little training, skills, and experience for employment, although it is not clear how much skills raise the productivity of the individual worker. Despite the stereotyping of the "low productivity" nature of these sectors, however, per-worker output has increased with managerial innovation, job redesign, job enrichment, and introduction of quality circle techniques as in the fast food industry, hotels and grocery business, and through new technology, such as laser readouts at supermarket cashier stations.[43] Both retail trade and personal services, however, are characterized by an internal job organization that is based on a routinizing of work, part-time work, and limited job and wage mobility. The earnings of black women in both sectors tend to be low and have wider gaps with white women on average than other industries.

Professional Services

Professional services, which include health, education, and social services, account for most of women's employment or over 30 percent. Black women are employed at nearly 33 percent in health and education alone. These are female-intensive sectors and have traditionally played the most important role of any in women's work. In 1980, women constituted 70 percent of the sector's employment compared to 43 percent of the total work force for all sectors. Other important characteristics that influence earnings structures relate to the extent of government role in setting the level of resources and occupational structure. Government influence is visible throughout the sectors. Professional services sectors are organized frequently under legislative authority and operate in highly regulated markets, even when resources are mainly private.[44] They benefit from significant underwriting of operating expenditures. Both health and education operate in public and private frameworks, but private institutions are exempt from most taxation and receive a variety of public resources. Included are grants to support professional staff, special programs, support for disadvantaged populations, and tuition assistance and student aid or consumer subsidies. Medicaid and Medicare insurance, for example, are key in supporting expansion of private medical care.[45] Government grants also support capital facilities, while sponsored research grants and other contracts contribute substantially to operating overhead in higher education and health care institutions. Another government influence on professional services sectors comes in the form of regulation and standard setting for operations and personnel. Licensing of professional staff and standard setting of fees influence salaries and wages for most personnel.[46] Licensing of activities is also extensive at the state level, particularly in the case of health and social services.

The health care industry has been particularly important as a source of employment for women and for black women, employing over 13 percent of all women and 18 percent of total black women's labor force in 1982. Sectors contrast in levels of earnings and between the sexes. As the occupational distribution for the largest employer categories in the health industry in 1982 as indicated in Table 6.9 based on 1982 data, convalescent home workers earn just over two-thirds of hospital workers' earnings on average. Other health care (which includes community-based clinics, group practice, HMO's, and laboratories) has slightly higher earnings as well as a far narrower gap between black and white women's earnings. One reason for the latter effect is that many outpatient services that dominate other health care have been recently established,[47] and black women have successfully found jobs in the new growth sector, as well as in the expanding community-based programs designed to serve low-income and minority neighborhoods.

In the occupational structure of earnings within the two largest sectors of the health care industry (hospitals and convalescent homes) illustrated in Table 6.8, the pay structure of the industry contrasts substantially. In the case of hospitals, the wage gap between black and white women in unskilled categories is narrow, if not nonexistent. By contrast, a large gap remains between earnings of the two groups in the top status categories. This suggests both bias in assignment of work responsibilities and possible ''overqualifications'' among black women at lower skills levels. In the case of convalescent homes, there are significant earnings gaps between black and white women throughout the occupational structure. But again, the widest gaps are at the top, among RNs and LPNs.

Table 6.8
Earnings in Selected Health Industry Occupations

Occupation	Median Annual Earnings: Full-Time Women Workers		Earnings Ratio
	White	Black	Black/White
Hospitals			
Prof/Technical	16,820.9	14,501.0	86.3
Managerial/Admin.	20,621.0	N.A.	N.A.
Operatives	8,656.7	10,458.3	120.8
Bookkeeper	12,783.8	5,936.0	46.4
Sec./Typist	10,860.8	11,078.7	102.0
Other Clerical	10,114.8	11,053.3	109.2
Cleaner/Janitor	9,011.2	8,052.1	89.4
Food Service	7,479.5	8,543.7	114.2
Health Services	10,239.9	9,703.5	94.7
Other Services	8,672.2	10,403.2	119.9
TOTAL	13,711.2	10,969.0	79.9
Convalescent Homes			
Prof/Technical	13,781.2	8,207.8	59.5
Operatives	7,452.6	8,336.8	111.9
Sec./Typist	10,367.4	5,200.0	51.7
Cleaner/Janitor	5,927.0	5,894.5	99.4
Food Services	6,172.7	5,986.2	97.0
Health Services	7,456.5	7,111.2	95.4
Other Services	7,584.5	5,000.0	92.2
TOTAL	8,230.0	6,905.0	83.9

Source: CPS 1982.

INDUSTRY COMPENSATION: WAGES AND BENEFITS

We have thus far examined earnings differentials for full-time workers for major industry groups where women work. Hourly wage rates are another measure of differences that would be useful, since hours actually worked could be taken into account to give a fuller picture of industry wage structure effects on black women. Owing to inadequate data for all occupational groups, wage rate

Table 6.9
Mean Hourly Wages for Women for Selected Industries

	Mean Hourly Wages ($)		Ratio
	Black	White	B/W
Industry Group			
Manufacturing: Durable	3.62	5.77	62.73
Manufacturing: Nondurable	3.98	4.18	94.74
Retail Trade	3.75	3.36	111.61
Finance, Banking, Insur.	4.00	4.74	84.39
Private Households	2.96	1.83	161.75
Personal Services	3.35	3.35	100.00
Professional Related	3.70	3.95	93.67
Mean Hourly Wages All Industries	3.63	3.67	89.91

Source: *CPS 1982*.

analysis by race from U.S. Census sources is limited. Some data, however, may be helpful.

Overall industry wage rates for 1982, as Table 6.9 shows, are relatively close for black and white women in primary hiring sectors of nondurable manufacturing, retail trade, and professional and personal services. White-collar services and durable manufacturing, however, show black women have substantially lower hourly rates than white counterparts.

Hourly Wage Rates

When occupational categories are examined within selected industries, as Table 6.10 illustrates, there are some surprising patterns. In health services, hourly rates differ considerably between professional and nonprofessional workers for the two races, with black women professionals earning higher rates than whites, while the opposite is true for nonprofessional categories. By contrast, white women working as operatives in manufacturing earn more than black women on an hourly basis. In personal services, white women earn more in cleaning services, but less in private household work.

Benefits: Group Health and Pensions

Wages and salaries constitute only part of the compensation gained from work. Over the past three decades, nonwage compensation has tended to grow faster than wages in many sectors of the economy, as collective bargaining and em-

Table 6.10
Hourly Wage Rates for Black Women in Selected Occupations

Industry	Mean Hourly Wage Rates ($)			Ratio
	Total	Black	White	B/W
Health				
-Health serv. workers (professional)	7.48	9.28	6.18	150.16
-Health serv. workers (non professional)	3.76	3.59	4.05	88.64
Retail				
-sales	3.56	3.87	3.53	109.63
Durable Manufact.				
-operatives	3.96	3.62	4.23	85.58
Non Durable Manufact.				
-operatives	4.08	3.98	4.18	95.21
Non-Farm Manufact.	4.50	4.65	3.75	124.00
Personal Services				
-Cleaning Services	3.71	3.59	3.76	95.48
-Priv. House. Workers	2.67	2.96	1.83	161.75
Occupations (all industries)				
Non retail Sales	4.00	4.00	4.00	100.00
Clerical				
-bookkeepers	4.22	3.60	4.34	82.95
-office machine oper.	5.45	---	5.45	---
-steno-typists	4.23	4.78	4.05	118.02
-other	4.12	3.88	4.18	92.82

Source: CPS 1982.

ployers alike have responded to demands by work forces for increased attention to measures to reduce costs of work interruption, prolonged layoffs, family needs, and life-cycle support requirements.[48] By 1987, while wages and salaries constituted 73.2 percent of the compensation paid by employers in private industry, the remaining 26.8 percent of payroll costs was paid in the form of various benefits.[49] The compensation of nonwage benefits, listed in Table 6.11, however, varies widely in industries and between occupational categories. Overall the largest categories were legally mandated benefits including social security, workman's compensation, and unemployment insurance, at around 8 percent; paid leave, including paid holidays and vacations at around 7 percent; and insurance and pensions, at around 11.5 percent.

Another contrast is between higher and lower status occupational groups. Compensation costs per hour averaged more for white-collar than blue-collar workers ($15.56 versus $13.43), while benefit costs were about the same for

Table 6.11
Distribution of Employer Compensation Costs

Category	% Total
Wages and Salaries	73.2
Legally Required Benefits	8.4
Insurance	7.9
Pensions and Savings	3.6
Paid Leave	6.9
	100.0

Source: Felicia, Nathan, "Analyzing Employer's Costs for Wages, Salaries and Benefits," *Monthly Labor Review*, October 1987, p. 5.

Table 6.12
Insurance Costs by Industry

Insurance	Wages & Salaries	Costs
Private industry	$ 9.83	$ 0.72
Transportation, Public utilities	13.77	1.32
Wholesale trade	11.24	.80
Manufacturing	10.77	1.06
Service	9.34	.53
Retail trade	6.07	.35

Source: Nathan, "Analyzing Employer's Costs," p. 5.

both at around $4.00. But compensation for service workers averaged $6.43 per hour and benefit costs were 22.8 percent or considerably below the 30 percent for blue-collar workers. Higher status occupations, such as managers and professionals, whether in the services industries or retail trade, however, equaled overall compensation costs for similar occupational groups in manufacturing.

Of the two benefits in the compensation package of most interest to women, insurance, particularly health insurance, and pensions show mixed patterns. Most health care in the United States is provided through prepaid group insurance plans in the workplace.[50] Health insurance extends beyond the individual worker, moreover. Most families are insured through subscription of a working head of family. In addition, health insurance increasingly constitutes paid compensation. As noted above, employers normally cover a proportion of total premium costs, as well as administrative costs that permit group discounts.[51] Table 6.12 contains estimates of current insurance costs by industry.

As the estimates in the table suggest, the availability and relative value of health insurance to workers depends strongly on the industry where one works. In addition, the level of the benefit depends on two other factors: (1) the amount of cost sharing by the employer, on premiums or contributions; and (2) the range of coverage offered. For example, a recent study of health insurance trends in cost control and coverage indicated that employers have tended to contain rising expenditures by increasing the cost to workers, particularly through raising levels of deductibles on hospitalization, extended care, and even some office visits.[52] The range of coverage shows additional trends, with more employers providing and encouraging employees to elect cheaper HMO plans, which emphasize prevention and lower cost outpatient care.[53]

Evidence examined on the patterns of coverage for black women show a generally mixed pattern. U.S. Census CPS data for 1982 indicate that only about one-third of black women workers have prepaid group health plans available where they work. Moreover, of those who do have plans available, only about 33 percent have premiums totally covered by employers, leaving about 56 percent subscribing to cost-shared plans and 10 percent who paid the entire costs of premiums. Data showed that black women were also more dependent than white women on publicly subsidized Medicaid to cover health insurance needs. About 25 percent of black women workers are on Medicaid, compared to around 16 percent of white women. This increases for women who are heads of households with children under 18 years old.

Table 6.13 also indicates that the impact of headship and dependent children among both white and black results in higher coverage rates. This suggests that some of the women who are not heads of households may be covered by plans of spouses. Even after taking this into account, however, an important residual of women who lack coverage altogether remains. Over half of black and white women with children and without spouses are not included in group health in the workplace, and the number of those without either workplace health coverage or Medicaid remains high—or about one-third for both races.

Pensions represent an additional problem for women workers in general and black women in particular. Only about one-quarter of all women had pensions available in the workplace in 1982, according to CPS data, and of those who did, a significant number (over one-third) were not included in pension systems where they worked. Although the value of pensions is less important in compensation than health insurance, it nonetheless represents an important pecuniary value, which can appreciate over time, and becomes more important for women than men because of longevity. Black women are slightly more likely than white women to have pensions available, although they are less likely to be included in pensions if they head households than white women. This may pose serious problems in old age, since black women are less likely to marry than white

Table 6.13
Employee Pension and Health Insurance Coverage

Type Benefit	All Women		All Heads Households	
	Black % T	White % T	Black % T	White % T
Pensions Available at work				
a) Yes	25.67	24.11	25.60	28.74
b) No	74.33	75.89	74.40	71.26
Included in pension				
a) Yes	70.81	57.62	64.56	70.15
b) No	29.19	42.38	35.44	29.05
Group Health Available				
a) Yes	34.65	33.14	38.48	41.66
b) No	65.35	66.86	61.52	58.34
Group Health Paid by Employer				
a) 100%	33.92	34.75	32.43	35.44
b) Part	55.74	56.26	52.98	58.53
c) None	10.34	8.96	14.59	5.63
Medicaid				
a) Yes	24.29	15.76	32.37	29.08
b) No	75.71	84.24	67.63	70.12

Source: *CPS 1982.*

women and therefore benefit from sharing in a husband's retirement plan. Since eligibility, contributions, and benefit rates paid vary considerably across industries and among work sites, it is difficult to assess the exact impacts of the current lack of coverage.

IMPACTS OF EARNINGS: CONSTRAINTS AND CONTRIBUTIONS TO FAMILY INCOME

A key disadvantage of black women in the workplace is a combination of three factors: low hourly earnings, fewer hours of work available, and little income from other sources for family support. The high rate of part-time and part-year work acts to drastically reduce annual earnings. An additional cost may be in health insurance coverage and retirement plans, generally restricted to full-time, year-around workers. Nonwage income, in the form of child support and public assistance, is also less available to black women than whites.

Blacks of both sexes and women of both races are more likely than white males to be forced to work part-time. As table 6.14, which shows the distribution of part-time employment by race and sex for 1985, indicates, black women are the most disadvantaged of the four groups in the extent to which they work part-time but would prefer to work full-time. Black women are also more likely than white women to usually work full-time rather than part-time.

Table 6.14
Part-Time Employment, 1985

	Percent Involuntary Part-Time*	Percent of Employed Usually Working	
		Full-Time	Part-Time
White	5.9	82.4	17.6
Men	4.4	90.2	9.8
Women	8.3	72.4	27.6
Black	10.4	84.0	16.0
Men	9.3	88.1	11.9
Women	12.0	79.9	20.1

*Includes those (a) working part-time for economic reasons who usually work full-time, (b) working part-time for economic reasons who usually work part-time.
Source: Thomas Nardone, "Part-Time Workers: Who Are They?" *Monthly Labor Review*, February 1986, p. 16.

Cause and Effects of Part-Time Work on Income

The cause of part-time work is clearly related to the industry where employment is concentrated. As Table 6.15 showing industry distribution of black and white women in full-time, part-time, and temporary work indicates, black women work at higher part-time rates than white women in some key employment sectors. Included are durable manufacturing, public administration, and services. When temporary full-time work is added, the disadvantage of black women worsens. Table 6.15 shows the industry impacts for detailed industrial sectors and illustrates how part-time involuntary work depresses annual earnings.

The impact of part-time work on the earnings of black women is considerable. Although on average they work more hours weekly and annually than white women, the level of part-time involuntary work by black women appears to depress annual earnings. Government statistics have only recently started to define part-time work more strategically, separating out those workers who elect part-time work from those who work less than 35 hours per week on an "involuntary" basis, or because of economic reasons, including inability to find full-time work; or who usually work full-time, but work part-time because of reduction in work hours, temporary layoffs, and other employer-defined status.[54] Beginning in the 1970s trends indicated substantial numbers of part-time jobs were generated in the economy overall. In fact, part-time employment grew more rapidly than full-time employment so that in the last quarter of 1987, national statistics reported over half of all jobs created were part-time.[55] As a result, in the 1983–1987 period, approximately 17 percent of all jobs were part-time (see Table 6.16).

Impact of Reduced Public Assistance and Child Support

We have noted throughout this chapter that industries where black women work pose severe constraints on incomes. In part, this is because earnings are

Table 6.15
Part-Time Women Workers by Sector, 1984

% Full/Part- time work:	Durable Manufact	Non Durbl	Util.	Whole- Sale Trade	Retail Trade	Fin., Insur., Real Es.
Full-time:						
% T Black	67.28	72.23	94.35	30.18	41.15	68.85
% T White	91.25	63.38	45.55	87.12	40.85	62.68
Part-time:						
% T Black	32.72	27.77	5.65	69.82	58.83	31.15
% T White	8.75	36.62	54.45	12.88	59.15	38.32
Temporary:						
% T Black	4.18	9.42	2.35	1.22	12.34	4.17
% T White	4.67	6.62	3.05	3.28	34.48	3.67

% Full/Part- time work:	Business Repair	Priv. House- hold	Pers. Serv.	Ent- ment	Prof. Relat.	Public Admin.
Full-time:						
% T Black	29.77	21.40	53.73	51.67	71.87	69.66
% T White	57.56	42.43	53.97	31.52	56.63	74.55
Part-time:						
% T Black	70.23	73.60	46.27	48.33	28.13	30.34
% T White	42.44	57.57	46.03	68.48	42.37	25.45
Temporary:						
% T Black	4.94	13.84	8.73	0.72	33.57	2.29
% T White	3.56	4.11	4.33	1.45	23.71	1.92

Source: CPS 1982.

Table 6.16
Part-Time Workers by Industry, 1983–87

	For Economic Reasons usually full-time	usually part-time	voluntary part-time
Total	100	100	100
Retail Trade	19.0	40.3	37.0
Services	22.4	35.4	42.6
Other Industry	48.6	24.3	20.4

Source: Nardone, "Part Time Workers: Who Are They?" p. 15.

low. A variety of workplace factors explain why earnings are depressed among black women compared to white counterparts, including concentration in low-wage industry, extent of lower compensation rates paid (including benefits), and occupational structure of the black women's work force within an industry. In many cases, however, median earnings are lower for black women working in

Table 6.17

Composition of Family Income for Women Workers by Race, 1982

Type Hshld.	%T Heads House hold	Wages Salary % T Income	B/W Diff	U.S. Govt % T Inc.	B/W Diff	Pub. Ass. % T Inc	B/W Diff	Chld Sup. % T Inc.	Sup. B/W Diff
Total Heads Household:									
White	100	78.23	105	1.12	192	12.3	85.5	8.33	39.1
Black	100	84.32	105	1.98	192	10.5	85.5	3.26	39.1
Heads NSP*									
White	95.7	80.68	107	1.22	170	13.2	82.0	9.05	28.3
Black	96.6	84.04	107	2.15	170	10.6	82.0	3.27	28.3
Heads House NSP*									
White	85.4	76.08	107	1.16	170	13.8	82.0	8.91	36.9
Black	79.4	83.08	107	2.14	170	11.1	82.0	3.70	36.9
Heads House NSP* Children < 5 years									
White	33.6	74.29	110	0.40	45	17.2	52.0	8.09	83.2
Black	27.2	83.32	110	1.81	45	9.06	52.0	9.06	83.2
Married Heads of Household									
White	4.32	96.09	73	--	--	3.45	143	0.42	--
Black	3.35	93.41	73	--	--	6.54	143	--	--

*No spouse present.
Source: CPS 1982.

similar occupations with white women. Seniority may explain some of these differences but not all. We have also noted that another disadvantage occurs when higher rates of involuntary part-time or temporary work are accounted for. For full-time workers, however, the lower income remains. An additional disadvantage is that black women compared to whites have far less available to them for family support from sources other than wages. As Table 6.17 illustrating the composition of family income for women workers for 1982 indicates, both child support and public assistance make up smaller proportions of total income for black families in all categories. Thus only 3.26 percent of the income of black women householders comes from child support from absent fathers, compared to 8.33 percent for white women households. Although the child support income improves somewhat for black women with young children, the disadvantage compared to white women remains.

In the case of public assistance, surprisingly black women also receive substantially less as a percentage of total family income or for all households—10.5 percent compared to 12.3 percent for white women, as Table 6.17 indicates. For women with young children, again black women have a severe disadvantage, receiving less than 10 percent of income from public assistance, compared to 17 percent for white women.

The causes for differences in supplementary household support payments between black and white families are not entirely clear. In the case of child support, one explanation may be the lower earnings and higher unemployment of absent black fathers. In the case of public assistance, reasons are less clear. The higher concentration of black women in states where payments are low, such as the South, may account for some of the difference.

NOTES

1. Bruce E. Kaufman, *The Economics of Labor Markets and Labor Relations* (Chicago: Dryden Press, 1986), pp. 207, 208.

2. James Heskett, *Managing in the Services Economy* (Boston: Harvard Business School Press, 1986). (This analyst provides an extensive review of the issues and evidence in productivity in the services industry, pp. 3, 91–96, and Appendix C, "Productivity," pp. 191–194.

3. Robert B. McKersie and Peter Cappelli, "Concession Bargaining," in Richard Rowan (ed.), *Readings in Labor Economics and Labor Relations* (Homewood, IL: Irwin, 1985), pp. 243–253.

4. Kaufman, *The Economics of Labor Markets*, p. 345.

5. Jack Stiebert, "Employment-at-Will: An Issue for the 1980s," in Rowan, *Readings in Labor Economics*, pp. 345–352, includes a review of trends in layoffs and discharges and legal protection as evident in current court cases and other negotiations and appeals.

6. For a review of trends in worker participation, see Charles Derber and William Schwartz, "Toward a Theory of Worker Participation," in Frank Hern (ed.), *The Transformation of Industrial Organization* (Belmont, CA: Wadsworth, 1988), pp. 217–228; and Ronald M. Mason, "Workplace Democracy," in Hern, pp. 205–216.

7. Karen Holden and W. Lee Hansen, "Part-Time Work, Full-Time Work and Occupational Segregation," in Clair Brown and Joseph A. Pechman (eds.), *Gender in the Workplace* (Washington, DC: Brookings Institution, 1987), pp. 217–237. Also Barry Bluestone and Bennett Harrison, "The Great American Jobs Machine: Proliferation of Low Wage Employment in the U.S. Economy" (Washington DC: Joint Economic Committee, U.S. Congress, 1986), p.4, suggest that many of the part-time jobs were the result of "redesign of full-time jobs," as well as reflecting an economic downswing in the creation of part-time and part-year work.

8. Thomas J. Nardone, "Part Time Workers: Who Are They?" *Monthly Labor Review*, February 1986, p. 15, reported that during the 1970s and early 1980s, part-time work grew more rapidly than full-time employment, or between 1968 and 1982, the proportion of employed persons who worked part-time grew from 14 to 18 percent.

9. Some explorations include: Patricia Gwartney-Gibbs and Patricia A. Taylor, "Black Women Workers: Earnings Progress in Three Industrial Sectors, 1970–1980," *Sage*, 3, no. 1 (Spring 1986), pp. 20–25.

10. Julianne Malveaux, "Comparable Worth and Its Impact on Black Women," in Margaret Simms and Julianne Malveaux (eds.), *Slipping Through the Cracks: The Status of Black Women* (New Brunswick, NJ: Transaction Books, 1987), pp. 47–62.

11. Ibid. There is a large literature in the field assessing the phenomena of occupational

segregation. See David Gordon, Richard Edwards, and Michael Reich, *Segmented Work, Divided Workers* (Cambridge: Cambridge University Press, 1982); Heidi Hartmann, "Internal Labor Markets and Gender: A Case Study of Promotion," in Brown and Pechman, *Gender in the Workplace.* Hartmann calculated indexes of segregation for occupations in an insurance firm and found stratification by race as well as sex (pp. 68–76). See also Francine Blau and Carol Justinius, "Economists' Approaches to Sex Segregation in the Labor Market: An Appraisal," in Martha Blaxall and Barbara Reagan (eds.), *Women in the Workplace: The Implications of Occupational Segregation* (Chicago: University of Chicago Press, 1976), pp. 193–195.

12. Hartman, "Internal Labor Markets and Gender."

13. See Carolyn Perucci, Robert Perucci, Dena B. Targ, and Harry R. Targ, in *Plant Closings: International Context and Social Costs* (Hawthorne, NY: Aldine de Gruyter, 1988), pp. 29, 30.

14. U.S. Census.

15. Kaufman, *The Economics of Labor Markets*, p. 207.

16. Ibid., p. 209.

17. George Silvestri and John Lukasiewicz, "A Look at Occupational Employment Trends to the Year 2000," *Monthly Labor Review,* September 1987, pp. 44–61.

18. George Stamas, "The Puzzling Lag in Southern Earnings," *Monthly Labor Review,* June 1981, pp. 27–31.

19. Kaufman, *The Economics of Labor Markets*, p. 209.

20. Gordon et al., *Segmented Work, Divided Workers.* See also Richard Freeman and Jonathan Leonard, "Union Maids: Unions and the Female Work Force," in Brown and Pechman, *Gender in the Workplace*, pp. 189–216. The analysts present data showing women are three times more likely to be unionized in the public sector than in private workplace settings. Women are also more likely to be unionized in blue-collar than white-collar jobs. They also find that unions do contribute to higher wages; this is particularly true of government jobs and white-collar workers (p. 197).

21. McKersie and Cappeli, "Concession Bargaining," p. 249.

22. Kaufman, *The Economics of Labor Markets*, p. 209.

23. Carl Barsky and Martin E. Personick, "Measures of Wage Dispersion: Pay Ranges Reflect Industry Traits," *Monthly Labor Review*, April 1981, p. 35.

24. Ibid.

25. Kaufman, *The Economics of Labor Markets*, p. 23.

26. Sally L. Hacker, "Sex Stratification, Technology and Organizational Changes: A Longitudinal Case Study of AT&T," in Rachael Kahn-Hut, Arlene Daniels, and Richard Colvard, (eds.), *Women and Work* (New York: Oxford University Press, 1982), pp. 249–250; and Kaufman, *The Economics of Labor Markets*, p. 375.

27. Heskett, *Managing in the Service Economy*, p. 191.

28. Bennett Harrison, *Education, Training and the Urban Ghetto* (Baltimore: Johns Hopkins University Press, 1972).

29. Stamas, "The Puzzling Lag."

30. Ibid. See also Bette Woody and Michele Malson, "In Crisis: Low Income Black Employed Women in the U.S. Workplace," Working Paper No. 131 (Wellesley, MA: Wellesley College, Center for Research on Women, 1986) for a discussion and data on regional effects on black women's earnings.

31. Barbara Bergmann, *The Economic Emergence of Women* (New York, Basic Books, 1986), pp. 63–64; and Julianne Malveaux, "Moving Forward, Standing Still: Women in

White Collar Jobs,'' in Phyllis Wallace (ed.), *Women in the Workplace* (Boston: Auburn House, 1982), pp. 101–130.

32. Renee Loth, "Jobs Go Begging in Human Services," *Boston Globe,* February 26, 1988; and Christine Robb, "Geneva Evans' Days: If Her Job Is So Important Why Don't We Value Her Work?" *Boston Globe Magazine*, November 8, 1987, p. 14. See also Coalition on Pay Equity, "Are Health Care Workers Paid What They Are Worth?" (Boston, 1987), p. 1.

33. Anne Kahl and Donald Clark, "Employment in Health Services: Long-Term Trends and Projections," *Monthly Labor Review,* August 1986, p. 17.

34. Malveaux, "Moving Forward," pp. 112–113; Woody and Malson, "In Crisis," pp. 3,4; Gwartney-Gibbs and Taylor, "Black Women Workers," p. 20.

35. Malveaux, "Moving Forward," pp. 101–130.

36. Kaufman, *The Economics of Labor Markets.* For a more detailed discussion of the causes behind this related to long-standing sex bias, see Rosabeth M. Kanter, "The Impact of Hierarchical Structures on the Work Behavior of Women and Men," in Kahn-Hut et al., *Women and Work*, pp. 234–247.

37. Nardone, "Part Time Workers: Who Are They?" p. 15.

38. Harry Wellington and Ralph Winger, "The Limits of Collective Bargaining in Public Employment," in Rowan, *Readings in Labor Economics,* pp. 278–290.

39. Bruce Dunson, "If All Women Were Men and All Blacks Were Whites, Who Loses?" in Bette Woody, Carolyne Arnold, and Jacqueline Fields (eds), *The Changing Economic Status of Black Women* (Detroit: Wayne State University Press, forthcoming). See also Julianne Malveaux, "Comparable Worth and Its Impact on Black Women," in Simms and Malveaux, *Slipping Through the Cracks*, p. 47.

40. Phyllis Wallace, *Black Women in the Labor Force* (Cambridge, MA: MIT Press, 1982), pp. 54, 55.

41. Ray Marshall, "Work and Women in the 1980s: A Perspective on Basic Trends Affecting Women's Jobs and Job Opportunities," in Rowan, *Readings in Labor Economics*, pp. 27–29. See also Gwartney-Gibbs and Taylor, "Black Women Workers," p. 20.

42. Valerie Personick, "Projections 2000: Industry Output and Employment Through the End of the Century," *Monthly Labor Review,* September 1987, p. 30; also see Steven E. Haugen, "The Employment Expansion in Retail Trade 1973–85," *Monthly Labor Review,* August 1986, p. 20.

43. For evidence on productivity gains in services industries, see Arthur Herman, "Productivity Continued to Increase in Many Industries During 1984," *Monthly Labor Review*, March 1980, pp. 11–14; Norman Sanders, "Economic Projections to the Year 2000," *Monthly Labor Review*, September 1987, pp. 10–13. For a description and evaluation of the effects of job-redesign and job enrichment on productivity, see David Hampton, Charles Summer, and Ross Webber, Organizational Behavior and the Practice of Management, 5th ed. (Glenview, IL: Scott, Foresman, 1987), p. 311.

44. See, for example, Dean Coddington, Lowell Palmquist, and William Trollinger, "Strategies for Survival in the Hospital Industry," *Harvard Business Review*, May/June 1985, pp. 129–135, which describes the level of control exercised by the federal government regulators on one end of the hospital industry, and by physicians on the other end. Both licensing (physicians, hospital facilities) and standard setting for care would be expected to restrict the flow of labor and possibly determine the direction in allocation

of resources. For a review of these latter economic effects, see Kaufman, *The Economics of Labor Markets*, p. 190.

45. Coddington, Palmquist and Trollinger, "Strategies for Survival," pp. 133, 134. See also Paul Ginsberg and Glen Hackbarth, "Alternative Delivery Systems and Medicare," in *Health Affairs*, Spring 1986.

46. Ginsberg and Hackbarth, "Alternative Delivery Systems," pp. 7, 8.

47. Ibid.

48. Kaufman, *The Economics of Labor Markets*, p. 345. See also Robert Frumkin, "Health Insurance Trends in Cost Control and Coverage," *Monthly Labor Review*, September 1987, pp. 3, 4.

49. Felicia Nathan, "Analyzing Employer's Costs for Wages, Salaries and Benefits," *Monthly Labor Review*, 1987, pp 5–7.

50. Bureau of Labor Statistics, "Employee Benefits in Medium and Large Firms," *Bulletin 2237* (Washington, DC, 1985).

51. Allen Blostin and William Marclay, "HMO's and Other Health Plans: Coverage and Employee Premiums," *Monthly Labor Review*, June 1983, pp. 28–33.

52. Frumkin, "Health Insurance Trends."

53. Ibid.

54. For an analysis of new U.S. Census definitions of part-time work, see Nardone, "Part Time Workers: Who Are They," p. 15.

55. Ibid.

CHAPTER 7

Profile and Personal Histories of Black Women

Despite myths about their motivation and dedication, there is surprisingly little documentation on the work behavior of.black women. The strength of commitment of women in general has been examined with the conclusion that psychological attitudes and behavior differ between the sexes and that for women there are trade-offs between family and paid employment.[1] This theory, however, has recently been challenged by evidence provided by the growth of women entering the work force. The presumed "competition" between work and family disappeared as the economic push and more attractive work opportunities grew. Thus, barriers to entry in the workplace, rather than attitudes toward work, may be the principal cause for the contrasting work patterns of women and men. Other contributing factors to the changing work behavior of women include birth control technology, reductions in the value and need for housework with a variety of labor-saving conveniences and innovation, and, finally, changing social attitudes toward women. But while society has accepted women working full-time, including those with preschool children, employers may have undergone an even greater change from resistance to aggressive recruitment of women workers as a principal component of the work force. Women workers appear to offer a high-quality work force. Women may also have temperament and skills more suited than men to the many new jobs created in the services economy.[2]

Social scientists and organizational experts widely agree that work constitutes a complex social activity that is equally influenced by motivation and behavior of the individual worker and by organizational settings, roles, other workers, superiors and subordinates.[3] Included in the definition of workplace setting are group processes that are considered to influence productivity and output in ways quite distinct from that of individual behavior. Thus, there is broad agreement that the individual worker brings skills, talent, and ability to the job and its component tasks. From the perspective of the organization, however, output is the product as much of the social organization of workers operating under rules, technology, managerial and control systems, and a work culture as it is of the individual worker.

To examine more fully how individuals may be motivated to achieve and how attitudes and interests are shaped by work, we conducted detailed personal interviews with four typical black women workers. The women selected met some mainstream profile criteria: they were from working-class or lower-middle-class backgrounds; they were the first in their families to achieve a college education and/or middle occupational status; they were experienced workers, having worked continuously for at least ten years; and all were in their 40s.

This chapter is organized in four parts. First the chapter examines individual characteristics, background, and life-cycle factors that influenced work histories of the women. Next work experience and work and task content of typical jobs are reviewed. The issues of supervisors and performance experienced by the workers are then covered. The final part looks at individual motivation, satisfaction, and expectations from work over the lifetimes of the women.

WORK HISTORY, EXPERIENCE, AND EXPECTATIONS IN THE WORKPLACE

Although we recognized there is no "typical" black woman worker, given the wide range of work experience patterns, occupational status, and age groups, we selected four experienced women workers in their 40s to interview for clues about individual perceptions about work and workplaces. All of the women interviewed had continuous work histories, dating from their mid-teens, thus giving each over 20 years in the work force. Some started at 14 years old and at least one had worked since she was 13, when she landed her first job as a restaurant waitress. The work histories of the women were remarkably similar. While all had experienced some unemployment and extended job search at one time or another, none had been unemployed for more than a few months. During periods of job search, the women would typically take temporary jobs. In a few of these cases, these jobs turned into more permanent work.

The one exception of work interruption was children. Children typically disrupted work for two to three years, with the mothers returning to employment when reliable baby sitting became available: One woman noted:

I always had to have child care. The last time I paid $90.00 a week, or one-third of my salary. I worked 9:00 to 5:00 so I had to have child care. When they were school age, I sent them to after-school programs.

Another noted that her return to work after her second child was two years old was facilitated by the presence of "good family day care" in a center across the street from where she worked.

Despite the relatively disadvantaged blue-collar backgrounds, all the women experienced mobility in the job market over their work lives and had obtained some postsecondary education and training. Backgrounds were modest. All came from homes where high school was the highest level achieved by their parents; and in some cases, they grew up in broken homes where they were raised by grandparents, other relatives, and occasionally had been placed with foster parents. Difficult backgrounds, however, seemed to exert only a slight influence, particularly on attitudes toward work and general ambitions. One woman stated that while she spent many years coming to grips with relating to a long-alienated mother, while growing up with a somewhat difficult and stern grandmother, she was reconciled to the fact that she had made a satisfactory life and that her family background posed no particular handicap to her own achievements, friendships, and support. Thus most women had started out with little encouragement other than support for working in very low-status, low-paid work. They went on to experience a number of degrading and unrewarding jobs, but managed to "stick it out" through a combination of personal drive and encouragement from outside the family.

A surprising finding was that the women developed moderately high ambitions early on and moved toward relatively high-status occupations, even if pay remained modest. Ambitions took three forms: changing jobs, pursuing college and graduate degrees, or going into business.

The earliest influences on the women were immediate family of both sexes, and community members, particularly those active in local affairs. Several women grew up in the U.S. South, where simple virtues, ethics, and morality, as well as personal responsibility for one's destiny, were influential in creating modest expectations for achievement as a norm. In some cases, the influence was mixed. One woman described the influence of her West Indian grandmother as no particular encouragement or discouragement, a kind of neutrality:

The issue of family objecting to work didn't come up. . . . My grandmother expected that I would work when I finished high school. College didn't come into the picture. I started at 16 during the summer and when I got out of school. I'm not certain when I got the idea about work. I just knew at an early age that I would be working for a lifetime . . . because my grandmother was working. Her last job was with the Whiting Boat Company . . . she was a cleaning lady there. She had all kinds of odd, sloppy jobs. She would go out at 3:00 and come home at 10:00 so that she was home when I got home from school.

For this respondent the lack of support for college or education represented a generational gap in approaches to children. Support for education was a value that simply never occurred to a woman of her grandmother's generation:

She had no expectations that I would go to college. In fact, in high school, it was always up to you. If you wanted an A or a C; my report card wasn't a big deal. If I made the honor roll, that was fine, if not, well that was O.K., too.

Another woman, a student in the third semester of an undergraduate degree program interrupted several times, had two early influences on her decision to work: her mother who supported the concept of work and communicated it to her four children, and a high school teacher:

My mother was important. . . . We had to work, you had work. If you made $25.00 when you were in school, you gave up $20. You got a "T" pass to go to school and what else did you need the money for?
   There is a teacher, bless her . . . I had this woman for typing and shorthand for two years straight. If the woman saw that you had potential, without a doubt, you could not leave her class without a B at a minimum. She probably doesn't realize the influence she had on me. Her style was good, she was always very neat. She had a nice personality. I was 18 or 19 at the time. She was a white woman, but she was very good, had a very big influence on me.

Despite the quality and pay of work available, most of the women appeared to have formulated early concepts of work as a "natural" if not a rewarding activity. One woman who had been raised in the South and started work as a teenager did so because "it was expected that I would go to work and there wasn't too much of a question about it." She added, "I really did enjoy getting out of the house and being 'grown up' with other people."

Typical work histories started with several job changes, but gradually assumed more formal career orientation as more and more attention was paid to the skills content of the job and to job satisfaction and motivation. The women appear to have undergone specific changeovers from "job" to "career," following much the same process as middle-class individuals. The change seems to have coincided with two events: a shift in responsibilities on the job and getting noticed and encouraged by someone of influence.

The break in responsibilities helped women without experience to conceptualize a higher level of achievement. In one case, an early childhood teacher, the turning point was getting hired as a paraprofessional teacher's aide after a series of unrewarding jobs. The woman noted that she discovered she was successful and rewarded in this experience in working with young children. She suggested that for the first time she knew that she could build a lifetime set of activities around early childhood education. In a second case, the change from job to career occurred when the woman was employed as secretary to the head of a social services agency. Given an assignment in public relations on behalf of the agency, her work was noticed by an influential member of the agency board of directors. This led to a recommendation to a job with full-time community relations responsibilities.

Despite a change in attitudes and ambitions about work, however, actual mobility for black women was restricted. Success in moving up was tied to two factors: nominations to jobs by others, particularly community leadership, and jobs in community-based organizations. Three of the women, for example, made their best progress while working for a day care center, a church, and a social services organization. Several of the organizations were black-run, which may have accounted for a greater degree of sympathy for success of black women. They also provided some role models, either on staff or on oversight boards.

As in the case of higher status career women, women interviewed reported few serious conflicts in balancing family and work life.[4] They tended to be highly organized and reported they were able to budget their days to include adequate family time, homework, and time for leisure, friends, and community. There appeared to be little pressure from home against work. One woman, for example, affirmed that her family "preferred" her to work, since they felt she was happiest on the job:

Work and family go well for me. In fact, my family likes me to work and they don't like me when I don't work . . . I'm grouchy. When I work, I am better with my kids, more relaxed. They love it particularly when I work close to home.

Despite modest beginnings, most of the women were ambitious with expectations for future achievements in career and work. One woman hoped to open her own child care center as a next career step. Another woman was considering changing jobs from that of an executive secretary to a nonadministrative career, training to become an education counselor. Still another described a "dream job" as working as a national lobbyist for adult education.

WORKING ENVIRONMENTS

The working environments experienced by black women were of a wide range, reflecting the diversity of the occupations held, the types of employers, and the domination of work by nonprofits and community-based organizations. The work environments were viewed by the women as providing a basic framework for their motivation and satisfaction.

As an example of general working conditions, one woman reported that conditions were excellent in her current job, which she described as in a setting that stimulated high morale, strong teamwork, and provided good job security. She contrasted her present job in a small government agency with previous employment in a community-based nonprofit organization, where conditions were poor, the bosses were numerous, the environment disorganized, and almost nothing worked. For others, similar contrasts were offered. One noted that her current part-time position had all the disadvantage of part-time status, such as little mobility. In addition, however, her employer, a suburban school system, was surprisingly neglected:

The worst part of the work is that the place is not clean . . . even compared to Boston Public Schools. There are a lot of janitors, but it seems to be patronage since there are dirty bathrooms even where the kids go. The janitors say "it's not my job." I have the impression that the professional staff is part-time to save money but it is unclear about the janitorial staff . . . I think they are unionized.

Similar inadequacies were described by a mid-level manager in an educational setting:

The working conditions here are deplorable with a capital "D"; there is no bathroom on the administrative floor; I have one of the "suites," which is more like a small closet; I cannot turn the thermostat on or off; the windows are all boarded up; mice run around and up and down scratching around . . . electrical wires are hanging down from the ceiling . . . about all they have done is remove the asbestos.

JOB CONTENT AND WORK SATISFACTION

Job content was seen partly as an opportunity and partly as a constraint by the women. In one case, for example, a high-mobility first job helped set the pace for subsequent experiences; this woman developed a personal approach to work that was based on mastering all jobs, including the undesirable ones, then using a good reputation to leverage more challenging assignments:

I had an insurance job back in 1965—you know, the kind of job black women get, low status, clerical. But I like to call myself "catfish Annie" because the catfish will clean up your aquarium. So I've taken the kinds of jobs that people don't like. It's not that I've sought them. But I haven't refused them and as a result, I have learned things; I've had exposure to things that other people didn't want to do. Clerical work for example, is not a black or white thing, but just a thing people don't like to do.

She suggested that making something out of an uninteresting work assignment, or routine work, helped advancement. It turned into a very-high-mobility career ladder at a large insurance company during the 1970s:

I've always found it a challenge [to do things people don't like to do]. People would say "Oh, she'll do anything," but I really didn't mind. Sometimes I think, here I go again, but in the long run, it turns out to be a good thing. By the 1970s I was a very highly paid junior underwriter without even a college degree.

The problems in job content and tasks as the women saw it were related to the traditional systems at work and to the lack of innovative leadership in making changes. One woman, for example, noted that her job had degenerated as the result of a change in leadership:

I enjoy work but now in this job there is a very different administration. I'm not opposed to change but my work style is to follow through. I have experience and I have excellent organizational skills. I'm not allowed to use them now and I'm a little frustrated. The responsibilities used to require skills, knowledge, and knowhow; now I'm asked to perform classified staff clerical things such as typing and correspondence.

In another case, job content and the internal tasks were chaotic and haphazardly organized, despite a job description that essentially made this woman an officer-manager of the organization. After noting that the organization, a nonprofit, seemed to have no understanding about how to use and compensate employees, this woman described a burn-out job:

It was very close to my home and that was one of the big advantages of being there. But it became a very stressful situation. It became a seven-day-a-week job because they wouldn't hesitate to call at night with what was office-related business. But they didn't see it like that. Then everything was done on an antiquated office machine, no computer, same rush-crush—Friday was awful. I did work on proposals for new equipment but everything took such a long time. It was very bureaucratic. It would take a long time and the stress level never diminished.

In jobs that involved services, discretion to plan and develop were even more important. A preschool teacher noted that skewing a services job toward the routine all but killed the possibility for performing well:

The worst thing about this job is that there is a limited amount you can do. They don't use the talent enough, don't use teamwork. For example, they bring in substitutes and substitutes cause problems. You need to plan and develop a routine. The substitutes have no plan and it just doesn't work.

Positive experiences with job content, in contrast to ''burn-out'' jobs, provided enough discretion and creative potential for women to exercise initiative but, at the same time, manage work to avoid stress. One woman noted that she was generally confident because of her experience, skills, and attitude:

I feel that I do the job well. I went in with an attitude that there are many things I don't know but I'm not going in with a guilt complex. Some things I can do very well, some extremely well, and those that I don't do well, I'll make it my business to find out.

Work motivation and satisfaction for most of the women was derived from a combination of job content and individual effort to achieve personal as well as organizational goals.

One woman felt that she had gained most of her confidence and motivation from her own experience and from developing a specific attitude toward work:

I have a natural ability to get people to believe that I care. I might get cranky clients who get to the bosses' office. I don't take these things personally. I say that all of the jobs I had previously trained me for the job I have today. I feel I have used practically every skill before and I started work almost 20 years ago.

The preschool teacher also confirmed the role of individual skills and self-confidence in achieving, despite the constraint of the particular job:

I enjoy working with young children. I've always been around them and it seems natural. I feel that I am most successful in preschool teaching. I am successful with kids and have a very good feeling about them. The worst thing is that I can't use my talent enough in my present job. This is despite my background experience and an associates degree from Wheelock College in early childhood education.

BOSSES, SUPERVISORS, AND CO-WORKERS

For the women interviewed, supervisory systems tended to be subordinated to some of the tradition of the organizations where they worked. In cases examined, supervisors tended to be either very controlled in management style or very loose. For women who were experienced workers, the more responsibility and control they were delegated, the lower their stress level. For one with a demanding but fair boss, loyalty and performance were assured:

The boss is partly Hispanic and handicapped. He is compassionate and doesn't take things personally. He is very direct. I think his attitude is good. There is a lot of talk, for example, about layoffs. I've witnessed him engineering as best he can against these staff cuts. If the employees have complaints, they can come right to him.

Her appreciation extended to his delegation of authority to his immediate staff and his setting a general pace with his subordinates:

My current direct supervisor is a very capable Hispanic woman. She is young, from Puerto Rico. I would rate her as good compared to other supervisors. Because this is a small office, she is very easy to work with.

For others, however, the problem of management style was extremely difficult. One woman found that an experienced new boss tended to work in a very traditional style, with a relatively rigid chain of command, to her dismay:

I think his style of management is more "classical" while my other bosses had a more behavioral management style. I think he has a problem with understanding the dynamics and the politics of this organization. I know that because of his rigid perspectives I'm not being used to my full potential.

While a combination of management style and work environment created negatives for some, very good bosses made major differences in career paths. In one case of an executive secretary in a large nonprofit agency, the boss led her to a decision to take the job:

I knew this Vice President from a job where I worked before. When she went to work in a new place, she called me and said she had heard I was looking for a job and would I like to interview with her. I jumped at the chance. She is an absolute jewel, a terrific person to work for—open, flexible and honest. Anyone can get in to see her. She is not autocratic.

In addition to the efforts made by the boss to extend and enrich her job with the addition of new tasks and projects, a general promotion of staff development characterized the supervisor's style and approach.

A principal disadvantage of working in smaller nonprofit organizations— churches, charitable organizations, and human service agencies—where black women typically work, was the absence of performance systems. Because many of the organizations were based on "volunteer models," there were few written rules regarding staff responsibilities, development, or even salaries and benefits. Another problem was in the executive roles established in these kinds of agencies. In many cases, executives had little formal discretion; they would then either respond in one or two ways: work as capitives of their agency oversight boards, or conceal most of the agency's business from the board and run the organization following an autocratic model. In either case, the problem for staff, particularly younger, more agressive and ambitious women staff, the agency offered a mix of mentoring and supervisory advantage and disadvantage.

Few of the women used the work setting for primary social relationships. In some cases, isolation in a small setting made peer friendships difficult. In other cases, jobs themselves were limiting. The women tended to work independently and not to view work as a place for friendship or social support. While none of the women mentioned having close friendships on the job, one made a rather typical response:

The staff here seem to be satisfied with their work. I get along well with them. I feel fairly close to the lawyer and my trust factor is high with my immediate supervisor.

JOB-RELATED STRESS AND JOB SATISFACTION

The women interviewed had generally modest expectations for the work world and tended to be extremely self-reliant, suggesting that self-sufficiency, self-motivation, skills attainment, and control over one's life were the best ways to manage work and life. Dissatisfaction was managed by quitting a job and moving on, or getting formal training for another position.

Job-related stress was described as the result of too much responsibility and a tendency to take on too many tasks. One example was a women who traded in one stressful job, director of a Head Start program, for another that was essentially administrative. In describing the job she left, she offered:

There were actually two programs in this Head Start program, each running between 9:00 to 5:00 daily. I finally left after 8 years because I was burnt out. I had 50 kids in the program and it was a model program, but I had to leave; it was killing me.

In taking a new administrative job, she hoped to manage under less psychologically stressing working conditions. She quickly found she had traded one kind of pressure cooker for another:

The City Hall job had its moments. It turned out to be very stressful. I had to read proposals, read quarterly reports, make site visits, examine programs to see that they modified what they were doing, evaluate staffing, and the like. But with my family demands and traveling all the time, it took a lot out. There were times when I really enjoyed it. But then there were times I only thought, I have to visit 30 sites each year.

Like this woman, most of the interviewees derived considerable satisfaction from work. All were highly motivated to begin with and, whether or not the job exactly fit, there was a personal expectation that somehow part of the satisfaction from living was inevitably derived from work, particularly if the work could be rationalized or changed to reflect some higher service ideal:

Work gives you a sense of being, of satisfaction. At the job before this, I took great pride in the newsletters that I put together. I had to say a lot in a small space. I enjoyed writing catchy phrases and being resourceful. I love being resourceful and putting something together with paste and glue or make a place look wonderful.

For another, satisfaction was derived in part from "mining" the work, or making the most creative thing possible out of the assignments given and in part from working with others:

This job is interesting. In one sense, you never know what next week is going to bring. I plan a dozen things to do in a day but in this particular job, something is always changing; there are new regulations, or maybe a new product developed. It always makes things more interesting. But of course, the best part of the job is the people I work with. I like the feeling that I've helped somebody. I like problem-solving.

The people orientation of the women, particularly in the kinds of lower middle management and direct services jobs typically held, were linked with job satisfaction because they were more often related to clientele and clients of agencies (i.e., students, customers, children, parents) than peers or other staff. Typical of this was this appraisal of job satisfaction and people:

My biggest satisfaction is in knowing I've helped somebody. Most of the jobs I have had, have involved helping someone. My first job out of high school was with the Boston Redevelopment Authority. I was a clerk typist. But I had contact with people. People came in to pay rent to the BRA. I also worked for a community neighborhood housing program and in a drug abuse program. In the drug program, I was very green and unaware; I learned what happens to people who go down the drugs path and I think there were people I did help.

A final issue related to people and satisfactions was the view stated repeatedly that networks and contacts, on and off the job, were important to getting the right job. Most of the women interviewed had benefited from contacts and they jealously guarded personal and professional networks for future job needs:

I was never afraid of unemployment. If I need to find a job tomorrow, my network will provide one without looking too long.

COMPENSATION, MOBILITY, AND CAREER EXPECTATIONS

The black women interviewed had typically gained a measure of job security and reasonable compensation after working a number of years. But at the same time, they were quick to note that compensation could be better, particularly after a lifetime of work averaging 20 years of experience. Job security and other benefits such as health insurance also were limited. For most, in fact, the current job represented a milestone in wage as well as nonwage benefits.

For the respondent now working as an executive secretary, there was considerable advantage over 20 years in various private-sector jobs:

My current pay is 25K, increased from last year. The raises are determined in set steps by the state with pay determined by seniority.

On the whole, she saw the low turnover in the agency as one kind of proof of job security. Health plans, a pension, and holidays definitely represented improvements of moving into the public sector:

The benefits of prepaid health are good. This is one of the reasons I wanted to work for the Commonwealth. Because at the last job, a nonprofit, I was naked in terms of coverage. ... It took a committee to decide to pick up half of a private health insurance plan and it was expensive and limited. I had no life insurance. I was at the grace of committees. Now I have Baystate; the costs are $5.00 a month.

For women, a good pension was extremely important:

The pension is 8 percent of my salary. With the nonprofit, for church workers and other organizations, there are big problems with pensions. They think of you in terms of "volunteers," constantly trying to treat you as this.

The regularity of traditional civil service and other protection offered by government was acknowledged by women to provide at least as much security as unions. Black women in general tended to view labor organizations somewhat suspiciously, although they acknowledged that collective bargaining was effective in raising compensation and improving working conditions. As one woman stated:

This is the first time in my life I've belonged to a union and I am not sure what it means. They take $5.00 per week in dues and I get dental benefits. I am curious as to how they [union representatives] get to be officers. Sometimes we are asked to vote, but I'm not sure who they are and where they come from.

She stated that she might have an interest in becoming active but she found it curious that in all the meetings that she had attended she hadn't seen any blacks involved. She did ask a female representative about this and was told that there was sort of an "old boy's club running the union." Another was even more candid in expressing the ambivalence that she felt about unions. After noting that they were in some ways helpful and probably responsible for negotiating her last pay raise, she stated that there were disadvantages. Unions seem to be "focused on seniority and tenure" and thus a new person has to wait for real benefits. She added that she should look into the union more and find out what it was all about.

The women interviewed were most interested in pay and pensions, rather than cafeteria benefits such as child care. Pay for all was limited, despite their seniority in the work force. For one who worked part-time, $8.50 was the hourly wage for the position of classroom aide. Since she was enrolled in school and lived at home, with a working husband and adult children (also in the work force), the issue of part-time work and reduced hours and pay did not arise as a hardship. But for the others, who were heads of households, income was a problem. In the case of one, a very low rent was especially critical, since a new car had really "broken her budget." For two others "moonlighting" was considered a necessity. One woman whose children were adults, and who worked as an administrator, found that a modest mortgage and upkeep on a ten-year-old car still forced her into a part-time second job. For another, a younger woman working as an administrative assistant in an office in a higher education institution with a teenage daughter to support, part-time work was a necessity when she could get it.

The black women interviewed were highly motivated to work with attitudes shaped early in childhood by relatives, parents, and family environments. In contrast to much of the literature on women's motivations, black women appear to have superior role models for work, where even lower status work is elevated as a goal because of its contribution to independence or to personal satisfaction. For this reason, expectations from work are independence and "betterment," as one woman suggested. But the role work plays in women's lives appears to extend beyond satisfaction to build future expectations for mobility, status, and good compensation. There are also expectations for more control over work lives and leisure.

One woman suggested that a combination of family and work experience had shaped her views about work. Of her current job she said:

My days are interesting, I don't have to be so sedentary and I get to meet a lot of people. This job has given me confidence on the road and even computer skills. I thought I was

Rip Van Winkle. I didn't know if I could catch up but I think my fellow workers are wonderful. I work with people who also like their jobs so I feel fortunate. It's uplifting.

She also found that important influences were a serious illness she experienced and encounters with disabled people. Following the illness, this woman gained a new appreciation about life: she was grateful to be alive. Second, handicapped people taught her how to use and exploit what skills she has:

People with disabilities can teach you a lot about life. They learn to use what they have and don't complain about what they don't have. The whole idea is how to have a useful life. That's a good philosophy in any life. . . . So many people say 'I can't.' I love the way that the handicapped look at life . . . they can joke about their disabilities or forget they are there.

Another woman expressed similar motivation for her future by reference to her background in the South and particularly the notion that ethics and work values outweighed any notion of welfare:

Growing up in the South, we were taught that welfare was just something that was a no-no. Southern people are proud people and what you work for you get. I think there are some people who need welfare and I think there are some people who are abusers of the welfare system. . . . I think the medical portion of the benefits are important.

This woman's expectations, however, are extremely high: in addition to having confidence about her ability to "get things done," her concept of mobility and expectations is tempered with education:

One thing emphasized in this work setting is advanced education. I want to get my graduate degree for professional growth. But it is difficult because the current boss doesn't respect this . . . release time from work is necessary to upgrade skills.

In terms of her long-range plans, she noted that while she had worked over the years in a variety of community-relations activities, her real ambition was in education:

I have a dream, to work on the national level as a spokesman for General Education Programs. I've been very interested in adult education and adult literacy. I have a sensitivity toward adults. I currently work as a general education program teacher but I see myself as a national spokesman. . . . If I retire I would probably go South, but I would always work, do some volunteer work, keep involved in adult education.

After struggling for several years to obtain her bachelor's degree on a part-time basis, another woman had made the decision to enter a graduate program to enable her to make a serious career change. The choice was influenced by her own life experience, but also by a volunteer effort to work with a pregnant teenager as part of a mentoring program.

I finally decided to get enrolled in a graduate program and get into a counseling job working with teenagers. . . . I feel that I have learned all that I can learn here on this job, and it is more and more difficult with the change in bosses to get support and understanding.

Another woman, who had been both an administrator and a teacher in preschool programs, had the objective of starting her own daycare center as a business:

I need to get a degree to get paid decently. I am currently studying for a degree. The reason I took this part-time job was to get back into school and get a degree. I need to plan; I want to know what is ahead. My long-term plans are to open my own day care center. I know how to do this, I can write proposals, I've learned a lot over the years and when I'm ready I will open the center. Probably in a year and a half.

Finally, despite having been in the work force from 15 to 20 years, none of the women envisaged retirement. Some noted that they would probably "go South" but remain active and working or volunteering. One woman stated that she wished to continue in the student financial aid field but as a counselor. She enjoyed the business of helping people and felt that she understood students and parents well. However, she viewed her life as extremely balanced:

I don't want to say some day, that I wish I had done that. I went to school for a semester in London. I really enjoyed that. It was the first time I had been away from my family and in another country. A friend of mine who worked in the financial aid office went to study for a year in Paris. I was getting bored so the boss said, why don't you think about going abroad so I looked at some brochures, found this semester in London and applied. She said, "if you get accepted you don't have to go." So I was accepted. I was ecstatic. It was no problem. I'm here, I'll make the best of it and it was a good experience. When I came back in 1977, I was really changed. I was always taught that opportunities don't come around often and I must say that I did do it; I have met a lot of nice people who have really helped me who have taken me under their wing. I will try to do the same thing with others; for example, serve as a mentor to others as has been done to me.

CONCLUSIONS

The work experiences of typical black women who have been employed for a decade or more show some surprising contradictions with typical stereotypes. First, the women are generally ambitious, and they have formed strong conceptions early on about work, both for what it offers in personal satisfaction and for the control over economic need. Social status was also seen as an important value: these women did identify with the type of organization in which they worked and organizational missions. They expect to work indefinitely, irrespective of other life changes. In response, the work world has been surprisingly receptive to them, providing positive feedback to an even greater extent than other sources of social power. For example, most of the women were devoted to work and felt they were doing a good job; these positive attitudes seemed to be rewarded and women did gain sponsors, mentors, and frequently supporters for better jobs, advancement, and higher pay. Such feedback was extremely important in solidifying the women's views of themselves over their work-career lifetimes.

While it is difficult to talk about careers for work that essentially is lower status than the normal definition of professional or managerial careers, these women generally did conceptualize their work as having both merit and status. This helps blur the distinction between "status" and "satisfaction." For example, most felt that their contributions to others was important. Their bosses and peers saw them as significant players in the group and people sought them out for help or opinions. Work was thus a far more enriching experience and one that had more in common with "high status" careers than lower status work.

NOTES

1. For a contemporary evaluation of the commitment of women to work, see Barbara Bergmann, *The Economic Emergence of Women* (New York: Basic Books, 1988); and Joseph H. Pleck, "The Work-Family Role System," in Rachael Kahn-Hut, Arlene Daniels, and Richard Colvard (eds.), *Women and Work* (New York: Oxford University Press, 1982), pp. 101–111.

2. See Bette Woody, "Black Women in the Emerging Services Economy," *Sex Roles,* 21, nos. 1 & 2 (July 1989), pp. 45–69. There is little research on the motivation of black women toward work, although literature abounds on such issues as welfare dependency and the lack of opportunity for black women to participate in the work force. For a recent examination of the latter question, see June Axinn and Mark Stern, *Dependency and Poverty* (Lexington MA: D. C. Heath, 1988). For good examples of current theory and evidence on individual motivation and work, see A. Bandura, *Social Learning Theory* (Englewood Cliffs, NJ: Prentice-Hall, 1977); R. Hampton, *Behavioral Concepts in Management,* 3rd ed. (Belmont, CA: Wadsworth, 1978); D. Nelkin and M. S. Brown, *Workers at Risk* (Chicago: University of Chicago Press, 1984). For a rare focus on behavior of lower status workers, see C. S. Telly, W. L. Franch, and W. G. Sort, "The Relationship of Inequity to Turnover Among Hourly Workers," *Administrative Science Quarterly,* 16 (1971), pp. 164–171.

3. See M. Patchen, *Participation, Achievement and Involvement on the Job* (Englewood Cliffs, NJ: Prentice-Hall, 1970); C. Pinder, *Work Motivation: Theory, Issues and Applications* (Chicago: Scott, Foresman, 1984); V. Vroom, *Work and Motivation* (New York: John Wiley, 1964); Edmond Schier, *Career Dynamics: Matching Individual Organizational Needs* (Reading, MA: Addison-Wesley, 1978); and George Ritzer and David Walczak, *Working: Conflict and Change,* 3rd ed. (Englewood Cliffs, NJ: Prentice-Hall, 1986).

4. Ibid.

CHAPTER 8

CHAPTER 8

Black Women in the Future Industrial Workplace

There is wide agreement that the twenty-first century poses massive challenges for the American worker in the form of increased competition from the rest of the world. There is reason to be pessimistic about the contributions labor will make to industrial output, as domestic producers continue a long steady decline. Structural change that characterized the 1960s in the United States has not been absorbed by the manufacturing sector, leaving large numbers of workers without jobs. At the same time, the services industry, which added considerably to the economy during the 1980s, has suffered severe cutbacks and failures contributing to a domestic recession by the early 1990s. Banking, insurance, and a variety of services dependent on consumer earnings growth—and in turn contributing to the growth of service businesses such as transportation, telecommunications, and business services—stalled and many collapsed with the slowing of economic growth. For labor, however, the problem is compounded by the problems of government and particularly the retreat from the welfare state and the declining role of government as employer of last resort.

Labor's role in the new economic order is more at risk because, in contrast to the past, both industrialized economies and Third World economic organizations are involved in the competition. On the one hand, new organizations such as the European Community's (EC) 1992 integration may constitute a new barrier as well as a stronger force, solidified by favorable production agreements across multiple borders. Europe is also still a major innovator in products and production processes. But as well, higher quality and efficiently produced goods may be another by-product of the EC. Second, however, the rapid rise of the Pacific Rim economies, with rapid gains not only in productivity but in growth of an educated work force, has increased competition for the United States. The Third World, led by industrial producers, Europeans, Japanese, and Americans, however, poses a threat to labor of lower wages, flexible working conditions, and, above all, a constant new supply to maintain both productivity and product flows. The general challenge facing all labor is the slowing growth of jobs and declining wages. For black women, this general picture has important implications.

In addition to global economic change and challenge, the future labor force status of black women is influenced in both short- and long-run terms by micro-level changes in the organization of the workplace and jobs and by the evolving subculture of low-wage work. On the one hand, black women may look forward to better job availability; but pay and benefits may be low and job security less and less. Adding to economic stress, however, is the continuing crisis of the black family. It can be anticipated that contraction of employment opportunities for black men, particularly in blue-collar jobs, will continue. As a result, black women will fall increasingly into a substrata of working poor with little hope to achieve economic self-sufficiency from earnings in the workplace.

The future challenge faced by the U.S. worker can be seen separately as individual and collective problems. For the individual worker, there is the dilemma of fundamental change in the nature of work and its relationship to the worker. Technological and managerial change and innovation have raised productivity but in the process have drastically altered work content. The traditional psychic awards derived from the personal and intimate relationships between work and worker in the form of individual satisfaction and self-worth, have eroded as man-machine relationships have changed and challenging tasks diminished. Job security and work status have also declined as job ladders have disappeared. Thus not only does the individual worker face a loss of control over work and job satisfaction, but also higher risks of layoff and loss of work status. The gains in productivity that economists laud may indeed point to future gains to the worker as consumer. But the typical worker would ask: What good are cheaper goods if there is no income to pay for them? More to the point, how can the individual influence the nature of work to ''contribute'' to and then gain directly from productivity in the form of income?

Direct declines in status and compensation, however, go further than having a job and cash in a salary envelope. The job security issue includes the larger value of the basic social contract forged in the past between labor and management: in return for loyalty and effort, there would be job security, a decent wage, and retirement. And with inevitable increases in the cost of living—health care and housing in particular—the position of the American worker's status has become even more precarious.

Finally, there is the risk of total unemployment or reduced hours or both. With the absolute decline in high-wage jobs in mainstream production activities, millions of workers have been pushed out of the workplace altogether, or into low-wage and marginal employment in unfamiliar industrial settings where mobility and wage growth depend on very sophisticated skills and advanced education. Thus, younger blue-collar workers are now unable to "get into the workplace" at all.

This chapter looks at the future of black women in the economy in three sections. We first examine several background factors that shape economic growth and the competitive position of the U.S. economy and their impact on domestic job growth. Next, demographic trends and work force participation rates are reviewed, along with current economic growth forecasts for the occupational and industrial structure in the United States. Finally, gaps and problems are summarized to provide a picture of the likely status of black women as a labor force.

FORCES SHAPING THE FUTURE ECONOMY

In part, problems for the individual worker are rooted in changes in the status and value of labor in the economy, but in part also in internal change in the composition of the labor force itself. Demand for the new worker is mainly from service employers for very different reasons than in the past with production activities. Labor, we have noted, is increasingly devalued as changes in technology and managerial innovation invade the workplace. But in contrast to traditional manufacturing employment, services are characterized by far higher managerial control over inputs that are mainly labor, are less closely monitored by government, and have few trade unions and collective bargaining to represent labor interests. But as well, the composition of the work force—increasingly nonwhite and female—figures prominently in this reshaping process. The work force has become increasingly fragmented and heterogeneous with fewer and fewer traditional mainstream workers with social status and power to set standards for working conditions and wages. In this vacuum, more and more managements determine how, when, and under what circumstances labor is deployed.

More than any force in the postindustrial twenty-first century, an emerging political economy of work organization where business and government overlap poses the most serious threat to the status of the bulk of wage earners. This link between business and government is particularly visible in shaping the future status of black women workers.

Over the past two decades, an interface has grown between key employment organizations, public policy in funding sources, and government regulations. While the aims of these linkages appear innocent, the effects are to subordinate the needs of the work force in subtle and indirect ways. Building on the eroding position of labor in the workplace with the rise of services, and reinforced by a growing weakness in organized labor, neoconservatives dominated the national political arena to set new agendas. The result was to disrupt attention to national economic growth as a matter of public policy. The reasoning behind this change-over was an objective to restore an unregulated market system assumed to be more efficient than government planning. The fledgling start by successive administrations toward the welfare state also ended with the Carter administration. Programmatic components of social policy, consisting of a national health insurance plan, family income floors, and full employment proposed by various Congresses, was the major casualty. Ironically, neoconservative policies also hurt corporate enterprise by eliminating or failing to evolve health insurance coverage and standards that would help reduce private-sector contribution costs to support the health care establishment. Such cost reductions would help bring the cost of American labor in line with that of other countries, as well as resolve some of the serious problems of part-time and irregular employment disadvantage to labor. Other somewhat more controversial social policies—such as family allowances, or tax deductions for dependents, or dependent care such as child care—might also promote economic growth and flexibility in broader ways, such as assisting smaller businesses and particularly new business starts.

Predictions of the future of the U.S. job economy are at best fraught with uncertainty of anticipating factors underlying broad trends in economic growth. Some are factor and product price trends, sales and market outlooks, and export trade and influences external to the immediate market such as the cost of borrowing. Demographic trends are also important, directly influencing the growth of the labor force and indirectly fueling the consumer economy. Employment prospects for black women are as dependent on these broad trends in the future as on specific characteristics of the work force and factors that figured prominently in past job growth.

In the short run, two kinds of trends will influence black women's employment. The first is demographic changes in shaping the size and composition of the work force. A second influence is job growth in the economy. On the demographic side are higher proportions of black women in the women's work force because of higher minority birth rates.

Official demographic trends forecast a reduction in the overall size of the working population. Black women will, however, grow as a proportion of the total female work force. A predicted continuing decline in black male labor force participation will also spur more black females, particularly in younger age cohorts, to enter the workplace to support families.

By contrast, expansion of available employment depends on industry growth and productivity trends. Predicted economic trends that will most influence the future job market are pessimistic for all labor force segments. There will be a continued erosion of goods-producing industries, particularly manufacturing, while services are forecast to expand at a slower rate than in the past two decades. Throughout the economy, future predictions are for accelerated restructuring, including downsizing, consolidation, and "shake outs" of primary firms in individual industrial categories. Services such as banking and financial services, insurance, health care, transportation and telecommunications that enjoyed spectacular growth in the recent past will likely undergo these changes. This in turn will influence the types of occupations available in job markets of particular sectors as well as the number of jobs.

For black women, job growth trends point to a mixed opportunity structure. They may benefit from a somewhat more competitive position as the size of the labor force overall contracts, but at the same time, fewer jobs and more high skilled occupations in the mix may hurt. Thus, marginal workplaces, low-skilled jobs, and part-time employment would be expected to face many black women breadwinners.

A final element influencing the future of black women in the workplace is government and public policy. During the 1980s, after a decade of progressive legislation and policy initiatives, a conservative administration in Washington successfully targeted and slowed government regulation of economic opportunity in the workplace. But a surprising number of corporate institutions retained mechanisms for fair hiring. Congressional, local government, and private actions in areas of comparable worth, minimum wage legislation, and unionization of women also contributed to some progress.

DEMOGRAPHIC TRENDS AND THE LABOR FORCE OF THE TWENTY-FIRST CENTURY

Demographic changes will continue to constitute the primary influence on the shape of the work force over the next two decades. Overall population decline in the post-baby-boom birth rate is the main cause of the anticipated contraction of the working-age population. Because of declines in white males, the portion of black men in the total population is predicted to rise by the year 2000, reflecting past growth. The black population grew 1.6 over the period 1972 to 1986, compared to 0.8 for whites. With the predicted growth rates, the proportion of whites in the total population 16 and over will drop from 86.4 in 1986 to 84.1 by 2000, while the black population 16 and over will rise from 10.8 to 11.8 over the same period.[1]

Work force participation, or the number of individuals actually working or seeking work, is a second factor influencing the overall supply of labor. Work force participation of men has declined overall over the past two decades, although more dramatically for black men than whites.[2] Among younger white men, extended education has been a primary explanation for these declines, but this does not hold true for black men, whose educational enrollments have declined. Particularly, the distance between black male teenagers and white counterparts has become so great as to raise serious questions about causes.[3] By contrast, work force participation of women of both races has been influenced by the growth in headship rates among women, with the increases in women heading households spurring growing entry into the work force. As the number of black families headed by men declined from two-thirds of all black families in 1950 to less than half by 1987, black women correspondingly grew as full-time breadwinners. At the same time, work force participation of black married women has declined recently, following patterns of white women in the past.[4] As in the case of black women, white women heading households grew to 18

Table 8.1
Changes in the Black Women's Work Force

	1972	%Black Women	1986	%Black Women	2000	%Black Women
Total Work Force	87,037	4.47	117,837	5.36	138,775	6.06
Total Women	33,481	11.63	52,414	12.04	65,631	12.31
Total Blacks	8,748	44.47	12,884	48.98	16,334	51.47
Black Women	3,893	100.00	6,311	100.00	8,408	100.00

Source: Harold Fullerton, "Projections 2000: Labor Force Projections: 1986 to 2000," *Monthly Labor Review*, September 1987, p. 25.

percent of all white families by 1987, and work force participation correspondingly increased. In the future, more white women, both married and single, are likely to enter the work force. Thus, the participation rates of white women 16 and over are forecast to grow from 55.0 percent in 1986 to 61.5 percent by 2000. This compares with an anticipated drop in participation rates of white men 16 and over from 76.0 percent in 1986 to 75.3 percent by 2000.[5]

The labor force participation rates of blacks are expected to both parallel and contrast with whites. High proportions of black women of working age will continue to enter the work force, reflecting continued growth of women heading households, although the rates of participation of black married women may fall slightly. While in the past black women (i.e., married women) have tended to work either to supplement earnings of black men to achieve family income goals, or to replace black male earners who were absent from the household, the future driving force behind employment patterns of black women will rest more with declining marriage rates.[6] Assuming that black women, particularly teenage girls, continue to improve skills and educational attainment, they will constitute a growing share of the women's work force. As Table 8.1 indicates, black women will make up a higher proportion of the total work force as well as passing the halfway mark in the black work force.

INDUSTRY, JOBS, AND BUSINESS FIRM WORK ORGANIZATIONS: TRENDS INFLUENCING BLACK WOMEN WORKERS

Industry has strongly influenced the work status and income of black women over the past two decades. Industry growth spurred a massive expansion of women's jobs and, in the process, provided vast new opportunities for black women prior to the accelerated entry of white women into the work force. Broad industrial growth will continue to exert a strong influence on the total number of jobs available in the future. Among factors most influencing industrial growth and the job mix are:

1. Trends in productivity and work output, including technological change
2. Growth of household income and consumption
3. Regional distribution of jobs, including overseas production trends
4. Public policy on: (a) employment and wages (b) social welfare for individuals and families (c) direct government expenditures

Industry growth in the future is difficult to predict because of uncertainty in such factors as raw material costs, labor availability, and prevailing wage and benefits costs, and such markets forces as trends in consumer income and spending that influence growth of retailing and personal services, and finally, competition from foreign producers. Most current economic forecasts for the next two decades project a continued slowing of growth for the U.S. economy. This translates into a general leveling of output and job expansion as well as a more selective sectoral expansion. Underscoring this is an anticipated decline in traditional production sectors, an increased productivity in contemporary production such as computers and high technology sectors, and a moderate growth in services.

Probably the most important factor influencing future job growth is the geographic distribution of jobs, and particularly the split between production located in the United States and the rest of the world. Adding to the complexity of this is the future split among developed and Third World economies, and industrial and nonmechanized production. As U.S. producers export products abroad, and foreign producers extend activities outside the United States and production inside the United States, important short-term changes in jobs in the United States will occur. As an example of the uncertainty in predicting these changes, there are current trends where services industries export routine clerical and paper-processing tasks to remote sites. Examples are found in the growth of offshore sites for satellite transmission of data and information by the insurance, airlines, and banking industries. Thus the expansion of the most routine, low-status and low-paid work to the developing world may accelerate in the future, because of labor cost differentials but also because technological innovation permits a broader range of production options. The entry of foreign competitors into the service industry, which has been protected through regulation and, further, locally organized, may increase and may also result in job losses. A Japanese bank, for example, might easily enter the consumer credit market in the United States by offering a new low-interest credit card while, at the same time, carrying out most of the transactions associated with customer service using remote and even offshore sites. Only a small "thinking" managerial end of such services businesses would be required in the United States, or even less than in the case of imports of Japanese automobiles and consumer durables. The drift of the production industry toward more service-type activities has also been seen as creating more, not less, use of offshore labor.[7]

In the workplace itself, job and task organization trends have generally shifted jobs from cognitive, human relations and invention-oriented skills to mere routine tasks. Following patterns set by manufacturing and other goods-producing industries, services will increasingly adopt "industrialization" techniques of breaking down tasks into minute routines, then combining them in ways to shift from high- to low-status jobs. Overall, the workplace can be expected to be restructured to reduce higher skills requirements and consolidate many tasks into low-status jobs, or into machine processing. The impacts of these changes on the growth of low-status jobs is somewhat unpredictable, since many jobs may be temporary, until technological innovation adapts to processing new tasks. In other large sectors of U.S. services activities, such as retailing, yet other innovation representing combinations of management, technology, and job restructuring is expected to continue at a rapid pace. This will cause an absolute reduction of certain job categories. In retailing, for example, the introduction of new workstations at checkout counters employing traditional cashier jobs now not only tally purchases but also debit inventories, credit sales, and order replacement merchandise via a sophisticated tracking system on a daily basis. These new systems, called just-in-time inventories, have served to reduce millions of warehouse and backroom inventory jobs, as well as clerical jobs associated with accounting systems, while at the same time producing impressive productivity gains in added sales volumes and profits. From the perspective of jobs that remain, however, the status and pay levels remain relatively low, such as in the case of the job of cashier. This salary level is based on characterizing the content of the work as essentially "routine," since most of the "thinking" is preprogrammed by computer. Because of these kinds of changes, a segment of the women's work force trained in routine work is most often employed in the job. Other management innovation in the organization of work has characterized other segments of the services industry, including activities historically considered "labor intensive" such as health care, hotels and restaurants, and maintenance services.

The impacts of increased productivity in services, resulting from higher revenue, reduced costs, or both, might be expected, as in the past, to be passed on to the work force in the form of increased compensation. One value of such profit sharing noted by an analyst would be to reduce turnover and motivate the work force to take initiative and learn more complex activities, all important for a company's productivity.[8] There is little evidence, however, that services productivity will be passed on in wages. Evidence from the manufacturing model suggests some of the reasons. While gains by manufacturing workers were passed on, this work force was largely male, with traditions of wage gains, and could depend on labor unions to negotiate wage settlements based on profitability of firms. Organized labor, which was strongly supported by both government and management in the male-dominated manufacturing sector in the past, was able to forge a lucrative social contract over time. By contrast, mainstream organized labor ignored women as a work force, and services sector management ruthlessly suppressed efforts to organize traditional women services workers in health care, education, and such sectors as the hotel industry. Such antilabor actions frequently enjoyed government support.[9] By contrast in private services industries where collective bargaining has succeeded, improvements in compensation and working conditions have taken place.[10]

Finally, public policy will exert direct and indirect pressure in several ways on both industry expansion and job growth trends. Included in policy directly affecting jobs are wage floors (both in general minimum wage standards, and through such prevailing wage standards as Davis-Bacon) and mandatory payroll taxes such as social security, unemployment, and the currently debated health insurance premiums. Payroll taxes, particularly those that fall on the employer such as disability and unemployment, can promote mechanization and job export as well as productivity gains by raising the cost of labor relative to capital. Wage floors (specifically the minimum wage in the United States) has a more complex impact. Evidence shows that raises in the minimum wage reduce part-time work, substitute part-time male employment for full-time female employment, and produce other business outcomes such as higher prices, shorter business hours, and smaller profit margins, as well as greater efficiency known collectively as "shock effects."[11] Other policies that will impact the size and productivity of specific industries are those related to federal spending, particularly social welfare programs. The health industry as well as education and government services are all influenced by particular government appropriations policy, and by rulemaking such as cost cutting strategies currently employed in association with insurance programs of Medicare and Medicaid.[12] Job growth as well as occupational structures and work organization are all affected by government actions, and anticipated changes to date are to reduce costs overall, to cut labor costs, and to shift more of the service burdens to consumers. With the decline in payroll as the work force contracts, pressures will be even stronger for such reductions.

Changes in the health industry have already started and serve to illustrate the innovations to reduce costs. Techniques to reduce health care costs include decentralization of patient care out of higher cost facilities, more self-administered treatment by patients, and expanded use of paraprofessional staff as a substitute for higher cost professionals.[13] Black women workers, heavily concentrated in low status jobs in health and education, may be negatively influenced by these trends. In government services where black women have made the most gains, particularly in clerical work, contraction is forecast at the federal level, and a slowing of growth in local government, with increased mechanization and contracting to outside, cheaper sources, is forecast for the future.

FUTURE INDUSTRY, JOBS, AND WORKPLACES

The U.S. economy is currently anticipated by most economists to continue moderate growth through the turn of the century. From a 2.9 percent growth in real domestic output experienced during the 1972–79 period, tapering to 1.6

Table 8.2
Output and Employment Growth, 1972–86; Projected to 2000

SECTOR	Employment (average annual rate of change in percentage)			Real Domestic Output (average annual rate of change in percentage)		
	1972–79	1979–86	1986–2000[1]	1972–79	1979–86	1986–2000
Total	2.6	1.4	1.3	2.9	1.6	2.4
Nonfarm Wages & Salary	2.8	1.5	1.3			
Goods Producing	1.6	-1.0	.0	2.3	0.8	-2.0
Mining	6.2	-2.8	-1.1	0.3	-1.4	-0.2
Construction	2.0	1.4	1.0	1.0	1.3	1.4
Manufacturing	1.4	-1.4	-0.3	2.9	0.6	2.3
Durable	2.1	-1.8	-0.3	3.1	0.5	2.7
Nondurable	0.3	-0.9	-0.3	2.6	0.8	1.8
Services	3.4	2.4	1.7	3.5	2.4	2.6
Transport, Util.	1.8	0.3	0.6	3.6	0.0	2.6
Wholesale Trade	3.4	1.4	1.7	3.1	3.6	2.7
Retail trade	3.4	2.5	1.7	3.2	3.0	2.4
Finance, Insur. Real Estate	3.5	3.4	1.7	4.1	2.5	2.6
Services	4.8	4.3	2.7	4.4	3.6	3.2
Government	2.6	0.7	0.7	1.7	1.8	1.5
Agriculture	-0.5	-0.6	-0.8	1.7	1.4	2.4
Priv., Householding	-3.4	-0.9	-0.1	-3.7	3.0	0.2
Nonfarm, Self- employer, etc.	3.0	1.8	1.3	—	—	—

[1]Moderate growth percent, equivalent to mid-range of ''low'' and ''high'' projections.
Source: Valerie Personick, ''Projections, 2000: Industry Output and Employment through the End of the Century,'' *Monthly Labor Review*, September 1987, Tables 1 and 2, pp. 32–33.

percent during the 1979–86 recession period, government forecasts have set a moderate 2.4 percent growth prediction over the period 1986 through 2000.[14] But in contrast to national output, employment expansion will slow considerably to an annual percentage increase of only 1.3 percent, down from 2.6 percent over the 1972–79 period and 1.4 percent between 1979–86.

Behind these forecasts of output and employment growth are several assumptions. First, the gains in real GNP reflect gains in productivity, particularly in the capital-goods-producing sectors that will allow production to expand without corresponding job gains. Output will also be helped by growth in exports that occur with a more favorable exchange rate. A second assumption is that the expansion of the labor force overall will slow, causing unemployment to level off to 6.0 by 2000.

The cumulative impact of growth on jobs will be a net gain of 21 million new jobs, to bring total U.S. employment to just over 133 million. New jobs, however, will be almost exclusively in services rather than goods-producing sectors. With no new net gains in goods production, most of the growth in manufacturing, for example, will be on the services side of the business: in R&D, engineering, marketing, and management. Manufacturing employment overall will fall from 19 million to 18.2 million between 1986 and 2000. Table 8.2 outlines government forecasts and distribution of real domestic output by major sectors from 1972 to 2000.

The following will review current output and employment forecasts for key

Table 8.3
Manufacturing Job Forecasts (in 000s)

	1979	1986	2000
Total	21,042	18,994	18,160
Durable	12,762	11,244	10,731
Nondurable	8,280	7,750	7,429

Source: Personick, "Projections 2000," p. 33.

industrial sectors for the year 2000, as well as occupational impact changes influencing the employment of black women.

When sectors are compared for output and productivity growth, it is clear that goods-producing industries will continue to outpace services. Goods-production industry "shakeouts" will result in the biggest contributions to national output overall, but as recent analysis indicates, the services sector will also shift radically, gaining surprising efficiencies compared to the past.[15] To illustrate how this occurs, we'll use the example of basic metals, an older declining industry. Competition from more efficient foreign producers helped shake out low performers and those plants and operations with very high energy and maintenance costs. The remaining industry was far more productive and able to recapture an important part of the basic metals market. The services industries, however, will to some extent follow patterns established a generation ago by manufacturing, with growth in output occurring in such sectors as white-collar, professional, and consumer services. The impact on employment, however, is a general slowing overall, with the most employment concentrated in restructured services such as banking and insurance and in newer contracted and consumer services such as credit agencies, business services, auto rentals, child care, and home-based health care.[16]

Manufacturing

Among goods-producing industries, manufacturing has proved the most important source of past employment for black women. Trends in productivity, however, will dampen opportunity for women in the future. Overall manufacturing output, for example, as Table 8.3 illustrates, is expected to expand at a moderate pace by the year 2000, with durable goods leading the pace at 2.7 percent annually, compared to 1.8 percent for nondurables. Employment, however, will fall by overall losses of −0.3 percent per year for an absolute loss of 834,000 jobs by 2000.

Output growth, particularly for durable goods, reflects several projected trends, including increased investment in capital equipment and growth of capital goods for export, as U.S. production becomes more price competitive with foreign production. As an example, 5 of the 79 durable goods categories not expected to grow are in primary metals groups and railroad equipment, where foreign producers have gained a leading edge. The cumulative effect, however, is to

Table 8.4
Forecast Changes in Manufacturing Occupations

	% Employment Durable		Nondurable	
All Manufacturing Occupations	1986	2000	1986	2000
Managerial, prof., tech.	19.9	23.4	12.8	14.7
Marketing, sales	2.2	2.3	4.1	4.6
Administrative support, clerical	11.3	10.2	12.6	12.2
Precision production	11.0	11.2	6.6	6.8
Other production jobs (mechanics, operators, assemblers, material movers, laborers)	47.3	44.9	55.5	53.6

Source: Personick "Projections 2000," p. 33.

reduce the number of jobs. A net decline of 513,000 jobs is expected in durables, compared to a drop of 321,000 in nondurables.

A second important trend influencing black women's employment is the internal occupational structure in manufacturing. As emphasis shifts away from production and assembly to professional, technical, and managerial functions, or more services-oriented activities within manufacturing, fewer blue-collar jobs will be available in the economy.[17]

The changes in manufacturing employment, as Table 8.4 indicates, will particularly affect three subsectors in durable manufacturing where black women have made important recent gains: computers, electronics, and automotive assembly. In nondurables, employment changes affecting black women are mainly in traditional blue-collar employment sectors of food products, apparel, and textiles.

Computers and office equipment have constituted one of the fastest growing sectors of U.S. industries over the past 25 years, and have contributed substantially to growth in women's blue-collar employment. Despite an anticipated increase in foreign imports, computers are expected to continue impressive output and employment growth in the future, making a principal contribution to the U.S. trade surplus. But internal domestic employment is expected to continue to shift radically from production workers to technical, managerial, and administrative support employment. Over 25 percent of employment is forecast for scientific and technical personnel alone of the total work force in computers, with only 35 percent in production work, compared to 68 percent production work employment in manufacturing as a whole in 1986.[18] Thus, 7.4 percent annual output growth is forecast between 1986 and 2000, and 85,000 jobs added to bring total employment for the sector to half a million by 2000. For this reason, the sector will add little to employment opportunity for women of both races in the future.

Growth trends are also anticipated for electrical and electronic equipment manufacturing, which currently provides approximately 2.1 million jobs. Employment is expected to remain stable while productivity gains will average about 5 percent annually. Because of the diversity of production, specialization in small production for high-value and customized equipment—such as X-ray machines, electromedical apparatus, satellites, broadcasting equipment, industrial laser systems, fiber optics systems—it is likely that most assembly jobs will remain in the United States and employ skilled labor.

Black women made particularly important strides in employment in transportation equipment manufacturing over the past 20 years, both in main assembly plants and in small parts contracting units. A slowdown is forecast for the future, however. The automobile industry slowdown will reflect a slowing of demand, as the absolute decline occurs in the size of the population aged 16–34, which accounts for the bulk of first-time car buyers. Domestic output of automobiles as a result is forecast to grow only about 2.0 percent per year from 1986 to 2000, compared to 2.4 percent for the GNP overall, with employment suffering a net loss, falling from 865,000 to 749,000 jobs over the period. This employment drop, coupled with productivity gains, will help raise growth to the 2.0 level. Productivity gains, for example, are predicted to reach an annual increase of 3.2 annually by 2000, mainly because of capital investments, particularly in new equipment such as robotics and other automation of production. Employment forecasts also assume that Japanese production in the United States will expand, to offset the rising value of the yen.

In nondurable manufacturing, black women have been employed primarily in food products, apparel, and textiles. In the future, food product production growth is expected to slow, mainly as a result of falling demand and demographic and consumer preference changes. For example, the demand for sugar-based products (confectionary, soft drink beverages, malt beverages) as well as dairy and meat products will decline with contraction in the number of youthful populations, which have constituted the main part of the market. As a result, employment in food products is expected to decline by approximately 161,000 jobs between 1986 and 2000. Apparel and textiles employment is also forecast to decline, but mainly as the result of continued foreign competition and cost-cutting. Clothing imports are expected to grow from 28 percent of the total sold in the United States in 1985 to 37 percent of the domestic market by 2000. Productivity increases resulting from cost-cutting will keep growth at slightly above 1.0 percent through the year 2000. As a result of labor cost-cutting, however, employment in apparel is expected to decline from 921,000 jobs in 1986 to 763,000 by 2000 for a loss of 158,000 jobs. These losses will affect blue-collar women particularly hard, where most of the employment is currently concentrated. Similarly, textile production output will continue to rise as in the past, through mechanization of production; following past patterns, where textile employment declined by 300,000 jobs between 1973 and 1986, an additional loss of 99,000 textile jobs is forecast by 2000.

Services Industries and Black Women in the Future

Some of the same trends that have influenced productivity gains in manufacturing are forecast for the services industries in the future. While by 2000 employment growth will be overwhelmingly concentrated in services, with 20 million of the 21 million new jobs forecast, the past dramatic rates of job creation will slow substantially. Key reasons are efforts to increase productivity to remain competitive, "shakeouts" in certain industries resulting in restructuring and cost cutting, and, finally, potential competition from abroad. Nonetheless, current government forecasts project that, by 2000, 80 percent of all wage and salary employment will be in one services category or another. The impacts of these trends on black women's employment will depend strongly on the internal occupational mix of services, on the rate of expansion of part-time work, and on trends in wages and other compensation. It is useful to look at selected subsectors more closely for output and employment changes along with occupational trends to predict impacts on black women workers.

Transportation and communications are two services sectors where black women made spectacular gains, both in employment and in compensation, in the recent past. The future, however, suggests that while productivity will increase and wages probably remain high, total employment will flatten considerably. In transportation, rapid recent expansion resulting from deregulation and increased competition has occurred with the entry of many new, smaller firms in the marketplace. Multiple firms stimulated price competition and job expansion. But already consolidation and takeover, along with employment cuts, have characterized the industry. With a continued consolidation predicted for the future, output is expected to grow 2.6 percent annually, but employment will flatten to only about 0.6 annually. Relatively high wages may be maintained, but this will reflect the fact that much of employment will be in higher wage managerial categories. A similar picture could be painted for the communications industry. Communications underwent similar growth with deregulation and the breakup of the telephone monopoly in 1983 and the entry of new competitors into the industry. As a result, no real output gains took place during the 1980s. In the future, output is expected to increase to 3.9 percent annually, primarily as the result of technological innovation and various consolidations and shakeouts in the industry. Employment is expected to decline by about 131,000, or a loss of about −0.9 percent annually.

The retailing industry has represented a mixed picture for black women in the past, from both employment and pay perspectives. While black women gained a significant employment, particularly in department stores, mail-order houses, and in the restaurant business, part-time employment was high. The numbers of hours and earnings for black women were thus reduced. Also, wage structures remained among the lowest in the economy. In the future, retail employment and wages may not change. Overall, output is expected to improve and reach 2.4 percent annually, or a level close to the national GNP. Employment will also increase by a modest annual increase of 1.7 percent overall. But the highest growth will continue to occur in the weakest part of the industry from the perspective of hours and wages—eating and drinking places—where employment growth is expected to increase 2.6 percent annually.

Part-time employment and wages have made retailing an employment "problem" as much as a solution for most black women. Overall 4.9 million jobs are forecast to be added, slowing somewhat from the past. Despite growth in demand for full-time work (particularly by women), part-time work is expected to remain a high proportion of total employment. Between 1973 and 1985, 40 percent of the increase in retail employment was in part-time work. Demographic changes, on the other hand, may limit the number of workers available for part-time work and may even push wages to advance somewhat. Teenagers, for example, who have constituted an important source of part-time workers, particularly in restaurants, will shrink from 6.9 percent of the work force in 1986 to 6.0 percent by 2000. Women, by contrast, have steadily reduced their share of total part-time workers in preference for full-time work. Declines in the number of women working part-time, for example, declined from 24.1 in 1976 to 21.7 in 1986. Thus, although the average weekly hours in the retail trade dropped from 35.6 in 1972 to 29.2 in 1986, it is expected that a shift will occur, increasing the number of full-time jobs in order to attract workers, particularly women. Subsectors where growth can be expected are in catering and contracted food services such as for hospitals, schools, residential institutions, airlines, and grocery stores, where an additional 600,000 new jobs will result from expanded hours and more labor-intensive delicatessan-type operations.

Banking, financial services, and insurance, along with government, constitute the bulk of white-collar services. Black women made impressive gains in this kind of employment during the past three decades, although they did remain concentrated in clerical jobs. The sector is forecast to make output gains at higher rates than in the past, but employment growth will slow. Principal reasons for this relate to consolidation and restructuring following a decade of deregulation of the financial services, banking, and insurance industry and the technological revolution that has mechanized thousands of operations. This raised productivity above the rate of national growth, while slowing employment. Thus jobs predicted for the next two decades will be fewer and more at the low and middle ranks. Clerical jobs will continue to grow, but are likely, as in the recent past, to expand on a "flexible" basis to permit short-run elimination or change.[19]

Business and Professional Services

Business and professional services and government, which led past employment growth, will continue to shape the biggest employment contributions to the economy. However, job growth will slow from past rates, as productivity gains are made and as spending slows from past levels, particularly in government and health care.[20] For example, while business and professional services constituted 23 percent of nonfarm wage and salaried jobs in 1986, and employment growth between 1972 and 1986 averaged 4.5 percent annually, employment growth in the sector is predicted to level to 2.7 percent between 1986 and 2000. Nonetheless, these sectors will gain as a proportion of total jobs, rising to 27 percent of all jobs by 2000, and adding 32 million payroll jobs.

Among business and professional services, business-related services will continue to expand most rapidly. Business services as defined by the U.S. Bureau of Census is complex, comprising both high and low ends of services. At the high end are professional/technical services such as computer systems design, scientific and technical services, legal services, advertising, professional, scientific temporary help and employment, credit reporting, and engineering. At the low end are nonadministrative categories of services such as building maintenance, equipment rental and leasing, security and guard services, as well as low-end temporary clerical and data processing services in the administrative area. A key reason for the recent phenomenal growth of business and professional services has been the growing practice of "contracting" out specialized services by business, government, and nonprofits such as health care. This explains the accelerated growth of such services as computer consulting and data processing businesses, building maintenance, equipment rental and leasing, and laboratory testing (materials, chemicals, and biomedical testing services). A second reason is the increasing reliance on temporary help agencies as a substitute for hiring in-house permanent staff. Temporary help agencies were initially organized for "office overload" to replace vacationing staff or to complete special projects involving routine, simple tasks such as inventories or infrequent paper-processing jobs. But with the growth in fringe benefits, employers have sought to reduce payroll costs by contracting labor. Another factor behind the expansion of temporary employee contracting may be for greater flexibility to phase out activities without having to lay off staff, pay unemployment benefits, and endure the discomfort of employee separation. As a result, temporary help agencies have grown into a billion dollar business, adding to clerical and office workers such new jobs as laborers, engineers, accountants, architects, nurses, and technical and scientific help.

The expanded use of contractors by government is predicted in the future for use in jobs from data processing to home nursing care for the elderly. The motives of government agencies include budgetary manipulations as well as avoidance of permanent civil service position growth and other public administration problems. The occupational mix that will grow out of these trends will result in declines in administrative support personnel such as stenographers, payroll and timekeeping clerks, typists and word processors, data entry keyers, and statistical clerks. Job growth is predicted for general health care workers, maintenance workers, security workers, paralegal help, and scientific and professional employment.

Health services began undergoing radical changes during the mid-1980s as a result of cost containment policies and subsequent efforts by providers to raise productivity. One result was a decline in hospital employment, and a corresponding growth in decentralized health care facilities as patient care shifted to outpatient care activities such as physicians' offices, emergency outpatient clinics, group practices, drop-in care clinics, and HMOs.[21] Future trends are expected to accelerate both decentralization and staff reductions, as growth occurs in cost containment pressures by private insurers, employer groups, and government.[22]

Thus, outpatient care is expected to grow by 4.4 percent annually, adding 1.4 million new jobs by 2000. At the same time, owing to the aging of the population, the demand for health care is expected to rise. The over-65 population will expand from 9.8 to 13.0 percent of the total population from 1986 to 2000. As the unit costs for patients over 65 more than double the costs of health expenditures compared to the population as a whole, costs overall will continue to expand. Employment growth, however, will be more pronounced in nursing homes and personal care facilities, as efforts are made to keep the lid on more expensive hospital confinement. Nursing homes are expected to increase employment by 3.8 percent between 1986 and 2000, while hospital employment will level to 1.0 percent annually.

The occupational mix in health services will also change, however, to reflect a downgrading of clinical professional tasks, and an expansion at the routine services end, following the reduced emphasis on costly hospital facilities for primary patient care. Lower skilled medical and nonmedical personnel (clerical, laboratory testing personnel, data processing) will grow, while the numbers of higher cost specialized medical personnel will decline. Reflecting the anticipated expansion of home-based care, early hospital release patterns and outpatient care, paraprofessionals, nursing aides, and LPNs will expand rapidly. Another trend forecast is the increased use of self-administered treatment utilizing new technologies and simplified packaging, following the patterns of diabetic patients. Another employment contraction, however, which will directly impact black women, and which will result from the decline in hospital employment, is a loss of low-skilled maintenance employment. These job losses include food preparation, laundries, janitors, and other maintenance workers.

Educational services and government are expected to remain stable and decline slightly in proportion to total employment. In both sectors, demographic change will have key impacts. Elementary and secondary education populations will decline dramatically over the next decade, extending into the postsecondary education population by the mid-1990s. A modest output rate of 1.8 is expected in education, with a 0.9 percent increase in employment over the 1986–2000 period. Government is also expected to be influenced by demographic change. As in the past, growth is predicted mainly for state and local government, with increases forecast to grow by 1.6 million over the period 1986–2000.

NOTES

1. Howard N. Fullerton, "Projections 2000: Labor Force Projections: 1986 to 2000," *Monthly Labor Review*, September 1987, pp. 19–29.

2. Andrew Brimmer, "Urban Young Lose Jobs to Suburbs," *Black Enterprise*, September 1987. See also Greg J. Duncan and Saul P. Hoffman, "Recent Trends in the Relative Earnings of Black Men" in Greg Duncan (ed.), *Years of Poverty, Years of Plenty* (Ann Arbor, MI: Survey Research Center, Institute for Social Research, 1984), pp. 139–152.

3. Bruce E. Kaufman, *The Economics of Labor Markets and Labor Relations* (Chicago: Dryden Press, 1986), pp. 285–287.

4. Barbara A.P. Jones, "Black Women and Labor Force Participation: An Analysis of Sluggish Growth Rates," in Margaret Simms and Julianne Malveaux (eds.), *Slipping Through the Cracks* (New Brunswick, NJ: Transaction Books, 1987), pp. 11–32.

5. Fullerton, "Projections 2000," pp. 18–19.

6. For a discussion on marriage rates among black men, see William A. Darity Jr. and Samuel L. Myers, Jr. "Does Welfare Dependency Cause Female Headship?: The Case of the Black Family," *Journal of Marriage and the Family*, 46, no.4 (November 1984).

7. James L. Heskett, *Managing in the Services Economy* (Boston: Harvard Business School Press, 1986).

8. Ibid.

9. See Richard Freeman and Jonathan S. Leonard, "Union Maids: Unions and the Female Work Force," in Clair Brown and Joseph A. Pechman (eds.), *Gender in the Workplace* (Washington, DC: Brookings Institution, 1987), pp. 189–212.

10. Ester Iverum, "Low Pay Cited in Decline of Day Care in New York," *New York Times*, February 7, 1988, p. 41 (article cites Council of Supervisors and Administrators, a union representing daycare administrators in New York City). See also Julianne Malveaux, "Comparable Worth and Its Impact on Black Women," in Margaret C. Simms and Julianne Malveaux (eds.), *Slipping Through the Cracks: The Status of Black Women* (New Brunswick, NJ: Transaction Books, 1987).

11. Kaufman, *The Economics of Labor Markets,* p. 231.

12. Edward S. Sekscenski "The Health Services Industry: A Decade of Expansion," *Monthly Labor Review*, May 1981, pp. 9–16.

13. *Boston at Risk* (Boston: Boston Foundation, September 1985).

14. Valerie Personick, "Projections 2000: Industry Output and Employment Through the End of the Century," *Monthly Labor Review*, September 1987, pp. 31–45.

15. Ibid

16. Heskett, *Managing in the Services Economy*.

17. George T. Silvestri and John M. Lukasiewicz, "A Look at Occupational Employment Trends to the Year 2000," *Monthly Labor Review*, September 1987, pp. 44–61.

18. Wayne Howe, "The Business Services Industry Sets the Pace in Employment Growth," *Monthly Labor Review*, April 1986. Another indicator of the shifting nature of the industry, as well as the blurring of distinctions between manufacturing and services, is the growth in scientific and technical services contracted from manufacturing. This reflects the organizational changes influencing manufacturing currently and a shift from

"hardware" to "software" in product markets. This trend not only influences computers (where it started), but instruments, communications equipment, imaging, publications, and other industry characterized as "manufacturing" in the past.

19. Heskett, *Managing in the Services Economy*. This analyst notes two likely patterns for financial services in the future: one involves expansion of back office operations at the expense of skilled and "thinking" jobs, with restructuring resembling patterns of industrial production processes where jobs are broken into minute tasks, then organized on a production process basis, with eventual mechanization likely. A second pattern, provided by an insurance industry example, is that after productivity gains are made by clerical staff, efforts turn to higher salaried managers and professionals. "By reorganizing the delivery of insurance services . . . it was found that underwriters were doing jobs that could be reassigned to clerical workers."

20. Sekscenski, "The Health Services Industry," pp. 9–16.

21. Ibid.

22. Health Insurance Association of America, "New Group Health Insurance" (New York, 1985); Pamela Jo Farley, "Data Preview Private Insurance and Public Programs: Coverage of Health Services in the United States, 1977," *National Health Care Expenditures Study* (Washington, DC: National Center for Health Services Research, U.S. Department of Health and Human Services, 1986).

CHAPTER 9

Employment Policy and the Future U.S. Economy

A new interest has recently emerged about the proper role of government in assuring a standard income and employment for its citizens. Following a decade of conservative political activism and ideologically based government actions to reduce the federal role in social needs areas, support for a more interventionist agenda is growing. However, under Reagan, considerable damage was done. The professional bureaucracies built up since the New Deal to mediate between the marketplace and the negative impacts of postindustrial structural change on the individual were dismantled. We have noted that the neoconservative grasp was firm for a decade and shaped less by the think-tank model of the Brookings Institution, the Urban Institute, and the universities that dominated the thinking of the Kennedy-Johnson administrations than by a new model of highly selective but ideologically bound conservative ideas, aimed to recruit a new and powerful if less sophisticated constituency from the emerging new South and West. While much has been made of the ideological laissez-faire and marketplace principles espoused under Reagan, the federal system became used for a vast new conservative patronage system that justified a massive redistribution of federal tax dollars. The new patronage was epitomized first by the Housing and Urban Development Department's "HUD Scam" and the Defense Department's "Wedtech Scandal." But an even more serious crisis was waiting in the wings, shortly after the end of the Reagan administration. Under deregulation of the banking industry, thousands of savings and loan companies were permitted to use discretion in lending vast sums of taxpayer-insured depositors' funds in unsecured and very questionable projects. The "free enterprise" exercise was proving by the 1990s to be nothing less than a vast redistribution of resources from the U.S. Treasury and a diversity of programs evolved over the decades, to a narrow group of deregulated institutions.

The elegant arguments of traditional conservatives such as Milton Friedman were replaced by the rough polemics of Charles Murray, Irving Kristol, Howard Lauffer, and the talent bank of the conservative American Enterprise Institute. Murray became the undisputed guru of Reagan's social policy, by arguing that social programs, not employment, were the cause of expanding poverty.[1]

Although more sympathetic to the plight of the poor, liberal critics looked almost exclusively to cash transfers and family social programs as the appropriate role for social policy.[2] As recently noted, however, the U.S. problem may be deeper than illustrated by the debate over programs. In stark contrast to other Western postindustrial states, the United States stands alone in the lack of an institutionalized welfare state. As an alternative, a set of fragmented programs has evolved that are isolated from macroeconomic planning and basic assumptions about the long-range employment picture. Rather than a coordinated social policy, government actions take place through a disconnected and incomplete set of programs that target special populations and needs. As well, the programmatic array that makes up policy tends to be initiated in spurts, following budgetary and political exigencies but, as often as not, fades quickly once in place. Cultural differences, class struggle, and, more recently, the decentralized nature of the American political system have been offered, in turn, as explanations for the failure of the United States to imitate Europe in developing a unified national support for a welfare state.[3]

European social policy history contrasts with the United States both in its historical origins and current scope. Most countries started early and initiated many of their programs beginning during the 1880s through the 1920s with pensions and social insurance for industrial workers. The British Liberal Party, for example, was responsible for passing workman's compensation and unemployment and national health insurance in 1911.[4] Similar patterns took place in Bismarck's Germany, beginning in the 1880s. Later during the 1930s and the 1950s post-World War II period, European programs were integrated and elaborated into comprehensive systems to include income support, social insurance, and family assistance, and were extended to entire populations. During the post-World War II period, the Scandinavian countries further integrated full employment with the welfare state in a coordinated social policy with Keynesian strategies of macroeconomic management and intervention in labor markets.[5]

By the 1970s, the United States lagged substantially in both macro policies and in programmatic development for social needs. In the mid-1970s, for example, the United States spent only 16 percent of its GNP for all education, income maintenance, and health expenditures, compared to more than 20 percent of the GNP by most European states.[6]

This chapter looks at the question of why the United States has lagged so far behind the rest of the world in policies to resolve social need and employment, and at the impacts this pattern has on the status of black women. Despite the long-standing goal of American democracy to assure equal opportunity, most government interventions have followed a roller coaster of peaks and valleys, rarely sustained or deep enough to respond to the needs of blacks and others discriminated against historically. Conservative principles continue to dominate actions with reassertions that poverty be solved by the efforts of the poor themselves in the "market system." The chapter first examines the framework of theory and policy on employment. Next, the history of two key policies (income distribution and employment) are reviewed for relevance to the case of black women workers.

EMPLOYMENT POLICY, MARKET REGULATION, AND EMPLOYMENT TRAINING PROGRAMS

Neglect and fragmentation of policy at the national level in the United States carried negative impacts on programs in the form of punitive and frequently costly "means tests" and other devices to screen and ration program benefits to individuals. The uneven eligibility rules and diverse benefit levels across states and among individuals also produce major inefficiencies, including very high administrative costs for the United States compared to other developed countries and Japan. Family assistance, for example, is locally distributed in the United States, but in other countries it is generally national, has uniform eligibility and grant levels, and frequently excludes means tests. Benefits thus can be higher with fewer costs to the state. Benefits currently range from 4.4 percent of average monthly earnings in manufacturing for two children in the United States to 16.2 percent in France.[7]

What are the reasons behind the U.S. failure to evolve a postindustrial welfare state and what does this mean for the U.S. work force and for a black women's work force in the next century? A recent study of U.S. social welfare policy offers an intriguing explanation in the form of a political development contrast. According to this thesis, the United States was characterized by decentralized politics, lacked universal suffrage, particularly for those most in need, and, finally, had an absence of a nationally organized political party with a principal working class constituency.[8] The fragmentation of the United States into local regionally dominated political units inhibited the growth of a professional bureaucracy at the national level. At the local level, however, welfare was generally subordinated to the interests of patronage-dominated party systems and suffered as well from the large regional division between North and South. Racial oligarchies held the South in a political stranglehold while patronage-dominated party systems ruled in the North. This checked the growth of liberal, labor-oriented, national party systems such as evolved in turn-of-the-century Europe. Second, the United States was one of the last industrial democracies to grant universal suffrage. Blacks were almost entirely excluded from voting until the 1960s, and this had the effect of splitting working class interests as well as to reinforce the power of southern oligarchies. Finally, the growth of ethnic politics in unreformed northern cities, coupled with balkanized trade unionism from the 1900s onward, impeded the growth of a unified liberal working class party. This political appraisal is supported by convincing evidence. In contrast to Europe, the U.S. working class came to divide loyalties and interests between local ethnic patronage politics, which was always distributive in nature, and national politics, where fiscal power was strongest but where particularistic politics were not possible.

Income Distribution Policy in the United States

Social policy in the United States evolved slowly and developed characteristics inherently marginal and temporary in nature. This was true for programs aimed at income distribution and those supporting employment. Not until the 1930s did attention focus on social needs at the national level. Passage of the 1935 Social Security Act started the process but also set up subsequent problems. Provisions covering unemployment insurance and old age and disability insurance were nationalized with uniform standards. But family assistance, the famous Aid to Families with Dependent Children (AFDC) or "welfare" as it came to be known, by contrast, was initiated as a "temporary measure" for widows until the more permanent Social Security and Disability Insurance (SSDI) program came into being. It included means tests and extensive local control. This legacy remains. AFDC is still a cost shared between states and the federal government and is largely administered by the states, which have considerable discretion on standards, eligibility, screening procedures, and grant levels.[9]

Genuine reform has been much debated, but opposition to stabilizing the program has remained remarkably effective over the years. National health insurance, which was specifically not included in the original act but was added during the 1960s (i.e., the Medicare program), continues to have eligibility linked to AFDC and thus covers very few of the working poor. The debate over social policy thus has failed to include a comprehensive policy and, instead, reflects sporadic bursts of legislative activities resulting in "add ons." Many of these are limited as they are targeted to specific problems and narrow population groups. This pattern may serve to increase costs, or at least make costs and beneficiaries highly visible and, thus, frequently attacked. Medicare, the health insurance program for the aged, has become very costly, while others such as employment and training have a history of drastic reductions.

The 1960s was marked by a sudden burst of program activities. Under the Johnson administration's Great Society, major additions were made to the Social Security Act with nationalization of old age insurance and the initiation of the Medicare health subsidy program for the elderly. Unemployment insurance was also expanded, with benefits extended to a broader group of workers. But because of the "targeting" of eligibility, particularly to the "worthy poor," such as the mainly white elderly, policy that would benefit broad sectors of the population in need, such as national health insurance and family assistance, remained decentralized and inadequate.[10] For the long-term unemployed adult, the working poor, and minorities, reforms brought little relief.

The first major reforms of the 1960s set the stage for subsequent efforts to change AFDC more fundamentally. Stimulated in part by the Civil Rights movement and urban unrest of the 1960s, plus the growing bloc of black voters in the South in particular, professionals and advocates pressed Congress and the Johnson administration for expanded benefits for family support and housing assistance.[11] Although housing assistance was quickly geared to the exigencies of the private market, other programs received negative reactions by big city Democratic Party machines who feared black political takeovers of city governments.[12] To maintain these constituencies, congressional and executive efforts retreated. Always controversial, AFDC reform continued to be dominated by conservative arguments that the "dole" would constitute a "disincentive to work" or "reward for failure," which won out over those critics favoring a new "income floor" as a "right." By the 1970s, Daniel Patrick Moynihan, then a member of the Nixon administration, was advocating a liberalizing of a basic grant for the all-but-forgotten working poor but, at the same time, balancing a conservative objective of work incentives. Moynihan argued that poverty and dependency could be resolved only by a program that encouraged families to remain intact and, above all, rewarded the able-bodied if they worked.[13] Continued political opposition from the South, on which the Republican Party increasingly depended, however, forced Nixon to retreat in face of objections of interruption of low-cost labor markets by the reform, particularly those reflecting agriculture wage standards.

By the 1980s, U.S. social policy was altered again, but this time to reflect neoconservative ideologies of the Reagan administration. Objectives this time were to dismantle programs entirely, rather than to reform them. AFDC was again targeted. Reagan first considered conservative Martin Anderson's strategy to focus on the "truly needy" by tightening eligibility, then switched to embrace the radical conservatism of Charles Murray, who argued that programs should be dismantled on the grounds that they "caused poverty." Ignoring the rise of unemployment and subemployment in ghettos, welfare rolls were slashed along with support programs such as health care, housing, food stamps, child care, and job training.[14]

U.S. Employment Policy in Perspective

As noted at the beginning of this chapter, the United States contrasts with most industrialized nations in the absence of policy that integrates social assistance and employment. A central reason may be the absence of macroeconomic outlooks and strategies that help plan and articulate employment goals. It could be argued that such policy needs are in the best interest of industrial capitalists as much as those of labor. As with social policy such as income distribution, the United States differs from Europe and Japan in a neglect of national economic planning, where monetary policy, capital investment, R&D, trade, and debt management efforts by private interests are coordinated to enhance expansion goals, raise productivity, and build a competitive position in the world market as well as at home.[15] This is more crucial than ever, since over the past decade world markets have demonstrated far greater influence on the domestic U.S. market than in the immediate postwar period, when the U.S. economy was highly self-contained. During that time, the United States held sway over the postwar world marketplace, and the dollar was a standard exchange. Further, much of U.S. productive capacity had little external competition.

In contrast to other Western economic organizations, however, U.S. business relies less on government policymakers and plans than their influence through indirect means. This kind of influence, mostly through special interest political lobbying, is at best an incremental manipulation of regulatory agencies' rules, tax law, and special legislation to obtain narrow favorable treatment for particularistic interests as the following notes.[16]

Conflicts within the ranks of American business are readily politicized and U.S. corporate interests have always found it difficult to provide unified support for national initiatives that might benefit the economy as a whole on terms favorable either to most sectors of business or to economically dominant sectors. . . . the losers can always go to court—or back to the legislatures, or to a new bureaucratic agency—for another round of battle in the policy questions, especially when government intervention in the economy is at issue. . . . to American capitalists, the U.S. state has seemed neither coherent nor reliable.

Absent a coherent, consistent plan such as that of the French or the hegemony of the Japanese Ministry of International Trade and Industry (MITI) between business interests and government, an industrial development-oriented national policy remains subordinate to regional and specialized business cleavages. The United States has resisted all but episodic foreign trade and debt interventions and maintained limited macroeconomic regulation of industry through tax expenditure, capital gains and depreciation tax treatment, and Federal Reserve money supply maneuvers to manipulate interest rates. Trade and other macroeconomic decisions are frequently no more than reactions to decisions and market trends outside U.S. borders rather than constructive initiatives.[17]

The lack of a macro policy by the United States hurt any move toward employment or labor policy. As noted, the 1930s economic failures caused devastating unemployment increases and dramatic falls in U.S. family income. Not until the mid-1930s, however, did the government react, and this was limited to unemployment insurance for some of the work force and the regulation of collective bargaining. An emergency public works job program was initiated; however, mobilization for World War II was widely credited with resolving the widespread unemployment in the United States. Moreover, in contrast to Great Britain, the vast expansion of the U.S. national defense industry failed to create conditions of centralized authority adequate to build a welfare state. Growth in privatization of defense production through contracting, particularly in the World War II aftermath, when government-owned shipyards and arsenals were turned over to private interests, may have been partly responsible for this. One by-product of the World War II mobilization was a massive growth of federal tax capacity that would remain attached in the postwar period to national defense through congressional appropriations.[18]

In the absence of coordinated national labor intervention in the 1930s, the postwar period was essentially an extension of sporadic and fragmented legislation and narrowly drafted programs at the federal level, which attacked several fronts but lacked coordination:

1. Minimum wage

2. Collective bargaining regulation through the National Labor Relations Board

3. Equal Employment Opportunity regulation

4. Emergency public works and employment and training programs

The overwhelming reliance on the "market system" to regulate wages, hiring, and jobs, reinforced by conservative business pressures, lies at the heart of objections to most labor policy and resistance to coordination. At the same time, other pressures from liberals and labor made possible some response at the national level. Most resisted of all was the minimum wage floor, which has been surrounded by controversy in the economic community as well as in the political arena since its inception as a part of the Fair Labor Standards Act (FLSA) in 1938. At that time, the wage standard was set at twenty-five cents per hour and coverage at only 43 percent of the work force.[19] Over the years, the minimum wage was gradually increased, along with the proportion of U.S. workers covered, in a sporadic fashion. By 1989, efforts to raise the minimum wage after the longest period without change (more than eight years) finally succeeded. The minimum was raised from the 1981 level of $3.35 per hour, with 86 percent of the workers covered, to $4.35 per hour, with a compromise of a two-tiered system to include a so-called training wage not to exceed the first six months of employment. But as recent analysis shows in Table 9.1, the minimum wage has remained consistently lower than prevailing average hourly wages in manufacturing.[20] Moreover, only twice in the entire history of the legislation—during the late 1950s and early 1960s,—did the minimum wage reach the prevailing hourly manufacturing rate.

The stated purpose of the minimum wage outlined in the original legislation was to maintain a minimum standard of living necessary for health, efficiency, and general well-being of workers. As a wage floor for the working poor, however, the rate has rarely fit any standard of living criteria in the U.S. economy.[21] Arguments against the minimum wage essentially were those against any government-established floor (agricultural subsidies, for example), that such floors tend to reduce employment levels in the covered sectors. While some argue that such effects would be to eliminate exploitation of the working poor by eliminating low-productivity, low-paid marginal jobs that might disappear

Table 9.1
Level and Coverage of the Minimum Wage, 1938–81

Date of Minimum Wage Change	Minimum Wage	Percentage of Employees Covered in Private Industry	Percentage of Minimum Wage Relative to Average Hourly Wage in Manufacturing	
			Before	After
October, 1938	$0.25	43.4%	--	40.0
October, 1939	0.30	47.1	39.6%	47.6
October, 1945	0.40	55.4	30.8	41.1
January, 1950	0.75	53.4	28.7	53.7
March, 1956	1.00	53.1	39.3	52.3
September, 1961	1.15	62.1	43.1	49.6
September, 1963	1.25	62.1	46.6	50.6
February, 1967	1.40	75.3	44.8	50.2
February, 1968	1.60	72.6	47.6	54.4
May, 1974	2.00	83.7	37.8	47.3
January, 1975	2.10	83.3	42.7	44.9
January, 1976	2.30	83.8	41.7	45.6
January, 1978	2.65	85.1	38.5	44.4
January, 1979	2.90	85.1	40.8	44.6
January, 1980	3.10	86.1	41.7	44.5
January, 1981	3.35	86.0	40.1	43.3

Source: Bruce E. Kaufman, *The Economics of Labor Marekets and Labor Relations* (Chicago: Bryden Pres, 1986), p. 227.

eventually, other evidence is mixed. Analysis suggests that the impact of minimum wage falls most on teenagers and other first-time job entrants, rather than adults, which contributed to the logic of a ''training wage.''[22] What is less clear, however, is the impact on household income. Traditionally discriminated workers such as women family heads and unskilled black male adults might also find job opportunity eroded, particularly in high unemployment regions such as Detroit. Moreover, one recent study found that many second household earners who contribute to family earnings to raise families above the poverty level would be hurt, reducing overall household earnings:[23]

The Kneiser study found that . . . only one fourth of low wage workers (earning $2.65 or less) were found to be living in poverty households. The reason for this discrepancy is that many low wage workers are not single earner heads of households but rather so-called ''secondary earners'' such as teenagers and spouses. . . . for example . . . 77 percent of low wage workers were either a daughter, son or spouse of a household head. In this case while the individual income of these low wage workers was quite low, total family income was often above the poverty line because of earnings of other family members, particularly male heads of household.

Thus, while a minimum wage in principle may help skilled, adult women heads of households, it may hurt the same household if a teenaged son or daughter is a wage earner contributing to family income.

COLLECTIVE BARGAINING AND TRADE UNIONS

Trade unions have lacked the central coordinated power interest of European labor groups that influence government directly through political parties in multiparty systems. The failure of unionization over the years also reflects the resistance of business interests and their legislative representatives, but also internal divisions within organized labor. A cause of the sometimes fierce competition among unions may be rivalries that developed among ethnic power bases in cities, particularly in the Northeast and Midwest where union power was strongest. The warring among working-class European immigrants and between ethnics and native-born American workers was intensified by connections made to city patronage and machine systems, which extended to state legislatures. This weakened the movement toward a national unified labor organization in the 1940s, as well as the decline in the Democratic Party as a representative of working-class interests in both employment and social policy such as the labor party interface of Great Britain and France. Most of all, however, large numbers of workers—blacks and later Mexican Americans—were excluded completely from trade union membership or, in the case of agricultural workers, from organizing efforts. Racist unionism coupled with the eagerness of capitalists to exploit high rates of unemployment among blacks and use strikebreaking techniques during some of the important periods of industrial unionization also hurt. The rise of industrial automotive manufacturing in the Midwest is an example of racial politics in unions that worked to thwart union growth.[24]

The fragmentation of union organization, rivalries between traditional craft and industrial unions, and explicitly racial policies explain the weak mobilization of regulatory power to enhance collective bargaining in the United States. Labor power reached its peak under the Roosevelt administration during the late 1930s, when the National Labor Relations Act (NLRA) or Wagner Act was passed in 1935 and created the National Labor Relations Board (NLRB) as the primary regulatory body for collective bargaining at the national level. Prior to the 1935 act, legislation was generally anti-labor. The Wagner Act for the first time guaranteed the right to organize and established collective bargaining rights. By codifying prior court decisions that legalized unions, the Wagner Act helped protect workers from discrimination and harassment, firing, demotion, or hiring bans if they engaged in union activities. Three specific rights were guaranteed: (1) prohibition against antiunion and unfair labor practices by employers, (2) establishment of union representation elections, and (3) establishment of the quasi-judicial National Labor Relations Board to administer and enforce the law. The act further covered all workers except those in managerial roles, government employees, workers in agriculture and domestic services, and those covered by the Railway Labor Act.[25]

Subsequent policy eroded NLRB power and reflected a seesawing commitment to support of trade unionism. Taft-Hartley (1946) prohibited secondary boycotts and closed shops, and permitted the executive branch to impose 80-day "back to work orders'' in national emergency conditions. Hearings into union corruption by the McClellen Committee during the late 1950s produced the Landrum-Griffin Act. Additional amendments were made under Landrum-Griffin to the original Wagner Act to force disclosure of union finance, membership, and other internal union structures, but also added guarantees of open union elections. Finally, in 1962, under President Kennedy's Executive Order 10988, the right of federal employees to join unions was granted although strikes were forbidden.[26]

Women and Trade Unions

Women of all races, like minority males, have had a poor history with trade unions in the United States. This, as with other failures of the labor system, has been attributed to the "defect" in female characteristics, or a "disinterest in collective bargaining." Evidence shows, however, a very different explanation. Organized labor has a dismal history in supporting the unionization of women in the workplace, even in industry dominated by women such as the apparel sector. The International Ladies Garment Workers Union (ILGWU) has a history of few women leaders and a reputation for cozy relationships with management in bargaining at the expense of the interests of its mainly female membership, including wages, job security, and better working conditions. More important, as in the case of minorities, women workers endured a long and vigorous opposition to their entry into much mainstream employment by unions themselves. Entry monopolies, apprenticeship programs, and closed shops were some techniques used to bar women from admission into lucrative crafts and trade occupations, including printing, construction trades, and skilled jobs such as machinists. Only with massive class action court decisions, such as the well-known AT&T case of the 1970s, did women manage to crack union strangleholds on many workplaces.[27]

A third and even more damaging union problem has been a near total failure of unions to attack the problem of organizing women in the rapidly expanding services and retailing sectors. Ironically, this expansion took place during the period when union membership was in rapid decline, beginning in the 1960s. Blue-collar women expanded as a work force rapidly in the retail sector, in hospitals and health care institutions, as well as in white-collar clerical work in insurance, finance, and education.[28]

As a result, union membership among women has been slow to develop. Women union members grew from 16 percent in 1954 to only 24 percent of the total women's work force in 1978, despite the fact that a substantial majority of jobs over the period went to women workers. Union membership by women also remained highly workplace-specific and concentrated in very few unions compared to men. In 1978, for example, 50 percent of all women members belonged to just 26 out of the 208 major unions in the economy. That same year, 18 unions reported no women members.[29] The eight unions listed in Table 9.2 accounted for about half the female union members in 1978.

Table 9.2
Women Union Membership

Teamsters	480,000
AFSCME	409,000
Retail Clerks	375,105
Clothing and Textile workers	330,660
Service employees	312,500
International Brotherhood of Electrical workers	303,510
Teachers	300,000
ILGWU	374,000

Source: Ray Marshall, "Work and Women in the 1980s," Richard Rowan (ed.) in *Readings in Economics and Labor Relations* (Homewood, IL: Richard D. Irwin, 1985).

Causes of Low Unionization Among Women

A number of efforts have been made to find the causes of low membership among women. One study found that occupational and industrial status accounted for most of the male-female union membership differential.[30] But this does not explain why women are not organized, or why sectors and occupations where women are concentrated are so devoid of union presence. One reason may be that unions have failed to recruit female union leadership and organizers to target women workers where they are most concentrated. Underlying these failures is the possible bias in the typical union agenda, which simply does not appeal to the special needs and problems women face at work. The success of the American Federation of State and Municipal Employees (AFSME) in recruiting women may in part be explained, for example, by the fact that this union has embraced a major part of the women's agenda, including the comparable worth pay equity issue.[31]

The National Labor Relations Board is another area where more attention to promoting collective bargaining and unionization among women would be effective. NLRB activities have rarely focused, for example, on low-wage industry. Retailing and the insurance and financial sectors are particularly notorious for resistance to labor relations regulation and attempts at organizing clerical workers. For example, efforts to organize insurance and higher education workers have rarely been supported by the NLRB.

As the primary institutional apparatus for supervising and assuring fair union elections, the NLRB has been identified as the primary cause for recent declines in unionization. This is even more true of the woman worker. In analyzing this, three weaknesses in NLRB processes were recently identified by economist Richard Freeman: (1) Some U.S. laws, which allow management to conduct lengthy, well-funded election campaigns against unions; (2) the Taft-Hartley law, which allows states to pass so-called right to work laws that effectively outlaw union shops; and (3) strong labor laws, which require collective bargaining, as in the case of public-sector laws requiring municipalities and states to bargain.[32]

WORKPLACE-RELATED POLICY: TRAINING AND EQUAL OPPORTUNITY

As noted earlier, government labor intervention to improve and upgrade skills of the work force has been limited to resources and program content aimed mainly at unemployed men. Further, work force retraining had few connections to overall employment policy. In countries such as Sweden and West Germany, by contrast, considerable focus is placed on setting training goals to correspond to changes in unemployment rates and regional disparities. There is also a contrast with the United States in the emphasis placed on youth and first-time job entrants. German employment training during the 1980s, for example, was linked to national "full employment" policy and thus included goals to guarantee all youth either employment or extended education and training to avoid adding to national joblessness.

Employment Training Programs

U.S. training programs were initiated first during the 1960s, after a major recession exacerbated rising unemployment caused by structural changes in the economy. As technological obsolescence, capital investment declines, plant closings, and erosion in sales of American products because of foreign competition were first felt, national employment training programs were introduced first to assist displaced white male workers. Even engineers displaced by government space and aerospace contract contractions as late as the 1970s participated in federal job training programs. With the rise of political unrest during the 1960s, employment training was expanded to include teenagers and unemployed adult males. The Job Corps and the Concentrated Employment Program (CEP) were introduced as a part of the Johnson administration's Great Society program package. Subsequently, however, job training was transformed and reduced in scope. By the 1980s, the Reagan administration scrapped existing programs and introduced a drastically reduced level of effort and placed training in private-sector hands. Program aims also changed to placement of those most able to secure employment with minimum cost and effort.

Major criticism has been leveled at job training for failing to address the needs of women, particularly the growing corps of women heading households. Evidence suggests that the highest unemployment rates are among women, particularly blacks and Hispanics who lack in education and skills. But job training systematically excluded women from the recruitment pool and steered women almost exclusively into training for low-paid clerical and service "women's jobs," ignoring the better paid technical and craft training.[33] The job training program included in the 1989 AFDC reform bill did not correct this defect but, rather, ignored the problems of improving wages for the jobs to which welfare recipients are typically hired.[34]

Finally, the need for other types of work-support programs remains neglected at the federal level. For work programs to be effective for low-wage women, an array of services would be required to at least resolve the absence in the workplace of such services. Chief among these are health insurance and pensions. In 1989, approximately 37 million individuals were estimated to lack basic adequate health insurance, with spiraling premium costs threatening to increase that number.[35] Pensions for women workers were even worse. In 1982, according to the Current Population Survey of the U.S. Department of Census, only about one-quarter of women workers reported pension benefits where they worked.

Equal Opportunity and Affirmative Action

In our examination of U.S. policy, we have seen both a downside and some solutions to improving economic opportunity for black women. An examination of the array of policies on social support and employment has reinforced the essential themes of the book that the future of opportunity for black women rests with a change in government strategy to respond to deeper ills of the U.S. workplace, and the massive structural change in the economy that has produced decline in industrial jobs and, with it, changes in wages and the composition of earners. With the evolution of work force characteristics to more female and nonwhite, very different government policy will be needed in the workplace and outside in the form of social assistance and income floors.

Black women now face a major dilemma. While they are working at higher rates than ever, they have become captive victims of the work system. The work that is available is for the most part low-paid, dead-end, and lacks the security and benefits of the social contract of the past forged between elite production workers and their employers through collective bargaining. Also, black women workers suffer the stings of political invisibility and powerlessness in government. Instead of help, they are stereotyped as welfare-dependent "free riders" who lack a work ethic and other mainstream values. But we have seen that opportunities, defined as the organization and policies of the workplace, are the main constraints on black women and that the labor market, including those areas with shortages that now characterize retailing and services, for example, do not raise wages in the case of women's jobs. Instead, new job systems have evolved around technology and various managerial organizations. Reinforced by the absence of government monitoring and regulation, a women's subculture has evolved that has become the principal marketplace for black women workers. Finally, while the women's work subcultures dominate the economic life of black women workers, work patterns, productivity, and outputs of these workers have also indirectly acted to substitute for men's work. This is particularly visible in substitution for the kinds of jobs held by a large segment of the black male population three decades ago in services and even some production work. This conversion of services from male to female, particularly blue-collar service jobs, coupled with the loss of other jobs in the economy, has severely eroded the number of jobs available to black men. The real social impact of this change, therefore, though scarcely acknowledged in policy circles and popular accounts, is the drop in male household heads from over two-thirds of all black families a mere three decades ago to less than half by 1990.

Notwithstanding these pessimistic trends and the underlying class, gender, and race structure of policies that have worsened the effect of economic structural change, it is nonetheless useful to examine some of the directions for change. Here we are faced with the usual dilemma of American politics. Should reform take full account of the political traditions, and support strategies that reward the privileged in order to accomplish change for those at the bottom? There are many who argue that in practical terms, it is a peculiarity of the American political system that only policies that reward or "buy out" the well off are feasible. This "trickle down" thesis, borrowed from housing economists of the 1960s, is now applied in the case of health insurance. The recent growth of costs to the middle classes, as employers increased deductibles in group health plans, now points to an opportunity to pass a national health insurance program. At the same time, there is the reality that inefficiencies and even a perverse income distribution could result from policies aimed at the broad middle of the American population. Agricultural subsidies instituted in the 1930s to help poor farmers, but broadly targeted to the entire agricultural community, and housing market subsidies such as the VA and FHA programs, rarely trickled far enough down to those most disadvantaged in the market system.

There are two areas of reform that merit at least a brief discussion: social welfare policy and employment opportunity regulation. Our evidence suggests that these comprise the least political and monetary costs and will help most in resolving the greatest problems for black women workers. The social welfare policy we have in mind carries some fiscal and budgetary costs, but if implemented universally and fairly, may reduce overall per capita costs from current combined federal-state welfare related expenditures. Much of cost reductions may come from improved efficiencies of administration. Some costs may be offset by tax contributions from workers and from a more progressive taxation and distribution from higher earners. Our arguments rely heavily on the models of Europe and Canada, which have worked through many of the fiscal and administrative problems yet to be fully tested in the United States. We can argue that the second policy, employment opportunity regulation, carries few fiscal costs. Instead, sound employment policy demands strategic leadership and agreement from business leadership to establish a reasonable and fair political consensus to make possible policy agreement with labor and other special interests. Such consensus is required for reform legislation.

POLICIES ON FAMILY ASSISTANCE AND HEALTH INSURANCE

U.S. social policy reform in recent history reflects a continuation of limited, incremental, and conservative change, reflecting the opposition of Southern and low-wage regional interests, as well as big business lobbying organizations such as the U.S. Chamber of Commerce. Arguing that reform of public assistance and other social legislation such as health poses inflationary cost threats, successive executives have failed to propose or support radical change. The most recent reforms, including the Family Assistance Act of 1988 (the first reform since the 1930s), was passed over the objections of the Reagan White House. In contrast to various proposed efforts, the legislation that finally passed represented a compromise between "liberalization" of job training and some benefits and more conservative work requirements for public assistance. The strategy of a "foot in the door," legislatively, reflects the continuing *realpolitik* of congressional compromise. Longer term goals, including uniform grant and eligibility standards for welfare recipients and other standards, were put off for a future time. As well, Congress continued a key role and funding responsibility for the states, as well as discretion in determining eligibility and other standards.[36] Despite these disadvantages, achievement of the incremental objectives may move AFDC closer to the liberal goals of nationalized family assistance and eligibility extended to the working poor.

Critics, however, have proposed more radical policy to solve current problems: nationalization of total program costs, as well as standardization of eligibility are the two main reforms. In approaching change, reform is concerned with the implementation process, and particularly the bias and unevenness in administration represented by the present state-dominated system. For example, many concerns center on the problems that have hurt the Social Security program, such as the need for automatic adjustments in the cost of living for inflation and interregional cost differences of such household consumption as housing. Other reform has focused on the fact that most poor households are headed by women as sole earners. Child care and other costs of holding a job (transportation, clothing, food), it is argued, should be included.[37] Thus the ideal reform most resembles a uniform income "floor" that is adjusted for incidental costs of work over time and includes at least four elements:

1. nationalization, including total funding and administration borne at the national level

2. uniform eligibility and program grant standards adjusted for interregional costs differences

3. invisibility: removal of the stigma of "welfare" by removal of references to race, class, sex, poverty, and other socially disability stereotyping

4. provision of incentives for education, employment training, and job search; reducing punishment for market problems such as available employment and wages that may be visible in turnover rates

The cash grant form similar to SSDI and European family assistance is generally favored over various in-kind subsidies such as food stamps and housing assistance or tax deductions, because of consumer and administrative efficiency and invisibility and ease of communication to those eligible. The political and social "stigma" of assistance, for example, is removed.

The move toward the welfare state, however, is far more likely to occur as the result of social policy more closely associated with the traditional workplace and the needs of the middle class. National health, retirement, and child care, are likely to receive more intense scrutiny for these political reasons, and for the simple reason that industry, particularly big employers, long has been a source of major subsidy to health care through cost sharing of employee premiums. With rapidly escalating costs, business groups have increasingly looked to a national plan to save direct costs and possibly control inflation in the health industry. Pensions have received less attention than health insurance by business groups. The current tax law provisions, which allow corporations to claim much of the "growth" in funds that accrues to retirement fund investments and avoid sharing or passing through such gains to employees, support arguments for national control over pensions to better represent consumer interests against employers. In addition to the issue of fairness in earnings, government supervision of private retirement funds would help in the problems of transferability, or facilitating transfer of retirement funds when employees change jobs.

As we have noted, social programs of the past have provided very little help to black women in their pursuit of work and economic self-sufficiency with cash grants failing to lift women out of poverty and health care and other subsidies (housing, child care) barely touching a small minority. Family assistance and income floor programs extended to working poor families would do far more to lift most black women out of poverty than the current grants even with reform. Current reforms do little other than perhaps extend some employment and training.[38]

TOWARD A NATIONAL EMPLOYMENT POLICY

As noted, the United States has yet to embrace the goal of a full employment policy that would then provide a framework for programs in a variety of work-related areas, from wage floors and unemployment insurance to equal opportunity enforcement, collective bargaining in the workplace, and employment training and education for the individual worker. Absent this, macro policies, which acknowledged the influence of major structural change on wages and employment levels as we have identified in this book, would constitute an important start in shaping programs more selectively.

The unique situation of black women as a discriminated work force, however, requires most work-oriented policies of necessity be specifically tailored to overcome the continuing effects of discrimination, if not ongoing exclusion based on sex or race. We believe that two areas are important: collective bargaining and equal employment opportunity enforcement. Strengthening of collective bargaining institutions at the national level will help mediate wages and working conditions, particularly in workplaces where there are high concentrations of low-wage female workers, while equal opportunity enforcement will help open opportunity to a full range of jobs not yet accessible to black women.

Growth in collective bargaining and unionization of women's work has enormous potential. In addition to the high concentrations of low-wage workers in many very large white-collar sectors and corporate workplaces such as banking, insurance, retailing, and services such as hotels, two other factors argue for unionization: (1) productivity increases forecast for the next decades as service managements streamline to increase efficiency and profits; and (2) continuing strong relationship of much job growth to government subsidies, notably health care and government.

Improvement in government support of collective bargaining through restructuring of the NLRB could take advantage of timing of productivity increases in services to force a passing on of savings and profits to women workers, as occurred in the past with male workers. In industries such as health care and education, where government already plays a strong regulatory and subsidy role, collective bargaining could be even more easily justified as was the case in the federal government under Kennedy.

The history of health care collective bargaining illustrates a strikingly dismal role of government in failing to support unionization of the work force. In fact, the exact opposite role of government is visible in tacit support of the health care establishment's resistance to the formation of trade unions in hospitals, nursing homes, and other institutions. Similar patterns are found in other parts of the human services industry. In education, for example, teachers have fared somewhat better in bargaining than nurses, with results of impressive gains in pay, pensions, and other benefits. Similarly, blue-collar jobs in education such as janitorial and maintenance have excellent traditions of unionization and wages. But the lower status clerical, paraprofessional, and services workers—such as food services, school crossing guards, and drivers—have been slow to unionize. This is also true of such job categories in the fields of mental health, child care, and services for youth and the elderly. Nonprofessional human services jobs have grown rapidly under public programs but workers, particularly women, have continued to work at very low compensation levels. These highly subsidized services, however, represent the same conditions that characterized government workers in the past, which have become successfully unionized with the aid of federal legislation and administrative rule-making.

Equal employment opportunity laws were still on the books in the late 1980s; however, regulation and enforcement were eroded during the decade of the 1980s through court decisions, including a series of Supreme Court rulings reversing affirmative action plans. Change in the composition of appointees to emphasize conservative, narrow constructionist jurists along with efforts by the justice department's division of civil rights to challenge enforcement were key factors.

Equal employment opportunity (EEO) enforcement was massively attacked by the Reagan administration under its ideologically motivated efforts to deregulate business and halt Civil Rights progress. Enforcement nonetheless continued through employer compliance. Employers maintained a high level of interest in EEO, particularly the large progressive corporate interests who wished to keep

EEO plans and reporting in place for three reasons. The first was practical; in corporate political terms, EEO provided employers with a mechanism for integrating work forces despite internal opposition from white male work forces.[39] Another was the fit of EEO to long-term interests of corporate human resources planners who wished to streamline hiring systems, set and enforce standards, apply training requirements, and monitor progress of all workers. Finally, many employers believed that government regulatory postures were cyclical and the decline would inevitably swing back in favor of EEO, leaving those employers who had dropped plans at a disadvantage.

Arguments could be made for a return to a strong regulatory framework for EEO in the future along with increased attention to sanctions for sex-typing and racial stratification using certain job groups in the workplace. The EEO goal of full equity in hiring is effective when it complements corporate planning to broaden the recruitment pool to include minorities and women.

Black women benefited from the combination of job growth and open hiring opportunity during the 1970s. But because of trends in stratification of jobs and within job groups, future mobility and earnings will depend on direct intervention measures. The debate over pay equity and comparable worth opened some of these issues to discussion. There is a need to equalize compensation between men and women, because of long institutionalized differences among occupational categories but also because, as we have seen, technological change results in expansion of low-paid jobs. In the future, such change will continue to transform skilled tasks into highly routine and mechanical jobs rather than build cogitative skills, learning, and organizational ability on which job mobility depends. Pay equity and comparable work actions as currently designed will not solve this problem. Equal opportunity enforcement and expansion of collective bargaining may. Maintaining the status of black women in the workplace will most of all help a long-ignored human resource to make a full contribution in the economy.

NOTES

1. Charles Murray, *Losing Ground: American Social Policy, 1950–1980* (New York: Basic Books, 1984).

2. For the liberal perspective on social welfare, see Frances F. Pivin and Richard Cloward, *Regulating the Poor* (New York: Vintage, 1971). An excellent analysis of shortcomings and impacts of current programs is offered by David T. Ellwood and Lawrence H. Summers, "Poverty in America: Is Welfare the Answer or the Problem?" In Sheldon H. Danzinger and Daniel H. Weinberg (eds.), *Fighting Poverty* (Cambridge, MA: Harvard University Press, 1986), pp. 78–104; and William Julius Wilson and Kathryn M. Neckerman, "Poverty and Family Structure: The Widening Gap Between Evidence and Public Policy Issues," in Danzinger and Weinberg, *Fighting Poverty*, pp. 232–259.

3. M. Weir, A. Orloff, and T. Skocpol, "Understanding American Social Politics," pp. 19–21, and A. Orloff, "The Political Origins of America's Social Welfare State" both in Margaret Weir et al. (eds.) *The Politics of Social Policy in the United States*

(Princeton, NJ: Princeton University Press, 1988). See also Diana Pearce and H. McAdoo, *Women and Children Alone and in Poverty* (Washington, DC. National Council on Economic Opportunity, 1981).

4. Weir et al., "Introduction: Understanding American Social Politics," in Weir et al., *Social Policy*, pp. 3–37. See also Lester Thurow, *The Zero-Sum Society* (New York: Penguin Books, 1981), pp. 203–207.

5. Weir et al., *Social Policy*, p. 12.

6. Harrell Rodgers, Jr., *The Cost of Human Neglect* (Armonk, NY: M. E. Sharpe, 1982), pp. 127, 128.

7. Ibid., p. 121. See also Harrell Rodgers, Jr., *Poor Women, Poor Families* (Armonk, NY: M. E. Sharpe, 1986), esp. Chapter 5.

8. Weir et al., *Social Policy*, pp. 3–37.

9. Sar A. Levitan, *Programs in Aid of the Poor for the 1980s* (Baltimore: Johns Hopkins University Press, 1980). See also Mary Jo Bane, "Politics and Policies of the Feminization of Poverty," in Weir et al., *Social Policy*, pp. 381–397.

10. Levitan, *Programs in Aid of the Poor.*

11. Weir et al., *Social Policy.*

12. Bette Woody, *Managing Crisis Cities* (Westport, CT: Greenwood Press, 1982).

13. Bette Woody, "Welfare Reform: A Summary and Analysis of Current U.S. Congressional Debate over the Family Security Act of 1988," *Trotter Review* (William M. Trotter Institute, University of Massachusetts/Boston), 3, no. 2 (Spring 1989), pp. 9–14. See also Daniel Patrick Moynihan, *The Negro Family: A Case for National Action* (Washington, DC: U.S. Department of Labor, 1965).

14. Bette Woody, "Black Women in the Emerging Services Economy," *Sex Roles*, 21, nos. 1 & 2 (July 1989), pp. 45–68.

15. Henry J. Aaron, *Why Is Welfare So Hard to Reform?* (Washington, DC: Brookings Institution, 1973). See also Thurow, *Zero-Sum Society*; Ira C. Magaziner and Robert Reich, *Minding America's Business* (New York: Harcourt, Brace, Jovanovich, 1982), pp. 261–268; and Robert Reich, *Tales of a New America* (New York: Vintage Books, 1987).

16. Weir et al., *Social Policy*, p. 22. For similar appraisals of the impact of an absence of national economic planning and commitment to full employment, see John Kenneth Galbraith, *The New Industrial State* (Boston: Houghton Mifflin, 1972), pp. 304, 357, 393. See also Magaziner and Reich, *Minding America's Business*, p. 5.

17. Thurow, *Zero-Sum Society.*

18. Ibid.

19. Bruce E. Kaufman, *The Economics of Labor Markets and Labor Relations* (Chicago: Dryden Press, 1986), p. 26.

20. Ibid.

21. Ibid., p. 228. See also Thomas J. Kniesner, "The Low Wage Workers: Who are They?" in Simon Rottenberg (ed.), *The Economics of Legal Minimum Wages* (Washington, DC: American Enterprise Institute, 1981), pp. 459–484; and Sar A. Levitan, and Richard Belous, *More than Substance: Minimum Wages for the Working Poor* (Baltimore: Johns Hopkins University Press, 1979).

22. See Bruce Dunson, "Effects of Minimum Wage on Black Teenage Employment," (Cambridge, MA: National Research Bureau, 1988), and Charles Brown, Curtis Gilroy, and Andrew Kohen, "Time Series Evidence on the Effect of Minimum Wage on Youth

Employment and Unemployment,'' *Journal of Human Resources*, Winter 1983, pp. 3–31.

23. Kaufman, *The Economics of Labor Markets*, p. 228.

24. Weir et al., *Social Policy*. For an excellent history of black unionism, see August Meier and Elliot Rudwick, *Black Detroit and the Rise of the UAW* (New York: Oxford University Press, 1979).

25. AFL-CIO, "A Short History of American Labor,'' in Richard Rowan (ed.), *Readings in Labor Economics and Labor Relations* (Homewood IL: Irwin, 1985), pp. 88–101.

26. Ibid.

27. See Phyllis Wallace, "Increased Labor Force Participation of Women and Affirmative Action,'' in Phyllis Wallace (ed.), *Women in the Workplace* (Boston: Auburn House, 1982), pp. 1–24; and Phyllis Wallace, *Equal Opportunities and the AT&T Case* (Cambridge, MA: MIT Press, 1976).

28. For appraisals of union resistance to women members of both races, see Brigid O'Farrell, "Women and Non-Traditional Blue Collar Jobs in the 1980s,'' in Wallace, *Women in the Workplace*, pp. 140–141; Richard Freeman and Jonathan S. Leonard, "Union Maids: Unions and the Female Labor Force,'' in Clair Brown and Joseph A. Pechman (eds.) *Gender in the Workplace* (Washington, DC: Brookings Institution, 1987), pp. 189–202; and Phyllis Wallace, *Black Women in the Labor Force* (Cambridge, MA: MIT Press, 1982), pp. 50–54.

29. Kaufman, *The Economics of Labor Markets*, p. 436.

30. Ray Marshall, "Work and Women in the 1980's: A Perspective on Basic Trends Affecting Women's Jobs and Job Opportunities,'' in Rowan, *Readings in Labor Economics*, pp. 139–141.

31. Richard B. Freeman, "Why Are Unions Faring Poorly in NLRB Representation Elections?'' in Rowan, ibid., pp. 139–141.

32. Ibid.

33. Lynn Burbridge, "Black Women in Employment and Training Programs,'' pp. 97–114, and Harriette Harper, "Black Women and the Job Training Partnership Act,'' pp. 115–130, both in Margaret Simms and Juliane Malveaux (eds.), *Slipping Through the Cracks: The Status of Black Women* (New Brunswick, NJ: Transaction Books, 1987).

34. Ibid, p. 141.

35. Allan Gold, "The Struggle to Make Do Without Health Insurance,'' *New York Times*, July 30, 1989, pp. 1, 22. See also Paul Starr, "Health Care for the Poor: The Past Twenty Years,'' in Weir et al., *Social Policy*, p. 106; and Diane Brown, "Employment and Health Among Older Black Women: Implications for Their Economic Status,'' Working Paper No. 177 (Wellesley, MA: Wellesley College, Center for Research on Women, 1988).

36. Starr, "Health Care for the Poor,'' p. 16.

37. Margaret Simms, "Black Women Who Head Families: An Economic Struggle,'' in Simms and Malveaux, *Slipping Through the Cracks*, pp. 141–151, provides an analysis of the composition of noncash assistance in total income of black women. See also Clair Brown, "Consumption Norms, Work Roles and Economic Growth 1918–1980,'' in Brown and Pechman, *Gender in the Workplace*, pp. 124–125, for an analysis of family budget expenditures by class of worker and race.

38. Woody, "Welfare Reform,'' pp. 9–14.

39. Bette Woody, "Executive Women: Models of Corporate Success'' (Wellesley,

MA: Wellesley College, Center For Research on Women, 1986). (This report was based on a summary of interviews with 36 corporate human resources managers.) See also Ruth Schaeffer and Edith F. Lynton, "Corporate Experience in Improving Women's Job Opportunities" (New York: The Conference Board, 1979); and Wallace, "Increased Labor Force Participation," pp. 1–20, and "Appendix: EEO Guidelines on Discrimination Because of Sex," pp. 215–219, in Wallace, *Women in the Workplace*.

Appendix: Employment Industry Change 1960–80 by Race and Sex

| | MALE WORKERS | | | | FEMALE WORKERS | | | |
| | WHITE | | BLACK | | WHITE | | BLACK | |
SECTOR:	1960	1980	1960	1980	1960	1980	1960	1980
AGRICULTURE,								
FORESTRY, FISHING	3,409	2,098	457	132	320	957	88	29
MINING	600	838	19	33	31	111	--	9
Coal Mining	--	247	--	6	--	14	--	1
Petrol., Gas.	8	397	--	17	--	76	--	6
Other	--	8	--	--	--	--	--	-
CONSTRUCTION	3,312	4,667	332	378	197	439	5	26
MANUFACTURING	12,122	12,923	932	1,353	4,156	5,782	219	810
Nondurable	4,779	4,224	336	503	2,484	2,839	149	437
Printing	825	822	48	59	288	565	11	41
Apparel	271	222	22	32	791	768	65	356
Durable	7,478	8,575	591	826	1,654	2,871	67	356
Stone/Clay	459	432	43	44	95	133	3	14
Prefab Metals	751	928	115	138	48	144	2	20
Fab Metals	1,011	974	53	83	214	276	8	27
Machinery	1,315	1,986	37	112	210	521	3	47
Elect. Equip.	944	1,118	31	79	489	775	18	99
Trans.	1,475	1,691	113	211	212	363	8	66
TRANS/COMM/UTIL.	3,487	4,558	301	587	742	1,446	25	240
Transportation	2,369	9,876	224	415	223	711	11	111
Communication	389	700	9	51	412	541	11	101
Utilities	729	982	68	122	107	194	3	28
WHOLESALING	1,693	2,778	109	192	429	1,018	17	68
RETAILING	5,395	6,809	394	515	3,686	7,183	229	521
Food	1,090	1,197	56	92	541	1,041	21	64
Eat, drinking								
establishments	673	1,384	88	147	939	2,178	116	193
General Merch.	459	450	35	54	1,035	1,101	44	115
FINANCE/INS., REAL								
ESTATE	1,417	2,226	63	163	1,188	3,005	34	287
Banking	965	438	12	43	533	1,037	8	117
Insuraance	952	763	51	41	655	937	27	105
Real Estate	674	---	--	61	---	615	--	35
BUSINESS REPAIR	1,217	2,370	89	210	324	1,195	14	130
Auto Repair	452	694	51	63	26	93	2	6
Bus. Services	449	1,313	26	34	270	1,046	11	122

| | MALE WORKERS | | | | FEMALE WORKERS | | | |
| | WHITE | | BLACK | | WHITE | | BLACK | |
SECTOR:	1960	1980	1960	1980	1960	1980	1960	1980
PERSONAL SERVICES	857	729	203	115	1,638	1,583	1,113	457
Priv. Household	109	42	75	17	816	343	900	258
Laundry, Dry								
Cleaning	226	309	45	47	245	507	69	102
Beauty/Barber								
Shops	138	--	14	--	450	--	35	--
Other	312	--	38	--	329	--	47	- -
ENTERTAINMENT	306	523	36	49	145	366	11	27
PROF. SERVICES	2,748	5,745	238	618	4,093	10,974	432	1,683
HEALTH	673	1,391	96	224	1,567	4,480	214	809
Physns. Office	--	380	--	10	--	799	--	32
Hospitals	--	783	--	176	--	2,651	--	578
Nursing Homes	107	--	24	--	758	--	159	--
Other	120	--	13	--	272	--	40	--
EDUCATION	1,149	2,540	97	273	1,940	9,629	185	639
Elem. & Second.	--	1,495	--	179	--	3,417	--	496
College, Univ.	--	956	--	84	--	983	--	120
SOCIAL SERVICES	--	189	--	43	--	633	--	161
Children	--	15	--	6	--	257	--	62
Residential	--	28	--	6	--	52	--	10
Other	--	146	--	32	--	323	--	88
PUBLIC ADMIN.	1,589	2,579	134	379	757	1,629	81	373
(excl. Postal)								
Federal	727	--	82	--	389	--	51	- -
State, Local	923	--	51	--	367	--	29	- -
Postal Service	468	430	71	94	60	123	7	97
TOTAL	41,315	44,994	3,278	4,641	17,480	35,072	2,268	4,651

Source: Census of The Population, Table 287 and Table 213.

Bibliography

Aaron, Henry J. *Why Is Welfare So Hard to Reform?* Washington, DC: Brookings Institution, 1973.

AFL-CIO. "A Short History of American Labor." In Richard Rowan (ed.), *Readings in Labor Economics and Labor Relations*. Homewood, IL: Irwin, 1985, pp. 88–101.

Axinn, June and Mark Stern. *Dependency and Poverty*. Lexington, MA: D. C. Heath, 1988.

Bandura, A. *Social Learning Theory*. Englewood Cliffs, N.J: Prentice-Hall, 1977.

Bane, Mary Jo. "Politics and Policies of the Feminization of Poverty." In Margaret Weir, Anna Orloff, and Theda Skocpol (eds.), *The Politics of Social Policy in the United States*. Princeton, NJ: Princeton University Press, 1988.

Barlett, Ellen. "Minimum-Wage Jobs Enable Survival, But Little Else." *Boston Globe*, March 29, 1987.

Barsky, Carl B. and Martin E. Personick. "Measures of Wage Dispersion: Pay Ranges Reflect Industry Traits." *Monthly Labor Review*, April 1981, p. 35.

Bass, Laurie J. and Orley Ashenfelter. "The Effect of Direct Job Creation and Training Programs on Low Skilled Workers." In Shelton H. Danzinger and Daniel H. Weinberg (eds.), *Fighting Poverty*. Cambridge, MA: Harvard University Press, 1986, pp. 133–150.

Bassi, L., Margaret Simms, Lynn Burbridge, and Charles Betsey. "Measuring the Effects of CETA on Youth and the Economically Disadvantaged." Washington, DC: Urban Institute, 1984.

Becker, Gary. *The Economics of Discrimination*, 2nd ed. Chicago: University of Chicago Press, 1980.

Bergmann, Barbara. *The Economic Emergence of Women*. New York: Basic Books, 1986.

Betsey, Charles. "Wage Gap by Race and Sex in Public Sector Jobs." *Policy and Research Report*, The Urban Institute, 15, no. 1 (July 1985), p.1.

Blau, Francine D. *Equal Pay in the Office*. Lexington, MA: Lexington Books, 1977.

Blostin, Allen and William Marclay. "HMO's and Other Health Plans: Coverage and Employee Premiums." *Monthly Labor Review*, June 1983, pp. 28–33.

Bluestone, Barry and Bennett Harrison. *The Deindustrialization of America*. New York: Basic Books, 1982.

———. "The Great American Jobs Machine: Proliferation of Low Wage Employment in the U.S. Economy." Washington, DC: Joint Economic Committee, U.S. Congress, 1986.

Boston at Risk. Boston: Boston Foundation, September 1985.

Brimmer, Andrew. "Urban Young Lose Jobs to Suburbs." *Black Enterprise*, September 1987.

Brown, Charles, Curtis Gilroy, and Andrew Kohen. "Time Series Evidence on the Effect of Minimum Wage on Youth Employment and Unemployment." *Journal of Human Resources*, Winter 1983, pp. 3–31.

Brown, Clair. "Consumption Norms, Work Roles and Economic Growth 1918–1980." In Clair Brown and Joseph Pechman (eds.), *Gender in the Workplace*. Washington, DC: Brookings Institution, 1982, pp. 123–125.

Brown, Diane R. "Socio-Demographic v. Domain Predictors of Perceived Stress: Racial Differences Among American Women." *Social Indicators Research* 20 (1988), pp. 517–532.

———. "Employment and Health Among Older Black Women: Implications for Their Economic Status." Working Paper No. 177. Wellesley, MA: Wellesley College, Center for Research on Women, 1988.

Burbridge, Lynn. "Black Women in Employment and Training Programs." In Margaret C. Simms and Julianne Malveaux (eds.), *Slipping Through the Cracks: The Status of Black Women*. New Brunswick, NJ: Transaction Books, 1987, pp. 97–114.

Cain, Glen. *Married Women in the Labor Force: An Economic Analysis*. Chicago: University of Chicago Press, 1966.

Cary, Max L. and Kim Hazelbaker. "Employment Growth in the Temporary Help Industry." *Monthly Labor Review*, April 1986, pp. 36–44.

Clark, Kenneth B. *Dark Ghetto*. New York: Harper and Row, 1965.

Clay, Phillip. "Housing, Neighborhoods and Development." In Phillip Clay (ed.), *The Emerging Black Community of Boston*. Boston: Institute for the Study of Black Culture, University of Massachusetts, n.d. [c. 1988].

Coalition on Pay Equity. "Are Health Care Workers Paid What They Are Worth?" Boston, 1987.

Danzinger, Sheldon H. and Daniel H. Weinberg (eds.). *Fighting Poverty*. Cambridge, MA: Harvard University Press, 1986.

Darity, William A. Jr. "The Human Capital Approach to Black-White Earnings Inequality: Some Unsettled Questions." *Journal of Human Resources*, 17, no. 1 (1982), pp. 72–93.

——— and Samuel Myers, Jr. "Public Policy and the Black Family." *Review of the Black Political Economy*, 13, nos. 1–2 (Summer–Fall 1985), pp. 165–187.

———. Book Review: "Losing Ground: American Social Policy, 1950–1980, By Charles Murray." In Margaret C. Simms and Julianne Malveaux (eds.), *Slipping Through the Cracks: The Status of Black Women*. New Brunswick, NJ: Transaction Books, 1987.

Daugherty, James R. "Black Women in the Military." *Focus*, Joint Center for Political Studies, 13, no. 7 (July 1985), p. 3.

Dempsey, Paul Stephen. "The Disaster of Airline Deregulation." *Wall Street Journal*, May 9, 1991, p. A14.

Dentler, Robert. *American Community Problems*. New York: McGraw-Hill, 1968.

———. *Major Social Problems*. New York: McGraw Hill, 1972.

Deutermann, William, Jr. and Scott Campbell Brown. "Voluntary Part Time Workers: A Growing Part of the Labor Force." *Monthly Labor Review*, June 1978, pp. 3–10.

Doeringer, Peter B. and Michael Piore. *Internal Labor Markets and Manpower Analysis*. Lexington, MA: Lexington Books, 1971.

Duncan, Greg J. and Saul Hoffman. "Recent Trends in the Relative Earnings of Black Men." In Greg Duncan (ed.), *Years of Poverty, Years of Plenty*. Ann Arbor: Survey Research Center, University of Michigan, 1984, pp. 139–152.

Dunlop, John. "The Development of Labor Organization: A Theoretical Perspective." In Richard L. Rowan (ed.), *Readings in Labor Economics and Labor Relations*. Homewood, IL: Irwin, 1985, pp. 58–71.

Dunson, Bruce. "Effects of Minimum Wage on Black Teenage Employment." Cambridge, MA: National Research Bureau, 1988.

Ellwood, David T. and Lawrence H. Summers. "Poverty in America: Is Welfare the Answer or the Problem?" In Sheldon H. Danzinger and Daniel H. Weinberg (eds.), *Fighting Poverty*. Cambridge, MA: Harvard University Press, 1986, pp. 78–104.

Farley, Pamela Jo. "Data Preview of Private Insurance and Public Programs: Coverage of Health Services in the United States, 1977." *National Health Care Expenditures Study*. Washington, DC: National Center for Health Services Research, U.S. Department of Health and Human Services, 1986.

Flora, Peter and Arnold Heidenheimer (eds.). *The Development of Welfare States in Europe and America*. New Brunswick, NJ: Transaction Books, 1987.

Freeman, Richard B. "Why Are Unions Faring Poorly in NLRB Representation Elections?" In Richard Rowan (ed.), *Readings in Labor Economics and Labor Relations*. Homewood, IL: Irwin, 1985.

Freudenham, Milt. "Volleyball on Health Care Costs." *New York Times*, December 7, 1989, p. D1.

Frumkin, Robert. "Health Insurance Trends in Cost Control and Coverage." *Monthly Labor Review*, September 1987, pp. 3–8.

Fullerton, Howard N. "Projections 2000: Labor Force Projections: 1986 to 2000." *Monthly Labor Review*, September 1987, pp. 19–29.

Galbraith, John Kenneth. *The New Industrial State*. Boston: Houghlin Mifflin, 1972.

Garrett, Gerald R. and Russell K. Schutt, "Working with the Homeless." Department of Sociology and Center for Communication Media, University of Massachusetts, Boston, 1990.

Garson, Barbara. *The Electronic Sweatshop: How Computers Are Transforming the Office of the Future into the Factory of the Past*. New York: Penguin, 1988.

Glenn, Evelyn Nakano and Roslyn Feldberg. "Degraded and Deskilled: The Proletarianization of Clerical Work." In Rachael Kahn-Hut, Arlene Daniels, and Richard Colvard (eds.), *Women and Work*. New York: Oxford University Press, 1982, pp. 206–207.

Gold, Allan. "The Struggle to Make Do Without Health Insurance." *New York Times*, July 30, 1989, pp. 1,22.

Gordon, David, Richard Edwards, and Michael Reich. *Segmented Work, Divided Workers*. Cambridge: Cambridge University Press, 1982.

Gwartney-Gibbs, Patricia. "Women's Work Experience and the 'Rusty Skills' Hypothesis." In Barbara A. Gutek, Ann Stromberg, and Laurie Larwood (eds.), *Women and Work*, Vol. 3. Beverly Hills, CA: Sage Publications, 1988, pp. 169–188.

———— and Patricia Taylor. "Black Women Workers: Earnings Progress in Three Industrial Sectors, 1970–1980," *Sage*, 3, no. 1 (Spring 1986), p. 20.

Hacker, Sally L. "Sex Stratification, Technology and Organizational Changes: A Longitudinal Case Study of AT&T." In Rachael Kahn-Hut, Arlene Daniels, and Richard Colvard (eds.), *Women and Work*. New York: Oxford University Press, 1982.

Hagstrom, Suzy. "Tax Breaks Offered UAL." *San Francisco Examiner*, May 7, 1991.

Hampton, R. *Behavioral Concepts in Management*, 3rd ed. Belmont, CA: Wadsworth, 1978.

Harper, Harriette, "Black Women and the Job Training Partnership Act." In Margaret Simms and Julianne Malveaux (eds.), *Slipping Through the Cracks: The Status of Black Women*. New Brunswick, NJ: Transaction Books, 1987.

Harrison, Bennett. *Education, Training and the Urban Ghetto*. Baltimore: Johns Hopkins University Press, 1972.

————. "Regional Restructuring and 'Good Business Climates': The Economic Transformation of New England Since World War II." In Larry Sawyers and William K. Tabb (eds.), *Sunbelt/Snowbelt: Urban Development and Regional Restructuring*. New York: Oxford University Press, 1984, pp. 48–96.

Hartman, Heidi. "Internal Labor Markets and Gender: A Case Study of Promotion." In Clair Brown and Joseph A. Pechman (eds.), *Gender in the Workplace*. Washington, DC: Brookings Institution, 1987, pp. 59–87.

Haugen, Steven E. "The Employment Expansion in Retail Trade, 1973–85." *Monthly Labor Review*, August 1986, p. 21.

————. "New Group Health Insurance." New York: Health Insurance Association of America, 1985.

Hern, Frank. "Beyond the Management Model of Industrialized Organization." In Frank Hern (ed.), *The Transformation of Industrial Organization*. Belmont, CA: Wadsworth, 1988, pp. 194–204.

Heskett, James L. *Managing in the Services Economy*. Boston: Harvard Business School Press, 1986.

Hesse-Huber, Sharlene. "The Black Woman Worker: A Minority Perspective on Women at Work." *Sage*, 3, no. 1 (Spring 1986).

Hillsman, Sally T. and Bernard Levenson. "Job Opportunities for Black and White Working-Class Women." In Rachael Kahn-Hut, Arlene Daniels, and Richard Colvard (eds.), *Women and Work*. New York: Oxford University Press, 1982, pp. 218–233.

Hine, Darlene Clark. "From Hospital to College: Black Nursing Leaders." *Journal of Negro Education*, Summer 1982, pp. 222–237.

Holden, Karen C. and W. Lee Hansen, "Part-Time Work, Full-Time Work and Occupational Segregation." In Clair Brown and Joseph A. Pechman (eds.), *Gender in the Workplace*. Washington, DC: Brookings Institution, 1987.

Horwath, Francis W. "The Pulse of Economic Change: Displaced Workers of 1981–85." *Monthly Labor Review*, June 1987, pp. 3–12.

Howe, Wayne. "The Business Services Industry Sets the Pace in Employment Growth."
    Monthly Labor Review, April 1986, pp. 29–36.
Iverum, Esther. "Low Pay Cited in Decline of Day Care in New York." *New York
    Times*, February 7, 1988, p. 41.
Jaynes, Gerald David and Robin M. Williams, Jr. (eds.). *A Common Destiny: Blacks
    and American Society*. Washington, DC: National Research Council/National
    Academy Press, 1989.
Jennings, James, "Race, Class and Politics in the Black Community of Boston." In
    James Jennings and Mel King (eds.), *From Access to Power*. Cambridge, MA:
    Schenkman Books, 1986, pp. 39–56.
———. "Race and Political Change in Boston." In Phillip Clay (ed.), *The Emerging
    Black Community of Boston*. Boston: Institute for the Study of Black Culture,
    University of Massachusetts, n.d. [c. 1988].
Job, Barbara Cottman. "More Public Services Spur Growth in Government Employ-
    ment." *Monthly Labor Review*, September 1978, pp. 3–7.
Jones, Barbara. "Black Women and Labor Force Participation: An Analysis of Sluggish
    Growth Rates." In Margaret Simms and Julianne Malveaux (eds.), *Slipping
    Through the Cracks: The Status of Black Women*. New Brunswick, NJ: Transaction
    Books, 1987, pp. 11–31.
Kahl, Anne and Donald Clark. "Employment in Health Services: Long-Term Trends and
    Projections." *Monthly Labor Review*, (August 1986), p. 17.
Kanter, Rosabeth M. "The Impact of Hierarchical Structures on the Work Behavior of
    Women and Men." In Rachel Kahn-Hut, Arlene Daniels, and Richard Colvard
    (eds.), *Women and Work*. New York: Oxford University Press, 1982, pp. 237–
    238.
Kaufman, Bruce E. *The Economics of Labor Markets and Labor Relations*. Chicago:
    Dryden Press, 1986.
Kilson, Martin, "Paradoxes of American Acculturation." Paper delivered at the Inter-
    national Symposium on Cultural Pluralism, University of Toronto, October 19,
    1985.
Kniesner, Thomas J. "The Low Wage Workers: Who are They?" In Simon Rottenberg
    (ed.), *The Economics of Legal Minimum Wages*. Washington; DC: American
    Enterprise Institute, 1981, pp. 459–484.
LeBaron, Dean and Lawrence S. Speidel. "Why Are the Parts Worth More Than the
    Sum? 'Chop Shop' A Corporate Valuation Model." In Lynn Brown and Eric
    Rosengren (eds.), *The Merger Boom*. Boston: Federal Reserve Bank, 1987,
    pp. 78–95.
Leon, Carol and Robert, Bednarzik. "A Profile of Women on Part-Time Schedules."
    Monthly Labor Review, October 1978, pp. 3–12.
Levin, Henry and Russell Rumberger. "The Low-Skill Future of High Tech." *Technology
    Review*, August–September 1983.
Levitan, Sar A. *Programs in Aid of the Poor for the 1980s*. Baltimore: Johns Hopkins
    University Press, 1980.
——— and Richard Belous. *More Than Substance: Minimum Wages for the Working
    Poor*. Baltimore: Johns Hopkins University Press, 1979.
Lewis, Oscar. *The Children of Sanchez*. New York: Random House, 1961.
———. *La Vida: A Puerto Rican Family*. New York: Random House, 1965.
Loth, Renee. "Jobs Go Begging in Human Services." *Boston Globe*, February 26, 1988.

Magaziner, Ira and Robert Reich. *Minding America's Business*. New York: Harcourt, Brace, Jovanovich, 1982.

Malveaux, Julianne, "From Domestic Worker to Household Technician: Black Women in a Changing Occupation." In Phyllis Wallace (ed.), *Women in the Workplace*. Boston: Auburn House, 1982.

————. "Recent Trends in Occupational Segregation by Race and Sex." Presented to the Committee on Women's Employment and Related Social Issues, National Academy of Sciences, Washington, DC, May 25, 1982.

———— and Susan Englander. "Race and Class in Nursing Occupations." *Sage*, 3, no. 1 (Spring 1986), pp. 41–45.

Marshall, Ray. "Work and Women in the 1980's: A Perspective on Basic Trends Affecting Women's Jobs and Job Opportunities." In Richard Rowan (ed.), *Readings in Labor Economics and Labor Relations*. Homewood, IL: Irwin, 1985.

McKersie, Robert and Peter Cappelli. "Concession Bargaining." In Richard Rowan (ed.), *Readings in Labor Economics and Labor Relations*. Homewood, IL: Irwin, 1985, pp. 243–253.

Meier, August and Elliot Rudwick. *Black Detroit and the Rise of the UAW*. New York: Oxford University Press, 1979.

Milkowich, George T. "Comparable Worth, the Emerging Debate." In Richard L. Rowan (ed.), *Readings in Labor Economics and Labor Relations*. Homewood, IL: Irwin, 1985, pp. 324–338.

Moynihan, Daniel Patrick. *The Negro Family: A Case for National Action*. Washington DC: U.S. Department of Labor, 1965.

————. *The Politics of a Guaranteed Income*. New York: Random House, 1973.

Mullins, Terry W. and Paul Luebke. "Symbolic Victory and Political Reality in the Southern Textile Industry: The Meaning of the J.P. Stevens Settlement for Southern Labor Relations." In Richard Rowan (ed.), *Readings in Labor Economics and Labor Relations*. Homewood, IL: Irwin, 1985, pp. 196–200.

Murray, Charles. *Losing Ground: American Social Policy, 1950–1980*. New York: Basic Books, 1984.

Nardone, Thomas J. "Part Time Workers: Who Are They?" *Monthly Labor Review*, February 1986, pp. 13–19.

National Committee on Pay Equity. *Pay Equity in the Public Sector*. Washington, DC: October 1989.

Nelkin, D. and M. S. Brown. *Workers at Risk*. Chicago: University of Chicago Press, 1984.

Newman, Debra Lynn, "Black Women Workers in the Twentieth Century." *Sage*, 3, no. 1 (Spring 1986), pp. 2–14.

Nilsen, Diane. "Blacks in the 1970's, Did They Scale the Job Ladder?" In Richard L. Rowan (ed.), *Readings in Labor Economics and Labor Relations*. Homewood, IL: Irwin, 1985, pp. 2–43.

Norwood, Janet L. "A Cyclical Rebound: The Job Machine Has Not Broken." *New York Times*, February 22, 1987.

O'Farrell, Brigid. "Women and Non-Traditional Blue Collar Jobs in the 1980s." In Phyllis Wallace (ed.), *Women in the Workplace*. Boston: Auburn House, 1982.

Orloff, Ann, "The Political Origins of America's Related Welfare State." In Margaret Weir, Ann Orloff, and Theda Skocpol (eds.), *The Politics of Social Policy in the United States*. Princeton, NJ: Princeton University Press, 1988, pp. 37–80.

Patchen, M. *Participation, Achievement and Involvement on the Job*. Englewood Cliffs, NJ: Prentice-Hall, 1970.

Pearce, Diana and H. McAdoo. *Women and Children Alone and in Poverty*. Washington, DC: National Council on Economic Opportunity, 1981.

Pecora, Peter and Michael Austin. *Managing Human Services Personnel*. Beverly Hills, CA: Sage Publications, 1987.

Personick, Valerie. "Projections 2000: Industry Output and Employment Through the End of the Century." *Monthly Labor Review*, September 1987, pp. 30–45.

Perucci, Carolyn C., Robert Perucci, Dena B. Targ, and Harry R. Targ. *Plant Closings: International Context and Social Costs*. Hawthorne, NY: Aldine de Gruyter, 1988.

Peters, Thomas and Robert Waterman. *In Search of Excellence*. New York: Harper and Row, 1982.

Pinder, C. *Work Motivation: Theory, Issues and Applications*. Chicago: Scott Foresman, 1984.

Pivin, Frances F. and Richard Cloward. *Regulating the Poor*. New York: Vintage, 1971.

Plunkert, Lois M. "The 1980's: A Decade of Job Growth and Industry Shifts." *Monthly Labor Review*, September 1980, pp. 3–16.

Polacheck, Solomon. "Occupational Self-Selection: A Human Capital Approach to Sex Differences in Occupational Status." *Review of Economics*, 58, no. 1 (February 1981), pp. 60–69.

Rainwater, Lee. "Crucible of Identity: The Negro Lower Class Family." *Daedalus*, 95, pp. 172–216.

Ravenschraft, David. "The 1980s Merger Wave: An Industrial Organization Perspective." In Lynn Brown and Eric Rosengren (eds.), *The Merger Boom*. Boston: Federal Reserve Bank, 1987, pp. 17–37.

Reich, Robert. *Tales of a New America*. New York: Vintage Books, 1987.

Ritzer, George and David Walczak. *Working: Conflict and Change*, 3rd ed. Englewood Cliffs, NJ: Prentice-Hall, 1986.

Robb, Christine. "Geneva Evans' Days: If Her Job Is So Important Why Don't We Value Her Work?" *Boston Globe Magazine*, November 8, 1987, p. 14.

Rodgers, Harrell, Jr. *The Cost of Human Neglect*. Armonk, NY: M. E. Sharpe, 1982.
———. *Poor Women, Poor Families*. Armonk NY: M. E. Sharpe, 1986.

Rottenberg, Simon (ed.). *The Economics of Legal Minimum Wages*. Washington, DC: The American Enterprise Institute, 1981.

Rowan, Richard L., Kenneth Pitterle, and Philip Misciamarra. *Multinational Union Organizations in the White Collar, Services and Communications Industry*. Philadelphia: Industrial Research Unit, The Wharton School, University of Pennsylvania, 1983.

Sawyers, Larry and William K. Tabb (eds.). *Sunbelt/Snowbelt: Urban Development and Regional Restructuring*. New York: Oxford University Press, 1984.

Schier, Edmond. *Career Dynamics: Matching Individual and Organizational Needs*. Reading, MA: Addison-Wesley, 1978.

Sekscenski, Edward S. "The Health Services Industry: A Decade of Expansion." *Monthly Labor Review*, May 1981, pp. 9–16.

Simms, Margaret. "The Choices That Young Black Women Make: Education, Employment and Family Formation." Working Paper No. 190. Wellesley, MA: Wellesley College, Center for Research on Women, 1988.

Squires, Gregory. "Capital Mobility Versus Upward Mobility: The Racially Discrimi-

natory Consequences of Plant Closings and Corporate Relocations." In Larry
Sawyers and William K. Tabb (eds.), *Sunbelt/Snowbelt: Urban Development and
Regional Restructuring*. New York: Oxford University Press, 1984, pp. 152–161.

Stamas, George D. "The Puzzling Lag in Southern Earnings." *Monthly Labor Review*,
June 1981, p. 27.

Strober, Myra and Carolyn Arnold, "Occupational Segregation Among Bank Tellers."
In Clair Brown and Joseph A. Pechman (eds.), *Gender in the Workplace*. Washington, DC: Brookings Institution, 1987.

Telly, C. S., M. L. Franch, and W. S. Sort. "The Relationship of Inequity to Turnover
Among Hourly Workers." *Administrative Science Quarterly*, 16 (1971), pp. 164–
171.

Thurow, Lester. *The Zero-Sum Society*. New York: Penguin Books, 1981.

———. "Building a World-Class Economy." In Frank Hern (ed), *The Transformation
of Industrial Organization*, Belmont, CA: Wadsworth, 1988.

Urisko, James A. "Productivity in Hotels and Motels, 1958–73." *Monthly Labor Review*,
May 1975, pp. 24–28.

Urquhart, Michael. "The Services Industry: Is It Recession-Proof?" *Monthly Labor
Review*, October 1981, pp. 11–13.

———. "The Employment Shift to Services: Where Did It Come From?" *Monthly Labor
Review*, April 1984, pp. 15–21.

U.S. Department of Commerce, Bureau of the Census. *Bulletin 2169*. 1983.

———. *Census of the Population, 1960, 1970, 1980*. Washington, DC: Government
Printing Office.

———. "Money Income and Poverty Status of Families and Persons in the United States,
1982." *Current Population Reports*, Series P–60, No. 140. Washington, DC,
1982.

U.S. Department of Labor, Bureau of Labor Statistics. *Current Population Survey, 1982*
(Micro Data Tapes). Washington, DC: U.S. Department of Labor, 1982.

———. "Employee Benefits in Medium and Large Firms." *Bulletin 2237*. 1985.

———. "Linking Employment Problems to Economic Status." *Bulletin 2169*. 1983.

Vroom, V. *Work and Motivation*. New York: John Wiley, 1964.

Waite, Stephen. "Discussion." In Lynn E. Browne and Eric S. Rosengren (eds.), *The
Merger Boom*. Boston: Federal Reserve Bank, 1987, pp. 38–47.

Wallace, Phyllis. *Equal Employment Opportunity and the AT&T Case*. Cambridge, MA:
MIT Press, 1976.

———. *Black Women in the Labor Force*. Cambridge, MA: MIT Press, 1982.

———. "Increased Labor Force Participation of Women and Affirmative Action." In
Phyllis Wallace (ed.), *Women in the Workplace*. Boston: Auburn House, 1982,
pp. 1–24.

——— (ed.). *Women in the Workplace*. Boston: Auburn House, 1982.

Weir, Margaret, A. Orloff, and T. Skocpol. "Understanding American Social Politics."
in Margaret Weir, Anna Orloff, and Theda Skocpol (eds.), *The Politics of Social
Policy in the United States*. Princeton, NJ: Princeton University Press, 1988.

———. "The Federal Government and Unemployment: The Frustration of Policy Innovation from the New Deal to the Great Society." In Margaret Weir, Ann Orloff,
and Theda Skocpol (eds.), *The Politics of Social Policy in the United States*.
Princeton, NJ: Princeton University Press, 1988.

Williams, Rhonda M. "Beyond Human Capital: Black Women, Work and Wages."

Working Paper 183. Wellesley, MA: Wellesley College, Center for Research on Women, 1988.

Wilson, William Julius. *The Declining Significance of Race*. Chicago: University of Chicago Press, 1980.

——— and Kathryn Neckerman. "Poverty and Family Structure: The Widening Gap Between Evidence and Public Policy." In Sheldon H. Danzinger and Daniel H. Weinberg (eds.), *Fighting Poverty*. Cambridge, MA: Harvard University Press, 1986, p. 252.

Woody, Bette. *Managing Crisis Cities*. Westport, CT: Greenwood Press, 1982.

———. "Executive Women: Models of Corporate Success." Wellesley, MA: Wellesley College, Center for Research on Women, 1986.

———. "Welfare Reform: A Summary and Analysis of Current U.S. Congressional Debate over the Family Security Act of 1988." *Trotter Review* (William M. Trotter Institute, University of Massachusetts/Boston), 3, no. 2 (Spring 1989), pp. 9–14.

———. "Black Women in the Emerging Services Economy," *Sex Roles*, 21, nos. 1 & 2 (July 1989), pp. 45–68.

Index

ABOUT THE AUTHOR

BETTE WOODY is Associate Professor of Sociology at the University of Massachusetts and a research associate and project director at the Center for Research on Women at Wellesley College. She is the author of *Managing Crisis Cities* (Greenwood Press, 1982).